D1195668

MODERN
BOAT BUILDING

MODERN BOAT BUILDING
Materials and Methods

International Marine Publishing Company
Camden, Maine

Published by International Marine Publishing Company
21 Elm Street, Camden, Maine 04843
(207) 236–4342

CONTENTS

ACKNOWLEDGEMENTS

Many people have helped with the production of this book in many ways, from providing technical information and advice to supplying photographs, correcting the text and offering moral support. Writing about a developing technology is always difficult since new developments occur with such rapidity as to make old theories and ideas quickly outdated. Moreover, the level of knowledge as to the properties and potential use of new materials lags behind their introduction, so there is always the difficulty of sorting out scientific data from personal beliefs and the 'witchcraft' of general supposition. To all those who have helped with this book I would like to say a heartfelt 'thank you' – without you it would not have been possible. In particular I would like to thank all the staff of Structural Polymer Systems Ltd for their help and enthusiasm, Magda Gulvin for checking the manuscript and, most especially, my family and friends for their support during the writing and research – thank you for your understanding.

Steve Sleight

Thanks are due to the following for permission to reproduce photographs:

Structural Polymer Systems Ltd	Borden (UK) Ltd
Fibreglass Ltd	Hexcell
Strand Glass Ltd	Marglass
Vetrotex (UK) Ltd	Carr Reinforcements
Ciba-Geigy	Amoco Chemicals
Du Pont	Dow Chemicals
Fothergill & Harvey Ltd	Unitex Ltd
Lonza Inc.	Cornelius Chemical Co. Ltd
Orcon	Firet
Permali Plasticell	Dufaylite Developments Ltd
Jotun	Amcell Ltd
Solarbo	Contessa Yachts Ltd
Baltek	Westerly Yachts Ltd
Scott Bader	Eric Lerouge

INTRODUCTION

During the last thirty-five years boatbuilding, by both professionals and amateurs, has undergone a considerable change as fresh materials and variations of established ones have made new techniques practical and possible. The development of waterproof synthetic resin glues during the Second World War led to the use of plywood for boat construction and marked the start of the boom in the pleasure boat industry. The introduction of GRP (glass-fibre reinforced plastic) as a boatbuilding material was also linked to that early development of synthetic resins but, while the availability of plywood had its greatest effect on the amateur boatbuilder, the introduction of GRP made its impact on the boatbuilding industry which adapted fairly quickly to take advantage of the new material.

Nowadays we are completely used to the idea of 'plastic' boats and the material now dominates the production boat market to the extent that a majority of owners do not give a second's thought to how their boat was built or the materials that went into it. A boat is, however, only as good as its components and its builder, and this is as true for a GRP boat as it is for one constructed by any other method. In the years since GRP first made its impact on boatbuilding, considerable knowledge has been acquired about the material and the methods of using it. Technology does not, however, stand still, and in the last ten years new types of resins and high-performance fibre reinforcements have been developed and used in industries such as aerospace, where the demand for stronger and lighter structures is never-ending.

Natural spin-off has resulted in the increasing use of a wide range of materials in 'plastic' boat construction, especially for high-performance craft where the extra expense can be more easily justified. By the nature of progress, the use of these materials will undoubtedly spread to production boatbuilders and, in some cases, to the amateur. Inevitably, when new materials appear, there is a period when their potential benefits and applications are not fully understood, and it is to that problem that this book seeks to address itself. In recent years words like Kevlar™, carbon fibre, Nomex, epoxy resins and vacuum-bagging have been added to the boatbuilder's vocabulary, but to most of the boat-buying public and, dare it be said, to some in the trade, these are mere buzzwords that convey little knowledge. The first part of this book is concerned with the materials such as fibre reinforcements, resin systems and core materials, that can be used by the builder to create a composite structure. In the second part is a review of a number of construction methods that are available to the amateur or professional builder.

Because of the increasing use of fibres other than glass fibres as reinforcement material, the term FRP (fibre-reinforced plastic) will be used as a general term throughout this book, although other abbreviations such as GRP and CFRP (carbon fibre-reinforced plastic) will be used when talking about a specific fibre reinforcement.

In recent years it has been realized that, while FRP materials have a number of advantages for boatbuilding, they are not totally immune to the marine environment. It comes as something of a shock to many boat owners to discover that FRP composites do absorb water which can, in time, affect the integrity of the moulding. Much publicity has been given to the causes of long-term deterioration in some boat hulls and it is now realized that the choice of materials and the care that goes into the construction has a considerable effect on the properties of the moulding. The last part of the book looks specifically at the problems of osmosis and examines in detail the question of damage from the marine environment and the ways in which it can be prevented.

The inclusion of chapters devoted to wood and its uses may seem out of place in a book that concerns itself mainly with resin systems and fibre reinforcements. Wood is still, however, one of the most versatile and cost-effective boatbuilding materials and, although traditional wooden boatbuilding is rarely seen today, new methods of working with wood now allow its use as a genuine structural engineering material. It is, in fact, a very sophisticated natural form of fibres held together in a resin matrix, and the design of a wooden structure has much in common with that of an FRP one. Wood is also used with glass and other fibres. It can be used, in its low-density varieties, as a core material with skins of glass or other fibres, or it can be used as a skin on the outside of a foam or honeycomb, or indeed a wooden core.

No apology is made for not including other materials used for boatbuilding such as steel, ferro-cement or aluminium. These and their construction methods are well understood and there are many excellent books devoted to them. Moreover, all three materials have a more limited range of use than does FRP. Steel and ferro-cement are both limited to the building of medium- or heavy-displacement boats of moderate to large size, but for this use both materials have their devotees. Aluminium results in a much lighter construction than either steel or ferro-cement and is found in a wide range of craft from knock-about dinghies to large power craft. It is also used to build some high-performance racing boats, both sail and power, but although there have been recent developments in the use of riveted and glued aluminium construction and in super-plastic aluminium, it is likely that this material will be largely superseded by developments in FRP technology.

The reader who hopes to be able to use this book as a step-by-step guide to boatbuilding will, I'm afraid, be disappointed. There are many excellent books available from which the amateur can obtain specific information related to his own project, and to attempt to include that information here would be superfluous. It is hoped that the information presented here will extend the interested reader's knowledge of the materials now commonly used to build a majority of boats and will enable the prospective boat buyer more easily to assess the quality of the craft he may buy.

It has to be said that the quality of production boats has, in the past, varied considerably. Thankfully this situation is now improving, but the difference between a well-built FRP boat and a bad one can be difficult for the average buyer to spot. Only by knowing the right questions to ask can a prospective purchaser assure himself of the quality of the product.

SECTION I
MATERIALS

1 FIBRE REINFORCEMENTS

Fibre-reinforced plastic (FRP) has, over the last thirty-five years, found an important place as a structural engineering material in a wide range of industries of which the marine industry has been one of the most important. The success of FRP in becoming the most popular material for production boatbuilding is due to the number of advantages that it possesses when compared with other possible materials. Fibre-reinforced plastic is unique in that it is usually formed in place during the fabrication of the hull, deck or other moulding. This feature gives the designer and builder the opportunity of adjusting the materials specification of parts of the moulding to tailor it exactly to suit the strength or stiffness requirements.

Because the material is formed in the mould, intricate shapes can be

moulded which would be difficult or impossible to achieve with any other material. This gives additional freedom to the designer to explore fully and utilize a variety of possible shapes. FRP has a number of other advantages when compared with alternative boatbuilding materials and these include the following:

– good strength-to-weight and stiffness-to-weight ratios
– easy-to-handle, light-weight material
– easy to maintain and repair
– good corrosion resistance
– good weathering properties
– easily coloured during manufacture and surface can be textured
– good resistance to abrasion
– immune to marine borers

Fibre-reinforced plastic is commonly referred to as a composite material because it consists of at least two discrete but thoroughly mixed components – the reinforcement fibre or fibres and a resin which is often referred to as the matrix. Unreinforced plastics have a low density, are easily processed, require no surface protection and have good weathering properties, but for structural uses they generally suffer from low stiffness and strength and creep under load.

Fig. 1.1 Not only pleasure craft are built in FRP. HMS *Wilton* is a GRP 157-ft minesweeper in service in the Royal Navy. (*Photo: Amoco*).

Fig. 1.2 A cross-section of the hull of HMS *Wilton*.

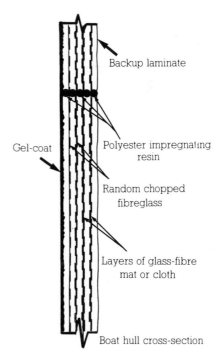

Backup laminate

Gel-coat

Polyester impregnating resin

Random chopped fibreglass

Layers of glass-fibre mat or cloth

Boat hull cross-section

It has long been known that very fine filaments of glass have a far higher strength than bulk glass because they possess fewer microflaws which act as stress points and cause early failure. Glass fibres, fibres of carbon, aramid (Kevlar), and others not used in boatbuilding such as asbestos and boron, have high strength and stiffness but are so brittle that their potential properties cannot be realized.

By combining a fibre reinforcement with a resin matrix, stress can be transferred into and between the fibres so that they can work together. The resin also serves to protect the surface of the fibres from damage which would reduce their strength.

Glass fibre

The history of glass fibre dates back to 1836 when a French weaver applied for a patent to cover the invention of 'weaving glass made malleable by steam'. By 1839 woven glass fabrics were on display at an exhibition of industrial products, and in 1840 that fabric received official recognition when it was used to make draperies for Napoleon's body before burial. The material soon disappeared, however, probably because of its high price and low resistance to abrasion, and it remained forgotten for a century until its re-emergence for use in the insulation of electrical conductors. The development of synthetic laminating resins in the 1940s provided a new use for glass fibres as reinforcement, and it is this application that has opened up a huge market for the material.

Glass fibres are produced from molten glass which is fed into a platinum bushing containing a number of holes through which the glass flows by gravity. As each filament emerges, it is drawn at high speed and cooled. By controlling the temperature and speed of drawing, continuous filaments of specific diameters can be produced. These newly formed glass filaments cannot be used in their virgin state because they lack cohesion and are susceptible to abrasion and attack by moisture. To overcome these problems the filaments are coated with size. The type of size used is determined by the use for which the glass fibres are intended. Fibres which are to be woven will need a high resistance to abrasion during the weaving process, while those fibres intended for direct use as plastic reinforcement may need to be adapted to suit the production process and to match a particular resin matrix.

When a fabric is intended for plastic reinforcement, it is usually necessary to remove the size that protected the yarn during weaving and then to apply a size that is compatible with the resin that will be used. Occasionally a size is applied to the original filaments that is a compromise between the textile and plastic size and is suitable for both weaving and resin bonding. The

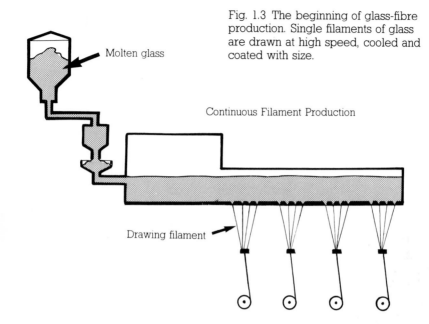

Fig. 1.3 The beginning of glass-fibre production. Single filaments of glass are drawn at high speed, cooled and coated with size.

Molten glass

Continuous Filament Production

Drawing filament

amount of size that is deposited on the fibres is small: usually between 0.3 and 3 per cent by weight, depending on the type and requirements. It must be capable of binding single filaments as they are brought together to form strands but, for most purposes, it must not stick to itself, otherwise when the strands are wound on to a 'cheese' they would set into a solid mass.

Once filaments have been sized and gathered together untwisted into strands, they may be subjected to a number of further processes which depend on the required form of the final product. Fabrics are formed by twisting strands of fibres into various types of yarn, while many of the most common reinforcements used in boatbuilding, such as chopped strands, rovings and chopped-strand mat, are made directly from the strands of sized filaments.

E glass

Glass fibre is produced in a range of types suitable for different applications. The original type, A glass, was made from standard window glass, but is now obsolete. Of primary interest to the boatbuilder is E glass which was originally required for its electrical insulation properties and is now produced in the largest quantities of all types, accounting for about 90 per cent of the total glass-fibre production. E glass is a low-alkaline glass (less than 1 per cent alkali content) which draws well and has good stiffness, strength and

Fig. 1.4 Sized filaments are gathered
into strands and then processed
according to the final product
requirement.

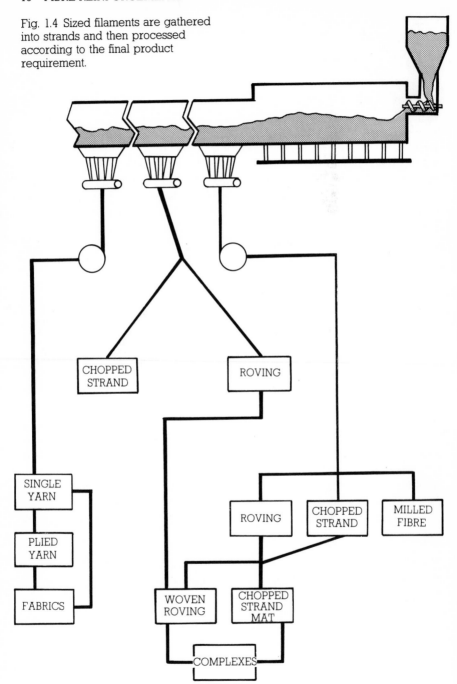

weathering properties. The filaments used for the reinforcement of plastic resins are commonly produced in diameters of between 6 and 15 microns (1 micron = 0.001 mm or approximately 0.00004 in), with the larger diameters being easier to make and hence more popular with manufacturers.

E glass is by far the most common fibre reinforcement used by builders of FRP boats, perhaps 95 per cent of all such craft making use of it. In their virgin form, E glass fibres have quite remarkable mechanical properties – their tensile strength, for example, exceeds that of more recently introduced 'exotic' fibres. Unfortunately, however, the properties of the virgin fibres are not retained in their mass-produced form which shows a typical drop in mechanical properties in the order of about 50 per cent, resulting in E glass, as used by the moulder, being the least strong of the fibres available to the boatbuilder.

This drop in properties during production is due in part to abrasion damage caused by the fibres rubbing against each other while being processed. The more the fibres are handled, the greater is the damage and the loss in strength. For this reason, woven fabrics which undergo several stages in manufacture tend to be less strong, weight for weight, than unwoven fibres. Because E glass fibres are produced in very large volumes and there is a need for the cost of the end product to be kept low, manufacturers cannot afford to use costly processing methods, such as are used for higher-performance fibres, or to use expensive sizes to reduce abrasion damage during processing.

Yet, despite these losses of performance during manufacture, E glass is still a very effective reinforcement, especially when it is compared with alternatives on a cost basis. The table, fig. 5, shows some mechanical properties for E glass but, like other figures in this book, these are intended as a guide to give the reader a feel for the order of magnitude of properties. Such data has been obtained from a variety of sources and inevitably covers a wide range of different products. E glass, in particular, is produced by many different manufacturers whose product specifications may vary significantly. The interested reader will find in Appendix 1 an explanation of terms, along with details of the units used for mechanical properties.

E glass is available to the boatbuilder in many more forms than any of the other reinforcement fibres used in boatbuilding and a description of these woven and non-woven materials will be found later in the chapter.

R glass and S glass

To cater for a demand, which came initially from the aerospace industry, for fibres with better mechanical properties than E glass, manufacturers in the USA and Europe separately developed high-performance forms of glass fibre. Owens Corning, an American producer, introduced S glass in the

1960s, while in Europe the French-based company Vetrotex developed its version known as R glass. Although S glass was developed initially for aerospace users, a lower-cost version, usually called S-2 glass or CS (Commercial S), is available for commercial applications that do not require the testing and certification demanded by aerospace and military customers.

The higher mechanical properties of S and R glass, typically from 20 to 40 per cent greater than E glass, depending on the particular property, are achieved by changing the composition of the glass. Specifically both R glass and S glass contain a higher proportion of both alumina and silica than is found in E glass, while other components of E glass are either missing or much reduced in the high-performance glasses. Experience with the production of E glass has also allowed the manufacturers to improve both the production processes used for S glass and R glass and the sizes used to coat and bind the filaments. The extra cost of these processes and sizes are acceptable in the production of the high-performance fibres despite the fact that the production volume is relatively low because the end cost can be higher due to its specialist use. Typical costs of R glass and S glass are five to nine times that of E glass.

Another benefit of using either R glass or S glass is the diameter of the drawn filaments. These are typically about half the diameter of E glass filaments which means that, for a given weight of fibre, S glass and R glass each have roughly twice the surface area to which the resin matrix can bond. This increases the adhesion between resin and fibre and further adds to the strength of the laminate.

For all glass-fibre laminates one of the major causes of loss of mechanical strength is attack by water, either in liquid or vapour form, and this problem is, of course, of concern to boatbuilders. Both R and S glass show a marked superiority to E glass in this respect, although the protection afforded by the resin is still of vital importance to the retention of physical strength of the laminate.

When mechanical strength and stiffness is important to the design, such as for high-performance racing power or sailing boats, R and S glass have many advantages when compared with E glass and, indeed, when compared with other more expensive fibres. Even in production craft where E glass would be the normal choice for reinforcement, the use of limited amounts of R glass or S glass in high-stress areas can be advantageous without significantly increasing the cost.

At the moment S glass is less readily available in the UK than is R glass, but it is expected that both will become more common in the future as the prices drop with more boatbuilders making use of these materials. As with E glass, both R glass and S glass are available in several woven and non-woven

Fig. 1.5 Comparative figures for the composition and basic physical properties of A, E, S and R glass. A glass – the original type – is now obsolete.

Composition %	'A'	'E'	'S'	'R'
SiO_2	72.0	52.4	64.4	60.0
Al_2O_3, Fe_2O_3	1.5	14.4	25.0	25.0
CaO	10.0	17.2		9.0
MgO	2.5	4.6	10.3	6.0
Na_2O, K_2O	14.2	0.8	0.3	
B_2O_3		10.6		
BaO				
BeO, TiO_2, ZrO_2, CeO_2				

Property				
Specific gravity	2.45	2.56	2.49	2.58
Single fibre tensile strength – GN/m^2	3.3	3.6	4.5	4.4
Young's Modulus of Elasticity – GN/m^2	69.0	75.9	86.2	84.8
Softening point – °C	700	850	–	990

forms, although they are not normally available in low-performance products such as mats where their improved mechanical properties would not be used to advantage. The table shows some of the important properties of S glass and R glass and allows comparison between these and the other possible choices of reinforcement fibre.

Kevlar™

Kevlar, the trademark of the Du Pont company, is the name generally used for aramid fibres (basically a form of nylon) of which the Du Pont product is the only one available at present. Kevlar was first discovered by Du Pont in 1965 when it was known as 'Fibre B'. After eight years of development Kevlar was first used for rubber reinforcement in radial-tyre belting. It was not long, however, before a wide range of commercial applications became apparent. Two forms of Kevlar are now made: Kevlar 29 for use in ropes, cables, friction materials and protective clothing such as bullet-proof vests; and Kevlar 49 for use as a reinforcement fibre for plastic composites.

The first users of Kevlar 49 were, naturally enough, the aerospace and motor-racing industries where the cost of exotic materials takes second place to strength and light-weight requirements. In the last few years, however, Kevlar fibre has started to become used in the marine field, especially in applications such as racing boats, both power and sail, where there is a need for stiff, strong and light building materials.

When compared on a strength-to-weight basis, Kevlar fibres show the highest specific tensile strength (tensile strength/specific gravity) of any commercially available fibre, being five times stronger than steel and twice as strong as E glass. This high strength-to-weight ratio means that a composite utilizing Kevlar fibres can achieve the same tensile strength as a composite of E glass at a fraction of the weight. Possible weight savings will be further considered in later chapters.

When the tensile modulus of fibres is considered (tensile modulus is a measure of the resistance of the fibres to stretching under a tensile load), Kevlar again scores over both E glass and S glass or R glass; and when the specific modulus (modulus/specific gravity) is measured, Kevlar's advantage is even more apparent.

Impact resistance, another important factor when a boat's hull is being designed, is also one of Kevlar's strong points, especially its ability to withstand repeated impacts. Linked to this strength against impact damage is a resistance to the propagation of cracks through a laminate incorporating Kevlar. Laminates reinforced with glass fibres allow the small cracks occurring in the resin and fibres after impact damage to spread, leading to further breakdown, but a Kevlar-reinforced laminate resists this crack propagation because of the non-brittle nature of the fibres.

When compressive strengths are considered, however, a laminate of Kevlar does not show the advantages over other fibres that it demonstrates under tensile loading. Under compressive loading, Kevlar does not behave in the same way as any of the other fibres discussed here, but rather demonstrates a low compressive strength and a metal-like behaviour, being elastic under low strain and almost perfectly plastic at higher strains. In practice this may mean either avoiding using Kevlar where compressive strength is important, or engineering the structure in tensile strength so that it can cope with the required compressive loading. This only applies in thick-walled structures, however, since when thin-walled laminates are considered, buckling failure will in any case limit the compressive resistance of the laminate. When compressive strength is important, an alternative to overbuilding a Kevlar laminate is to use a hybrid incorporating Kevlar with another fibre that shows the required compressive properties. The use of hybrids will be discussed later in this chapter and in Chapter 6.

Kevlar is available in a wide range of fabrics, and the fibre has the advantage that it takes the weaving process very well with negligible damage being caused to the fibres. Kevlar fabrics are usually supplied scoured and dried with no coating, but at least one manufacturer (Fothergill and Harvey Ltd) now supplies fabrics with a proprietary finish to improve the bond when polyester or vinylester resins are to be used.

Claims have been made that Kevlar fabrics are difficult to wet-out with resin, but experienced FRP users should not find this to be a problem. Like all of the high-performance fibres, the properties of the resultant laminate are very dependent on achieving a high fibre-to-resin ratio, though this depends very much on the techniques of wetting-out that are used and the actual lay-up methods. This subject will be dealt with much more extensively in later chapters. Unlike glass fibres, Kevlar does not become transparent when fully wetted-out; instead the colour changes from a bright yellow to a deep gold when sufficient resin penetration has been achieved. It is certainly true that different fabric weaves of Kevlar or any other fibre differ greatly in the ease with which they can be wetted-out, but this is more a function of the tightness of the fabric weave than the type of fibre.

As with other fibres, the costs of Kevlar reinforcement will depend to some extent on the form of reinforcement that is chosen, but as a guide the cost is in the region of ten to twenty times that of E glass on a weight basis.

Carbon fibre

Carbon fibre is, along with Kevlar, a term that some boatbuilders and designers use to impress their customers and convince them that their products are what has come to be known as 'the state of the art'!

Like Kevlar, carbon fibres have been around for some time, their high strength and modulus properties first ensuring their use within the aerospace industry. Here their excellent physical properties and light weight allowed composites using these fibres to outperform metals in many applications. Exactly the same properties have resulted in some boat designers and builders making use of carbon fibre-reinforced plastics composites (CFRP) primarily to improve stiffness properties in high-performance racing craft.

Carbon fibres are now made world-wide by more than a dozen manufacturers whose products vary in their physical properties according to the process used for production. Most fibres are made from polyacrylonitrile (PAN), a special acrylic fibre, although some are pitch-based. The production process involves separate stages of oxidation, carbonization and graphitization, the properties of the resulting fibre depending on its carbon content.

Carbon fibres are generally classified in four groups depending on their properties: high strength (HS), very high strength (VHS), high modulus (HM) and ultra-high modulus (UHM). UHM carbon fibres are processed at temperatures in excess of 3000°C and have a carbon content of 99 per cent, while the carbon content of the other classes is generally between 91 and 95 per cent. Because of the high-temperature processing, UHM fibres are generally more expensive than the other types and usually have a lower

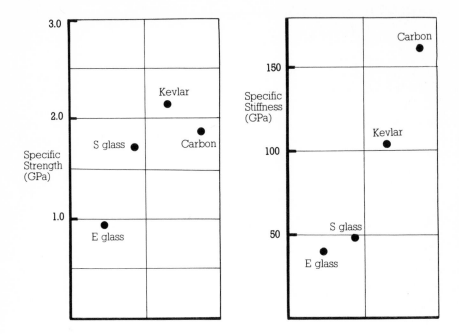

tensile strength. The surface of the fibres is lightly oxidized to improve the bond between the fibres and resins for laminating, and a surface coating (typically of an unhardened epoxy resin) is used to make handling easier. This surface coating is compatible with all the resin systems that are normally used with carbon fibres.

Filaments of carbon fibres, with typical diameters of between 7 and 11 microns, are gathered together in tows with up to 40,000 filaments in a tow. These tows are either twisted into yarns or used untwisted to make a wide range of woven and non-woven fabrics for reinforcement purposes. Fabrics used in boatbuilding generally have between 3000 and 12,000 filaments per tow, with the higher filament counts being less costly on a weight-for-weight basis.

The density of carbon fibres varies slightly across the range but falls between those of glass and Kevlar. Its tensile strength approaches that of S glass or R glass, and when specific strength is considered carbon fibres are second only to Kevlar. They are, however, superior to any other fibre where stiffness (tensile modulus) is concerned and have, when laminated, excellent compressive strength. Carbon fibres also have good fatigue and vibration resistance and show low friction and wear characteristics. They are, however, very brittle fibres and develop their excellent strength at the

Fig. 1.6 Comparative fibre properties. The properties of laminates using the various fibres will vary depending on fibre content and resin type, etc.

Fig. 1.6(a) A comparison of the various fibres showing specific strength, specific stiffness and impact strength.

Fibre properties

Fibre	*Tensile strength* GPa	*Tensile modulus* GPa	*Specific gravity*
Polyester	1.0	11	1.38
E-Glass	3.4	75	2.54
S-Glass	4.5	86	2.54
Kevlar 49	3.6	130	1.45
Carbon HS	3.1	227	1.74
Carbon HM	2.1	390	1.81

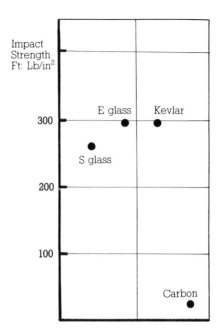

lowest elongation of any of the fibres under consideration. Because of this, they are usually used together with another fibre such as S glass, R glass or Kevlar, in order to improve the impact resistance of the laminate which would otherwise be low.

Another reason for not using carbon fibres alone is that they are the most expensive of all the fibre reinforcements. On a weight basis, carbon fibres cost from twenty-five to one hundred times the cost of E glass, depending on the type of carbon fibre and the type of reinforcement fabric that is used.

Polyester fibres

Polyester fibres are not generally considered for resin reinforcement because there is usually a requirement for good stiffness in the finished laminate. Although stiffness is not one of polyester's advantages, it does have excellent resistance to impact damage and this property has led to an increase in its use for the building of canoes and kayaks which need to be able to withstand hard impacts without damage. In such an application the shape of the canoe provides all the stiffness that is necessary.

Forms of reinforcement

A great many types of reinforcement mats, fabrics and tapes are now available to the boatbuilder. Some incorporate only one type of fibre, while others make use of the properties of two or more fibres woven together in a variety of ways.

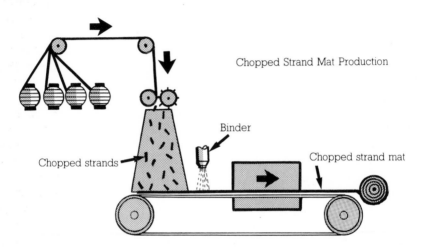

Chopped Strand Mat Production

Chopped strands

Binder

Chopped strand mat

Fig. 1.7 The production process of CSM – the most commonly used reinforcement material.

Fig. 1.8 A roll of CSM.

Chopped-strand mat (CSM)

By far the most common form of reinforcement currently used in FRP boatbuilding is chopped-strand mat (CSM). This consists of chopped strands of E glass, normally between 1 and 1¼in (25 and 30 mm) in length, which are allowed to fall in a random pattern on to a moving belt where they are impregnated with a binder to hold them in position. Two types of binder are used in CSM production: a polyester resin powder and an emulsion usually consisting of polyvinyl acetate. The emulsion-bound mat is less stiff than the powder-bound one and therefore is easier to handle, drapes well and is slightly easier to wet-out with resin. It has been shown, however, that the emulsion binder is much more sensitive to moisture than the powder binder and it is strongly recommended that only mats with powder binders are used for boatbuilding.

The advantages of CSM are primarily ease of use and cheapness. It is usually easy to wet-out as the mat absorbs resin well, although this will not be true if too heavy a mat is used. Because CSM is bulky, it thickens the laminate and this is an advantage as the stiffness of a laminate is a function of the cube of its thickness so the use of CSM allows the required stiffness to be built up cheaply. The other main advantage in using CSM is that it results in a laminate which has approximately equal properties in all directions in the plane of the laminate. This quasi-isotropic property is not shared by woven or non-woven fabrics since in these the fibres are arranged in one or two

Fig. 1.9(a) Surfacing tissue.

Fig. 1.9(b) An alternative form which uses no binder is continuous filament-stitched mat.

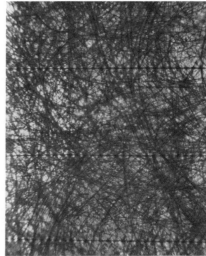

directions. In practice, however, even CSM may have fibres arranged with some preferential orientation as a result of the method of manufacture which tends to result in more fibres lying in one direction than any other. Because of this the wise boatbuilder will build up a laminate with alternate layers of mat laid at right angles.

Although CSM is the most popular form of reinforcement among production boatbuilders, it does have several disadvantages which make it unsuitable for strong but light structures. Using CSM results in the weakest laminate of all reinforcements, partly because it consists of discontinuous fibres which cannot give the strength properties of continuous fibres, and partly because it is impossible to achieve a high glass content in a laminate of CSM. Because the resin component of a laminate is relatively weak compared to the reinforcement, it is vital to have a high fibre content to achieve high strength. When using CSM a typical achievable glass content would be 20 per cent by volume or 30 per cent by weight. By using more efficient forms of reinforcement fibre, contents as high as 65 per cent by volume or 80 per cent by weight can be achieved depending on the method employed for construction.

Surfacing tissue

Surfacing tissue is a very light-weight mat made of thin layers of discontinuous glass fibres or filaments held together with a binder. It is used as the last, and sometimes the first, layer in a laminate to give a smooth surface finish. Used on laminates of CSM, it can sometimes be employed to advantage in other forms of reinforcement.

Rovings

As explained earlier, rovings of glass consist of a number of strands, up to about 120, gathered together and wound on to a spool. Rovings are usually classified into two main types: those for chopping and those for weaving. Rovings for chopping are often used in boatbuilding when spray-up moulding is employed. In this system a chopping head is mounted on a spray gun and rovings are chopped, mixed with a resin and hardener and sprayed directly into the mould, removing the need for mat or other reinforcement to be cut and laid. The same disadvantages as the use of CSM apply to this method, however, the only advantages being a faster and cheaper operation.

Rovings for weaving will be dealt with under 'Fabrics' (below) but it should be mentioned here that weaving-quality rovings are occasionally used directly for hand lay-up to reinforce selected areas of a moulding. Glass rovings can be of E, S or R glass, the first being by far the most commonly used in boatbuilding at present.

Fig. 1.10 A roll of rovings for spraying.

Fig. 1.10(a) A comparison of the price of woven fabrics using the range of fibres available.

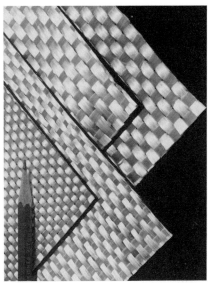

Fig. 1.11 A range of weight of E-glass woven rovings.

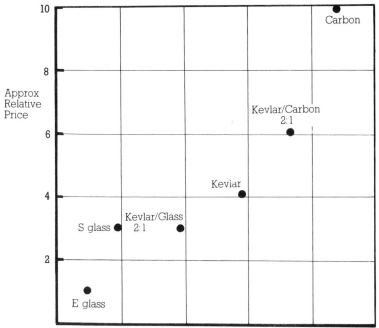

Relative Price for Woven Fabric 200g/m²

Fabrics

For high-performance laminates, i.e. ones designed to be light but strong, the best form of reinforcement is a woven fabric since these allow a high fibre-to-resin ratio to be achieved, give a thin laminate and enable the designer or builder to tailor the strength properties of the laminate to the end use.

Fabrics can be made from any of the fibres previously discussed, either singly or in any combination of fibres. Fabrics made from E, S or R glass can be made either from yarns which consist of two or more strands twisted together or they can be woven from rovings comprising groups of untwisted strands. Glass cloths made from yarns are usually at the lighter end of the fabric range, while heavier fabrics are nearly always made from rovings and are often referred to as 'woven rovings'. E glass woven rovings are, after CSM, the most common form of reinforcement used by boatbuilders.

Cloths produced from twisted yarns are easier to produce than woven rovings since the twisting of the yarns makes them more stable in the weaving process, but they are not as strong, weight for weight, as woven rovings. This is because twisted yarns involve more stages of production than rovings and hence expose the fibres to further abrasion damage. Twisted yarns are also harder to wet-out with resin due to their construction, and this can result in a weaker laminate because of the presence of voids.

Kevlar and carbon fibres are available in woven forms similar to glass fibres. Kevlar is nearly always woven in untwisted form or with only a couple of turns per metre twist, while carbon fibres are woven in both twisted yarn and untwisted rovings forms. In the case of twisted carbon fibre yarns, the amount of twist will vary up to about fifteen turns per metre.

Consistency in weight is a great advantage of woven fabrics over other forms such as CSM. Fabrics are also consistent in thickness and free from holes that can weaken a laminate. Because the yarns or rovings in woven fabrics are arranged in precise directions, more fibres can be contained in a given volume which results in superior strength properties when compared to mats. Fabrics are also easier to work with since they are usually easy to position and to cut, even when wet.

Fabrics are composed of yarns or rovings running in two directions, usually at right angles to each other. Warp threads (either yarn or roving) are the longitudinal ones, while the threads running across the width are known as the weft. Warp threads are often referred to as 'ends' and weft threads as 'picks'. Fabrics are distinguished by the pattern of the weave: that is, the way in which the warp ends and weft picks cross each other; the number of warp ends and weft picks per square inch or centimetre; and the weight of the fabric in oz/yd^2 or g/m^2 which depends on the construction and the type of yarn or roving being used.

Other features usually quoted are the width of the fabric, the way in which the edges are finished – raw, bonded or woven, for instance – and the type of finish or size that is applied. As we have already seen, glass-fibre fabrics may have a size applied suitable for weaving only, or may have one that is compatible with resins used for laminating. Fabric sizes will need to be burned off after the weaving process and a new, plastic size applied to suit the resin system that will be used. Kevlar fabrics are usually left unsized except for the previously mentioned proprietary finish used by one manufacturer when a polyester resin system is to be used. The size applied to carbon fibres before weaving is resin compatible and no further finishing is required.

Weave patterns

Fabrics are available in a variety of patterns, each of which will have differing characteristics. The type of weave affects the ease with which the fabric can be wetted-out with resin and the facility with which it can be draped around curves of varying tightness. There is also a definite increase in the strength of laminates made with more open-weave fabrics which is a result of the lower crimp of the yarns or rovings.

Plain weave   The simplest weave pattern is a plain weave in which each warp end and weft pick passes under one pick or end and over the next.

Plain weave fabrics do not distort easily but tightly woven ones can be difficult to wet-out. The high crimp caused by the tight interlacing results in a reduction of strength properties compared with other styles, but the plain weave is easy to handle and gives a consistent laminate thickness.

Twill weave   In fabrics with a twill weave the interlacing of warp ends and

Fig. 1.12 Plain weave – very stable.   Twill weave – good drape and handling.

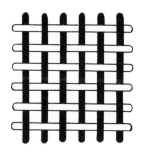

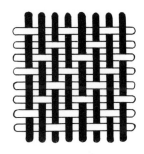

PLAIN WEAVE   TWILL WEAVE

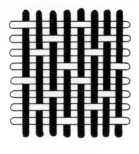

SATIN WEAVE

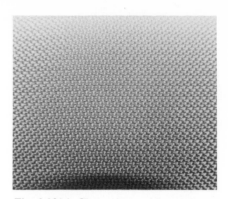

Fig. 1.13 Satin weave has excellent mechanical properties but needs careful handling.

Fig. 1.13(a) Close weave 4 harness satin of S glass.

weft picks can be varied to give twills of different constructions such as 2 × 2 or 2 × 1. In the 2 × 1 construction each warp end passes over two weft picks and under one pick while each weft pick passes under two ends and over one. Twills are much easier to wet-out than plain weaves and are more easily contoured to follow curved shapes. The crimp is less than a plain weave, giving a flatter fabric with superior mechanical properties.

Satin weave   Satin-weave fabrics are similar to twill weaves but have fewer intersections because the number of ends and picks that pass over each other before interlacing is greater. A typical designation would be '5 harness satin' or '5 end satin', which means that each warp end passes over four picks and under one while each pick passes under four ends and over one. The terms 'harness' and 'end' are interchangeable in this sense. Sometimes a 4 harness satin is referred to as 'crowsfoot weave', usually by American producers.

Satin-weave fabrics are very flat, with one side consisting mainly of warp ends and the other of weft picks. This flatness gives excellent drapability and ease of wetting-out as well as very good mechanical properties because of the low crimp. The use of satin weaves also results in a laminate of minimum thickness with a smooth surface, but against these advantages must be offset some difficulty in handling due to the looseness of the weave and a danger of disturbing the lay of the fibres while wetting-out.

Matt weave   In a matt-weave fabric two or more threads are woven as a single thread in both the warp and weft directions. It is used especially with Kevlar, which is available for weaving in relatively small yarns, and the style has the advantage that heavy, relatively cheap fabric can be woven from small individual yarns. Matt-weave fabrics can be produced in plain, twill, satin or other weave styles. American producers sometimes refer to matt

MATT WEAVE   UNIDIRECTIONAL WEAVE

Fig. 1.14 Matt weave – two or more threads woven as a single thread.

Fig. 1.15 Unidirectional weave.

weave as basket weave.

Construction

The most common form of construction is a balanced one in which the warp ends and weft picks are approximately equal in number and size. This balanced construction gives equal strength properties in both warp and weft directions. It must be realized, however, that even a balanced weave does not possess equal properties in all directions in the plane of the fabric.

As has already been mentioned, a chopped-strand mat has isotropic properties within the plane of the mat but a woven fabric has its strength properties concentrated along the lines of the fibres. Thus, while a balanced weave shows high strength properties when subjected to stress along the warp or weft, these properties will drop markedly if the stress is directed along, say, a direction at 45° to the warp or weft.

By varying the number or size of the ends or picks used in the construction, strength properties can be concentrated along either the warp or weft direction to suit various applications. Although a balanced construction is the most common, bi-directional fabrics can have the properties concentrated up to about 70:30 warp/weft or weft/warp directions.

Unidirectional weave When 70 per cent or more of the properties of the fabric are concentrated into one direction the weave is known as unidirectional. Unidirectional fabrics or tapes – narrow widths are more common for these materials – are generally made from rovings held together with an occasional fine thread at right angles to the main fibres and woven into them or glued or knitted to one side of them – the latter method having the advantage of eliminating kinks and easing wetting-out. This form of reinforcement has extremely pronounced directional strength properties, being very weak in any direction but along the line of the fibres. It does,

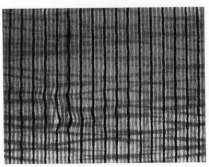

Fig. 1.16 Unidirectional carbon tape with glass traces and weft. These show when full wetting has occurred and keep the carbon rovings in line.

Fig. 1.17 UD glass and carbon with stitched random weft fibres to hold UD fibres in place.

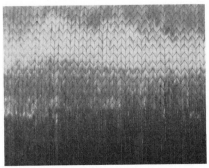

Fig. 1.18 Non-woven UD carbon tape.

Fig. 1.19 UD stitched glass cloth. Stitching holds the UD fibres parallel and causes no kinking.

however, make it possible to reinforce selected areas of a moulding by adding high strength to those areas where the loading is limited to one determinable direction.

It is also possible to construct a laminate from unidirectional tapes or fabrics by varying the orientation of successive layers. An advantage of this approach would be the minimum thickness of the resulting laminate and a possible fibre-to-resin ratio that could, in theory, exceed that obtainable by using a woven fabric.

Unidirectional tapes are, on the other hand, more difficult to handle than a woven fabric and more susceptible to disturbance during wetting-out.

Hybrids   When used to describe a fabric, the term 'hybrid' means that the material has been woven from two, or possibly more, different fibres. The advantage of incorporating two different fibres into one fabric is that the

Fig. 1.20 Five types of hybrid cloth. *From left to right:* (1) 2 Kevlar/1 carbon balanced twill. (2) 2 carbon/1 Kevlar balanced twill. (3) Unbalanced twill carbon weft, Kevlar warp. (4) 4 harness satin, Kevlar/carbon. The bi-plane construction gives mostly Kevlar on one side and mostly carbon on the other. (5) E glass Kevlar 2 × 2 twill.

Fig. 1.21 A 2 × 2 twill of Kevlar/carbon.

Fig. 1.22 A coarse Kevlar/glass satin stitched to glass mat.

properties of that fabric, and hence the laminate in which it is used, can be adjusted to fall anywhere between the properties of the individual fibres.

If, for example, it was necessary to achieve a stiff laminate with good resistance to impact damage and the lowest possible weight, the designer might choose to use a hybrid fabric of carbon fibres and Kevlar. In this case the carbon fibres would provide the stiffness, the Kevlar would contribute impact resistance, and the use of both in preference to, say, S glass would allow weight savings to be made.

In much the same way, any combination of E glass, S glass or R glass, carbon fibres or Kevlar may be used to optimize any chosen properties, including price.

Hybrids of all the above fibres are now available to the boatbuilder in the full range of styles already described.

Pre-pregs

The most recent material to find its way from the aerospace industries to boatbuilding is pre-impregnated fabrics and tapes, commonly known as 'pre-pregs'. The term covers any woven or non-woven reinforcing fibre that has been impregnated by the manufacturer with a catalysed resin. The resins used on pre-pregs suitable for boat construction are nearly all epoxy and are designed to cure fully only under conditions of high temperature and pressure.

The resin is applied to the fabric by rollers and is carefully controlled to give the optimum fibre-to-resin ratio for the type of fabric and the end use. Pre-pregs intended for bonding to honeycomb cores have a generally higher resin content to allow for good adhesion, while pre-pregs for laminating will have a lower resin content to give the optimum fibre volume and hence strength properties. Although the resin used is pre-catalysed, the shelf life of most pre-pregs is several months. The required storage conditions vary from a cool, dry environment to refrigeration.

Pre-pregs are covered on both faces by protective coverings and these should not be removed until the fabric has been cut to size and is ready for use. Pre-preg fabrics and tapes are usually tacky to some degree, which is an advantage, since it means that the fabric, when cut to shape and placed into the mould, will retain its position. It is best if the degree of tackiness is not too great or it will be difficult to adjust or re-position pieces as necessary. Should the fabric not be tacky enough to hold its position on a highly curved mould, a warm-air blower can be used to increase the tackiness.

The use of pre-pregs has many advantages, not least the fact that they are clean and relatively easy to handle, and can provide an optimum strength laminate because of the strict control over fibre-to-resin ratio. Unfortunately their use does demand the application of pressure and an elevated temperature, both of which are beyond the capabilities of the majority of boatbuilding yards at the present time. However, their use is bound to increase, initially for the construction of high-performance boats where cost is no object, and the methods of using pre-pregs are further described in Chapter 7.

2 RESIN SYSTEMS

If the full potential of any FRP laminate is to be achieved, the role of the resin matrix used to encase the reinforcement fibres is as vital as the role of the fibres themselves.

Three different resin systems are commonly available for marine laminates: polyester, epoxy and vinylester, although many other systems are used for different FRP applications. Of the three of interest to us, polyester resins were the first to be used and remain by far the most common type, accounting for perhaps 95 per cent of the total resin usage.

All three types come into the class known as thermosetting resins, setting, when suitably catalysed, into a hard, largely insoluble and infusible solid, unlike thermoplastic resins which can be melted and re-used by the application of heat.

Although the strength properties of any of the resins are many times lower than the fibre part of an FRP laminate, their role is a vital one. For our purposes a suitable resin must be able to protect the fibre reinforcement fully from the external environment, in particular against water absorption, abrasion and chemical damage, and it must also be able to adhere strongly to the individual fibres of the reinforcement. For the fibre part of the laminate to do its job, the resin matrix which surrounds and protects the fibres must be able to transmit any applied stress equally amongst the reinforcement fibres, and this property is dependent on the adhesive bond between resin and fibres. If, under stress, adhesion breaks down at any point, the matrix is no longer fully able to pass the stress throughout the laminate, cracks will occur and the weak spots formed will reduce the strength of the laminate.

Although the mechanical properties of resins are low, they are still important in their effect on the behaviour of the laminate as a whole. Unfortunately, the many different chemical variations possible even within a given class of resin make it impossible to talk in anything other than very general terms about resin properties.

It is, however, true to say that the ideal resin should be 'tough', that is, it should have a high ultimate tensile strength (UTS) but, at the same time, it should have a reasonable elongation at break. However, these two properties are, to a certain extent, difficult to reconcile since a high UTS usually

Fig. 2.1 The fibre reinforcement may be the element that gives a moulding its strength, but it is the resin system that forms the matrix, and also provides the good finish.

Fig. 2.1(a) Resins and their hardeners can be bought in various quantities. Here an epoxy resin and hardener available in small amounts to suit the small maintenance job comes with handy pumps to aid dispensing and measuring.

results in a brittle resin while good-elongation resins often exhibit low strength, a low heat-deflection temperature (HDT) and poor water resistance.

The heat-deflection temperature mentioned above is a measurement of the temperature at which a standard bar of cast resin under a defined load undergoes an arbitrary deflection. In other words, the HDT figure is a rough guide to the temperature range over which the physical properties of the resin can be expected to remain constant. For some high-temperature FRP applications, the HDT is an important factor, but for boatbuilding, where the finished product is unlikely to be subjected to high temperatures, the HDT is of less importance although a resin with an HDT of less than 140°F (60°C) should be avoided.

Although, as stated above, a relatively high UTS and a good elongation at break are among the most important of a resin's physical properties, the long-term properties are also very important if a laminate is to have a reasonable working life. Therefore a good resin should exhibit good fatigue resistance, particulary under regularly recurring stress cycles. The resin should be able to be stressed to a high proportion of its UTS but still be able to recover without permanent distortion when the stress is removed. In addition, the resin must not have a critical failure mode, i.e. the resin must resist the spread of cracks and fibre/resin adhesive failure within the

laminate. When looking for a boatbuilding resin suitable for a high-perform-ance laminate, a UTS in the region of 60MPa and an elongation at break of about 2.5 per cent plus should be aimed at.

Water resistance and, to a lesser extent, chemical resistance, is a primary requirement of a resin designed for marine use. It has been, for many years, a widely held misconception that plastic resins as used in boatbuilding are impervious to damage from water or water vapour. Indeed, one of the strongest selling points for 'plastic' boats has been their immunity to damage from the environment. Now, twenty-five years after FRP made its first real impact on production boatbuilding, it is widely recognized that it can be, and often is, damaged through the absorption of water. This problem is covered in detail in Chapter 11, but it should be mentioned here that the type of resin chosen for a laminate has an important influence on the water resistance of the moulding.

In addition to the choice of resin, other factors such as the type of fibre reinforcement, the moulding process, the resin/glass ratio and the surface finish will all affect the weather resistance of the finished moulding. When a high-performance laminate is required, problems can arise in reconciling the needs for high mechanical properties with the requirement of good resistance to environmental damage. For the laminate to show high mechanical properties, the ratio of fibre to resin must be as high as possible;

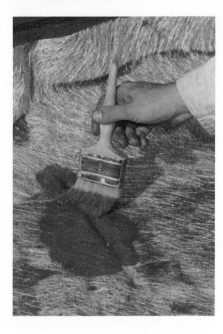

Fig. 2.1(b) Whatever resin is used it must be able to wet-out the reinforcement quickly and thoroughly with a minimum of effort.

Fig. 2.1(c) Good site-ventilation is important when working with all resin systems. In the production moulding shown here an extractor is used to remove fumes from inside the mould.

while for weather resistance the laminate should have a high resin ratio, at least in the outer layers. When these two requirements have to be reconciled, it is very important that only a top-performance resin system is chosen.

Despite the importance of mechanical and weather-resistant properties, there are other properties that the resin must exhibit if it is to be suitable for use by the boatbuilder. Primary among these is the ease with which the resin can be worked and its suitability for the production process chosen by the builder.

It is important that the resin is able to wet-out the fibres quickly and thoroughly, but this ability is as much a function of the fibre type, surface size and type of fabric weave as it is a function of the resin. However, the viscosity of the resin will greatly affect the ease with which wetting-out can be achieved and the effort that the laminator has to put into the consolidating of the resin and fibres. Typical viscosities for suitable resins are in the region of 400–800 cps, but it must be remembered that resin viscosity is temperature dependent, so a low working temperature can make an otherwise accept-able resin difficult to work with. It cannot be emphasized enough that thorough penetration of the fibres is essential if the laminate is to perform up to its design requirements. It is impossible to prevent voids occurring completely, but every effort should be taken to reduce them to a minimum because it has been shown that, for each 1 per cent void content, the

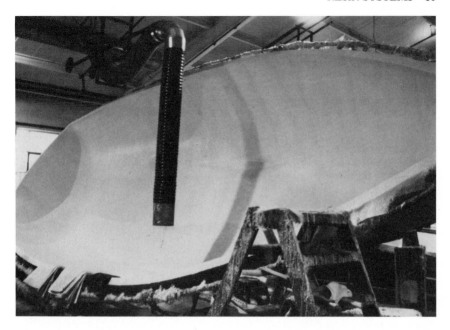

interlaminar shear strength of the laminate is reduced by about 7 per cent up to about 4 per cent total voids.

Resins of low viscosity are easy to work with but can often result in drainage problems on vertical or near-vertical surfaces, particularly in laminates with high resin-to-fibre ratios. To overcome this problem, thixotropic resins are normally used. With these resins the viscosity remains low when the resin is brushed or rolled but rapidly increases when brushing is stopped to prevent the resin sagging and draining off the surface. All the classes of resins are available in thixotropic or non-thixotropic forms or a thixotropic filler can be added to the resin to give this property. It has to be accepted that a thixotropic resin will be slightly less good at wetting-out the fibres, but without this property more serious effects of resin starvation would occur on sloping surfaces.

Of primary importance to the boatbuilder is the ability of the resin system to achieve good mechanical, chemical and weather-resistant properties after being cured at room temperature. There are many resins available that can give superb results after being cured at high temperatures, but few boatbuilders have the facilities to cure mouldings at these temperatures. If these resins are used for room-temperature cure, the results will be far lower than expected and less good than if a resin designed for room temperature is used. It must be said, however, that for a high-performance, light-weight laminate the best results can be obtained only when the moulding can be post-cured (matured) at an elevated temperature.

Whatever system of moulding is used, be it hand lay-up, a spray system, resin injection or vacuum systems, and whatever type of fibre reinforcement is used, it is very important that a resin system suitable for that particular application is chosen. Since most boatbuilders cannot afford to keep a chemist on the staff, the resin manufacturer should be consulted and his recommendations followed exactly.

Finally, in this introduction to the requirements of a resin system, we must not forget the importance of cost and toxicity. Although cost is obviously of importance to any builder, it should never be placed above all other considerations or the performance of the finished moulding is bound to suffer. When resin systems are compared, many people dismiss a high-performance system because of cost. This can be seen to be a short-sighted view when one realizes that the difference in cost between a cheap, low-performance system and the more expensive but better resin is a tiny percentage of the cost of the whole boat yet the moulding is one part of the boat that cannot be replaced. The hull and decks of any yacht are no place for cost cutting.

The toxicity of all materials connected with FRP boatbuilding must always be considered, and here again the best plan is to follow the recommendations of the individual manufacturers. Different classes of resins and individual resins within those classes can vary considerably in the degree and nature of possible toxic effects. Some resins, and more particularly their hardening systems, may cause dermatitis in sensitive individuals, and once sensitized the individual may not be able to tolerate even the briefest exposure to the material without symptoms recurring, although such extreme sensitivity is unusual. In all cases prevention is better than cure, and suitable protective clothing, barrier creams and site ventilation should be used to reduce the exposure to these materials to a minimum.

Laminating resins

Polyester resins

Polyester resins, by far the most commonly used class, comprise an extremely varied group with physical properties that range from strong but brittle to extremely flexible, each with their own particular application. Continual improvements in the choice and use of raw materials and a range of curing systems have provided the user with a class of resin of great versatility suited to a wide range of process requirements.

The resins referred to here are the unsaturated polyester types produced by reacting a combination of saturated and unsaturated organic acids

SCHEMATIC MANUFACTURE
OF POLYESTER

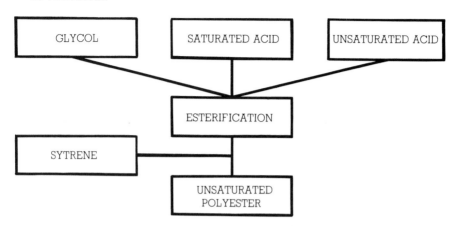

Fig. 2.2 The manufacture of polyester resin. The properties of the finished resin may be altered by varying the proportions of the components and by using different acids and glycols. Additives may also be used to give different properties.

(commonly phthalic and maleic anhydrides) with a glycol such as propylene glycol or ethylene glycol, and dissolving the mixture in a reactive monomer, a modifying agent, that is most commonly styrene.

Besides dissolving the polyester resin, the styrene monomer has the important property of reacting with the unsaturated acid during the curing process, cross-linking the polyester molecules and forming a co-polymer of polyester and styrene. Thus the monomer is not a solvent in the usual sense of the word but is an active part of the resin.

Several different acids, glycols and modifying agents can be used, depending on the required physical properties of the resin. Indeed, because of the wide range of acids and glycols available to the formulator, it is possible to tailor-make a polyester for specific purposes.

The curing process

To produce an FRP laminate the polyester resin must first gel and then harden, and this curing process is achieved by the addition of a suitable catalyst, sometimes called an initiator. Catalysts for polyester resins are usually organic peroxides in paste or liquid form mixed with suitable diluents to about 50 per cent in solution. The most common catalyst is Methyl Ethylketone peroxide (MEK peroxide) which, being a liquid, is easy to measure volumetrically in small quantities. The amount needed is usually 1 or 2 per cent. No less than the minimum level of catalyst should be used – or the laminate may not cure. MEK peroxide gives an even and complete cure and there are several variations for different applications. Another peroxide sometimes used for a fast cure is Acetyl acetone peroxide, but because of the heat build-up generated by a fast cure, this catalyst is not normally used for laminates thicker than about $\frac{1}{6}$ in (4 mm).

Catalysts are inflammable in most forms and hence care must be taken in their handling and storage; they are also caustic, so skin contact should be avoided. Peroxides can lose their strength with age, so old catalyst should be tested on a small sample before being used for laminating.

Curing begins as soon as catalyst and resin are mixed, but the rate of cure is too slow for practical purposes. The process can be speeded up by the application of heat or, far more commonly, by the addition to the resin of an accelerator to promote the reaction at room temperature. Many chemical compounds can be used as accelerators, but the most common types are based on cobalt soaps or tertiary amines. As with catalysts for polyester resins, only small amounts of accelerator are needed, typically 1 or 2 per cent. Unfortunately, the substances used for catalyst and accelerator will, if mixed directly together, react explosively. For safety purposes it is, therefore, far better to use only resins that are pre-accelerated by the manufacturer and require only the addition of the catalyst. There are no practical disadvantages to using pre-accelerated resins; the effect on shelf-life is insignificant, and although the working temperature range of the resin may be somewhat reduced, that too is not usually a problem. If, by any chance, it is necessary to add both accelerator and catalyst yourself, the accelerator should be added first and thoroughly mixed before the catalyst is added. At all times bottles containing the two substances should be kept well apart and a different mixing container used for each.

As with the other thermosetting resins considered here, the curing process is exothermic – heat is generated within the resin during the curing process – and the temperature of the resin could reach a level of 302°F (150°C) or more in a solid casting, depending on the level of unsaturation of the resin and the speed of the reaction. In a laminate, on the other hand, the exotherm temperature will be much lower because of the large surface area usually available to dissipate heat.

The curing process can be split into three separate stages. First is the gel time of the resin – the time between the mixing of catalyst and resin and the point when the mixed resin sets to a firm gel when the exotherm begins. The period just after the resin has set firm – its 'green stage' – is, incidentally, the best time for trimming the edges of a laminate since the resin is then rubbery and can be trimmed with a sharp knife. Both gel time and hardening time are considerably dependent on temperature. After the gel time comes the hardening time: the period necessary for the resin to achieve a hard cure when it will be rigid enough to remove from the mould if necessary. The final stage is the maturing time, during which the moulding develops its full hardness and stability. The maturing process is a vital part of the curing of the laminate and may take days or even weeks depending on the temperature at which the moulding is kept. This should certainly be no less than room temperature if a good result is to be obtained, but when the optimum properties of the resin are to be obtained it is necessary to postcure the laminate at an elevated temperature. In general, the higher the temperature at which postcure takes place, the quicker the time taken for the moulding to reach full hardness, but the temperature should always be kept safely under the heat-deflection temperature of the resin.

One of the reasons why polyester resins have achieved such popularity with boatbuilders, apart from their ready availability, is their general ability to be used at room temperature. This does not mean, however, that the best performance can be had out of a polyester resin if it is used in cold conditions. The boatbuilder should aim for a temperature in the moulding shop of 64–68°F (18–20°C) and the moulding should be kept at this temperature (or preferably a higher one) until it is fully cured. Although the moulding can be removed from the mould before it is completely matured, it is advisable, where practical, to mature the laminate in the mould so that no distortion can take place.

Properties

The ready availability and comparatively low price of polyesters make them an obvious choice for boatbuilding and indeed their cured properties are perfectly adequate for a whole range of marine uses, but it must be said that these properties are not always acceptable for the moulding of high-performance laminates.

Among the properties that are open to doubt for high-performance use are poor elongation at break, high shrinkage on cure and questionable adhesive- and water-resistant properties. Elongation at break is important since, if the resin matrix is to transmit applied stress throughout the fibre reinforcement, the resin must be able to stretch to at least the same extent as will the fibres under load. If the resin breaks down before the fibres have stretched to the point where they are taking their full share of the load, the laminate will fail at a lower stress than the reinforcement is capable of resisting. A typical figure for elongation of polyester is 2 per cent, well below the elongation at break of all the reinforcement fibres except carbon.

Adhesion of the resin matrix to the individual fibres of the reinforcement is also vital if resin and reinforcement are to work together efficiently. While the adhesion of polyester is perfectly acceptable for most purposes, this property is not as good as in some other resin systems such as epoxy and may be a limiting factor in the design of high-strength laminates. One of the reasons for this is the relatively high shrinkage that occurs when a polyester

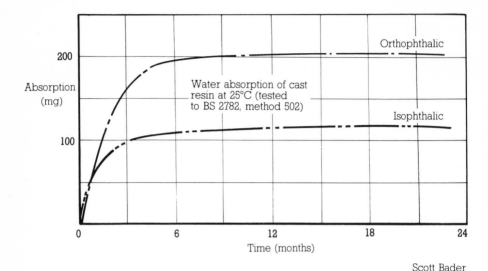

Scott Bader

Fig. 2.3 A comparison of the water-absorption of cast resin at 25°C. Isophthalic polyester is clearly superior to the orthophthalic type.

Fig. 2.4 Isophthalic polyester also scores on flexural fatigue tests.

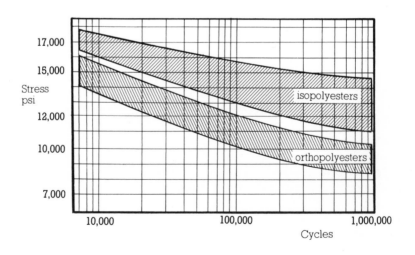

cures, typically around 7–8 per cent, which results in built-in stresses in the moulding and a less resilient laminate.

The water resistance of a laminate is, for marine use, of obvious importance. While this property is dependent on many factors (see also Chapter 11), the resistance of the resin matrix to water penetration is of critical importance. The correct type of polyester resin in a well-cured laminate is usually perfectly acceptable from this point of view, but if a high fibre-to-resin ratio is used, such as in a high-strength laminate, problems may still occur.

The original demand from the boatbuilding industry was for a general-purpose polyester resin of low cost. In those early days only orthophalic acid-based resins were available and these are the polyester resins that have been most commonly used. In recent years, however, polyester resins based on isophalic acids have become available and these have several advantages over the older type.

In particular, isophalic polyesters show a marked improvement in their resistance to absorption of water and water vapour. They also exhibit increased strength, flexibility and abrasion resistance, and a laminate moulded with this type of polyester will have an improved impact resistance and fatigue performance. For these reasons it is recommended that only isophalic polyesters be used for marine laminates that need to show good performance and a long life. Because this type of polyester costs slightly more than the general-purpose type, there has been some reluctance amongst builders to use them as a matter of course. Prospective buyers should, however, insist on the use of this type if polyester is chosen since, as has already been noted, there is little excuse for penny-pinching at the moulding stage.

Additives

A variety of additives are available which can improve specific properties of polyester resins, modify their characteristics and/or reduce their cost. The most obvious additive is pigment used to colour the resins. A pigment additive usually comes in paste form and only enough should be added to achieve the required density of colour. Usually 10 per cent by weight is sufficient. Too much colour pigment, like other fillers, can harm the physical properties of the resin, especially the water-resistant properties.

Ready-pigmented resins are now commonly available and have many advantages. In particular, colour matching is made possible – if mixing your own pigment you are unlikely to be able to repeat the exact colour in subsequent batches. While gel-coat resins are usually pigmented, it is best to use unpigmented resin for laminating up to the final topcoat on the inside of the laminate. Using a clear resin for laminating allows the laminator to see deficiencies and voids in the moulding which gives a better chance of their being corrected.

When polyester has cured at room temperature it is noticeable that the side of the laminate exposed to air is sticky to the touch. This is because the presence of air has the effect of inhibiting the curing process. To counteract this, a waxed resin is used for the final coat. The wax settles on the surface, excludes the air and allows a complete cure. It is important that a waxed resin is used only for the final topcoat, not inside the laminate, otherwise the adhesion between the layers of resin will be weakened.

Other additives available for polyester resins include thixotropic agents, flexibilizers, and fire-retardant agents. The trend nowadays is towards resins designed for specific purposes with all the necessary additives incorporated by the manufacturer. This is far better than the user having to mix the additives into the base resin since it removes the possibility of error and makes for more consistent results.

Epoxy resins

Epoxy resins, sometimes called epoxide resins, are a class of thermoset resins with a very wide range of possible starting materials that give them extreme versatility in both their end uses and the techniques used to process them. In one form or another epoxy resins can be used as laminating resins, adhesives, sealing compounds, paints and varnishes, casting resins, dipping compounds, moulding powders and floor-surfacing resins. Because of their versatility and their many advantages over other resin systems, they have found uses in a wide variety of applications ranging from satellites, bridges, roads and commercial and military aircraft to sporting equipment and, lately, many types of boats.

The development of epoxy resins dates back to the 1920s, but it was not until the early 1960s that the exploitation of their properties really began. Since then progress has continued at an increasing pace, with much work taking place in the development of the resin systems and especially in the development of new curing systems.

The chemistry of epoxy resins and their hardening systems is very extensive and varied and the correct choice of system is vital if the end product is to suit the user's process requirements. Because of the complicated chemistry of epoxies, the following description of this class of resin must be necessarily brief and general. For the professional user it is important to build up a good working relationship with a supplier who formulates resins suitable for one's needs.

Epoxy resins may be defined as those in which cross-linking occurs through reactions of the epoxide group which is the chief centre of their reactivity. In their basic state the resins can be either liquid or solid and are, at this stage, thermoplastic, with the ability to be softened by heat and hardened by cooling. Their conversion into a solid thermosetting plastic occurs through a process of polymerization brought about by the addition of a reactive hardener. Once the hardener has been added, a non-reversible change takes place during which the resin molecules are cross-linked together by strong covalent bonds.

Unlike polyester resins in which the proportion of catalyst to resin is usually in the order of 1–2 per cent, the epoxy-resin-to-hardener ratio can vary considerably, depending on the system used, sometimes being as high as 1:1. While it is possible to vary the amount of catalyst added to a polyester resin in order to control the gel time of the resin, the process of curing of an epoxy does not allow this, and the correct ratio of hardener to resin must always be used. Because of this, control of the gel time of the resin can only be achieved if the ambient temperature can be controlled or if a choice of slow, medium or fast hardeners is available. Where room-temperature systems are concerned, it is becoming more common for a range of hardeners to be sold for different working conditions. As with polyester, the curing reaction is exothermic and the comments made earlier apply equally to an epoxy resin. In particular, the user should avoid mixing a large amount of resin and hardener in a small pot or the temperature rise due to the exotherm will noticeably shorten the pot-life of the mix.

Although some users will see the inability to control the gel time by varying the amount of hardener as a disadvantage, it should be realized that gel times, and hence pot-life or working time, vary considerably with the choice of system, and epoxy resins can be had with gel times as short as a few seconds or as long as several weeks. For laminating, a working time of forty-five minutes to one hour at 68°F (20°C) is typical. Assuming that the user chooses a resin formulation appropriate to his needs and realizes the influence of temperature on the cure, few problems should arise.

Additives for epoxies

Since the basic resin-and-hardener combination alone is unlikely to provide a material with all the necessary properties for a given application, a range of additives can be used by the formulator to modify the basic properties. Typical additives might include a combination of diluents, inert fillers, flexibilizers, accelerators and fire-retardant agents.

Diluents are liquids used to reduce the viscosity of the basic resin and are necessary for a laminating resin in order to allow it to be easily worked and to give good wet-out properties. Diluents can be either non-reactive or can react chemically with the resin and hardener and are used in quite small amounts, typically 5–10 per cent by weight.

There are a variety of inert fillers available to the formulator to make a resin cheaper and to alter the physical characteristics of the cured resin. Such fillers can be used to increase the hardness of the resin, improve compressive strength or to impart thixotropic properties to the resin.

Because the cured resins are hard but brittle, flexibilizer additives are often used to give a more flexible resin which will be better able to withstand applied stresses. This property can be achieved by using a flexible epoxy resin or hardener or a reactive additive to give a long, flexible molecular chain on cure. Alternatively, a non-reactive additive may be used to give a flexible long chain molecule that remains unreacted on cure of the resin.

To alter the rate of reaction between the epoxy resin and the hardener, it is possible to add small quantities of a cure accelerator. Although this may help cure the system quickly at low temperatures, it does have the disadvantage, for our purposes, of tending to enbrittle the cured resin.

For some purposes it is necessary for the cured resin to exhibit fire-retardant properties and this can be achieved with epoxy systems by the choice of certain base resins and hardeners or by the use of certain fillers or diluents.

Properties

Although the excellent properties of epoxy resins have been known for a long time, they have, in the past, suffered from a lack of ready acceptance by boatbuilders who have pointed to the extra cost and difficulty of working with them as reasons for avoiding their use. This attitude is understandable, if somewhat unfair. Due to the high cost of the raw materials and their processing, the cost of epoxies is higher than that of a typical polyester. An epoxy resin suitable for the marine laminator will cost three or four times that of a polyester but, as has already been noted, this is a very small part of the total cost of most boats and, where a high-performance laminate is being considered, is a small price to pay for a significantly increased laminate performance.

The argument that epoxies are difficult to work with is based on the assumption that all epoxies have high viscosity and require a high-temperature cure. Nowadays this argument no longer holds true since marine laminating epoxies are generally available, are designed for room-temperature curing and have working properties similar to those of polyester.

Epoxies generally exhibit several significant advantages in terms of cured properties which are responsible for making them, as a class, the most popular for true high-performance laminates. For instance, their ability to adhere to a wide range of materials is of paramount importance in a laminate where the resin matrix must be able to adhere strongly to the fibre reinforcement in order to transmit the applied stresses throughout the laminate. It has been shown that the performance of epoxy at the resin/fibre interface is superior to that of the other resins available, which makes epoxy the obvious choice from this point of view. In laminates which make use of core materials, the adhesion of the resin to the core is also of vital importance, and in this case too epoxy scores.

The low shrinkage on cure of epoxies is another important point in their favour. Unlike polyester and vinylester resins which have only a 50–60 per cent solids content, epoxies are 100 per cent solids and have a shrinkage on cure in the region of 2 per cent compared to 7–8 per cent for polyesters. This low shrinkage reduces the stress built into the laminate with the result that a more resilient composite is obtained. In addition, laminates built with epoxies exhibit improved long-term fatigue resistance in comparison with polyesters because of the lack of the styrene configuration in the former.

Another advantage of epoxies is the potential for formulating a resin with excellent mechanical properties. In particular, the resin toughness described earlier is an improvement on polyester since an epoxy can be formulated to have excellent strength properties and an elongation at break in the order of 3 per cent or more. Indeed, if the strength properties of the resin can be reduced, it is possible to obtain an epoxy with an elongation at break up to about 6 per cent. This factor makes the epoxies better able to translate fibre properties into laminate properties since the resin is less likely to break down before the fibre is at full elongation and taking its full share of the applied loading. The strength properties of this type of resin also help reduce the possibility of interlaminar shear failure, which occurs between layers of reinforcement when the resin matrix breaks down under load.

Epoxies also exhibit excellent resistance to abrasion and, most importantly for marine laminates, superior resistance to water absorption. In fact, the water resistance of epoxies is better even than polyurethane paints which, in turn, are superior to polyester resins. This ability, coupled with their adhesive properties, is the reason why epoxy-based paints are now commonly used on large industrial structures such as ships, bridges, etc., which have to withstand severe conditions.

The water-resistant properties of epoxy are important when a high-performance laminate is to be used since this type, having a high fibre-to-resin ratio, cannot afford the luxury of a high-resin-content outer layer simply to resist damage from the environment. In fact, with the many recent instances of osmosis in production craft, there is some case for the use of an epoxy system for even this type of boat.

Although high-performance epoxy resins have always been associated with high-temperature cures, it is now possible to obtain epoxy laminating resins formulated specifically for marine use which give excellent performance when cured at room temperature. However, the most benefit can be obtained, even from these resins, by following the initial cure at room temperature with a maturing postcure at a higher temperature. When this

Fig. 2.4(a) These two tables show the increase in resin properties given by a postcure at an elevated temperature. The resin is an epoxy laminating system designed for boatbuilding (*courtesy SP Systems Ltd*).

Mechanical properties of a clear casting cured for 14 days at 23°C

Property	Test method	S.I.	Imperial
Tensile strength	ISO R527	62.0 MPa	8,990 psi
Tensile modulus	ISO R527	3.35 GPa	4.858×10^5 psi
Elongation at break	ISO R527	2.85%	–
Flexural strength	ISO R178	101.2 MPa	14,674 psi
Flexural modulus	ISO R178	3.65 GPa	5.29×10^5 psi
Compressive strength	ISO 604	121.6 MPa	17,630 psi
Compressive modulus	ISO 604	4.7 GPa	6.81×10^5 psi
Coefficient of linear expansion (linear/°C $\times 10^{-6}$)	ASTM D696	56.7×10^{-6} linear/°C	
Deflection temperature	BS 2782 121A	55°C	

Mechanical properties of a clear casting cured at 25°C for 16 hours, followed by 80°C for 8 hours

Property	Test method	S.I.	Imperial
Tensile strength	ISO R527	82.1 MPa	12,000 psi
Tensile modulus	ISO R527	3.34 GPa	4.84×10^5 psi
Elongation at break	ISO R527	–	6.81%
Flexural strength	ISO R178	122.6 MPa	17,800 psi
Flexural modulus	ISO R178	3.52 GPa	5.1×10^5 psi
Compressive strength	ISO 604	119.2 MPa	17,280 psi
Compressive modulus	ISO 604	3.92 GPa	5.68×10^5 psi
Coefficient of linear expansion (linear/°C $\times 10^{-6}$)	ASTM D696	–	5.2×10^{-6} linear/°C
Deflection temperature	BS 2782 121A	–	78–80°C

Fig. 2.4(b) Unlike polyester resin, *above*, vinylester resins only have reactive positions at the ends of the molecular chains. This makes vinylester more resilient. Vinylesters also have less ester groups, thus they are less susceptible to water than polyesters. The portion within the brackets is repeated three to six times in polyester; one or two times in vinylester.

POLYESTER

n = 3 to 6

VINYLESTER

n = 1 to 2

Crosslinking

can be done, and any builder who intends to build high-performance craft should attempt to do so, the strength, elongation, heat-deflection temperature and water resistance will all be improved and the properties of the laminate will be optimized.

Many epoxy resins are quite toxic, although later systems have reduced this factor quite considerably. The most common problem from them, and in particular their hardening systems, is the dermatitic hazard. The best approach for the user is to avoid skin contact altogether by the use of suitable protective clothing, rubber gloves or a good barrier cream recommended by the resin manufacturer. Once an individual is sensitized to the resin, it may become impossible for him to be exposed to it without suffering recurrent symptoms. It is, therefore, best to avoid initial sensitization by taking the recommended precautions.

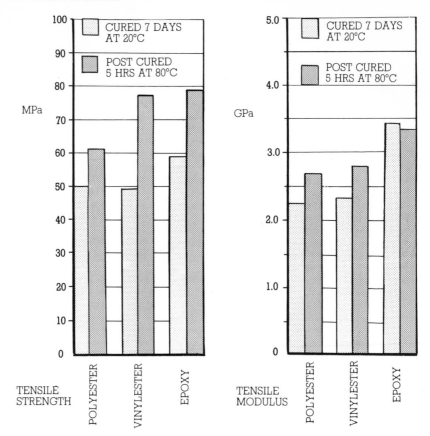

Fig. 2.4(c) Polyester, vinylester and epoxy resins compared for tensile strength and tensile modulus. Comparison shows systems cured at 20°C and 80°C.

Vinylester resins

A resin system relatively new to the boatbuilding world is vinylester resin, which owes its development mainly to the requirements of the chemical industry. Vinylester resin is similar to polyester in that it is reacted with styrene by a chain-reaction process initiated by the addition of catalyst and accelerator. Unlike that of a polyester, however, the reactive positions of a vinylester molecular chain occur only at the ends of the chain. The effect of this is to make vinylester a more flexible or resilient resin since the entire length of the resin chain is able to elongate to absorb shock loads.

The location of the ester groups – the reactive positions – at the end of the molecular chains only, also means that a vinylester chain has less ester groups than a polyester. Since it is the ester groups that are susceptible to attack by water, vinylester resins are more resistant to water than are polyesters.

Vinylesters, in fact, fit fairly neatly between polyester and epoxy resins when the three are compared in terms of mechanical properties, adhesion, water resistance and price. At the time of writing there appears to be a trend towards the use of vinylester resins for the building of high-performance one-off boats, but the reasons behind this may be suspect. It is true that vinylesters show improved performance when compared to polyesters, though some published figures for mechanical properties are more than a little misleading since they give figures for resin cured at an elevated temperature of up to 280°F (120°C). Working on these figures one could be led to believe that it is possible to achieve properties comparable with an epoxy system, whereas these properties can only be achieved at a postcure temperature that is unrealistic for the moulding of large marine laminates.

In particular, the good elongation properties of vinylester are often quoted as the reason for choosing such a system – figures given range from 3 to 7 per cent, depending on the particular resin, but these figures could not be achieved at room-temperature cure. Indeed, at normal curing temperatures the elongation properties of vinylester are unlikely to be significantly higher than those of a typical polyester.

The real reason why vinylester resins seem to be popular at the moment is probably that, while designers and builders recognize the need to upgrade the resin system for high-performance mouldings, they are reluctant to take the logical step of using epoxy, preferring instead to use a resin system similar in many ways, such as in the use of catalysts and accelerators, to the well-known polyesters. Also, of course, vinylester is somewhat cheaper than epoxy and this, no doubt, has an influence on the choice, which is out of proportion to the real extra cost of using an epoxy system.

The foregoing is not meant to suggest that vinylesters have no place in boatbuilding, but the fact is that their greatest strength, their high resistance to chemicals, is of little interest for marine purposes. If a vinylester is to be used, it must be remembered that, for the maximum properties to be obtained, the curing schedule must include an elevated-temperature postcure.

Gel-coat resins

The gel-coat is the outer resin layer of a female-moulded FRP laminate and its purpose is to protect the inner laminate from moisture and chemicals and to give the moulding the glossy, smooth, coloured finish that is the hallmark of

Fig. 2.5. A comparison of NGA isophthalic gel-coat and conventional gel-coat.

Mechanical/physical data in cured state

Properties	NGA-gelcoat	Conventional gelcoat	Unit	Test method	
Tensile strength	48	57	N/mm²	ISO/R	527–1966
Tensile elongation	2,7	2,9	%	ISO/R	527–1966
Flexural strength	90	85	N/mm²	ISO	178–1975
Flexural modulus	3,700	3,600	N/mm²	ISO	178–1975
Impact strength (Charpy)	8	7	mJ/mm²	ISO/R	179–1961
Volume shrinkage	6	6	%	ISO	3521–1976
Hardness, Barcol	35–40	35–40	934–1	ASTM D 2583–1975	
Heat distortion temp.	98	66	°C	ISO	75–1974
Water absorption after 28 days	71,6	78,4	mg/t.piece	ISO/R	179–1961

FRP. When a moulding is produced from a female mould, the gel-coat is the very first layer to be applied and will faithfully reproduce the detail and finish of the mould surface. When a male mould is used, the moulding is produced from the inside out with the outside surface the last to be applied, and in this case it is usual to paint the surface after fairing, filling and sanding rather than to use a gel-coat.

Virtually all gel-coat resins used in boatbuilding are polyesters and the comments made earlier about this class of resin apply equally to gel-coats as to laminating resins. The particular requirements of a gel-coat resin are that it should be highly water-resistant, scratch-resistant, flexible and impact-resistant and have good colour stability and gloss retention. A gel-coat resin must also be thixotropic in order to remain in position on the surface of the mould without running or sagging on vertical surfaces.

Polyester gel-coats can be produced from orthophalic polyesters but these are noticeably inferior to the isophalic polyesters, especially in water resistance and impact resistance, and cannot be recommended for marine use. A type of isophalic polyester incorporating neopentyl glycol has been shown to be superior to conventional isophalic polyester gel-coat resins and is to be recommended for all gel-coats where long-term water resistance, impact resistance, colour stability and gloss retention are of importance.

Another type of polyester gel-coat that should not be confused with those used for mouldings is tooling gel-coat. This is used to coat the surface of moulds to give a smooth, hard finish which is resistant to the heat that can be produced during laminating. Thus tooling gel-coat is based on a special heat-resisting polyester that gives the required properties for this specialist application, but would be unsuitable for use on a moulding.

If a vinylester laminating resin is to be used in the moulding, there is no need to use anything other than a polyester gel-coat, since the two systems are quite compatible. If an epoxy laminating resin is to be used, however, the situation is not quite as simple. When a polyester gel-coat is applied to the mould and allowed to cure, its surface will remain tacky which, although ideal for bonding with subsequent layers of polyester laminating resins, can cause problems of styrene migration into an epoxy laminating resin and result in an unsatisfactory bond. One way of overcoming this problem is to use a wax additive in the gel-coat which prevents the air inhibiting the cure of the polyester. In this case, though, the wax must be removed before laminating can proceed. This complication is one of the major reasons why production laminators are often reluctant to use epoxy laminating resins, despite the advantages to be gained from such systems.

The reader may, at this stage, be wondering why epoxy is not used as a gel-coat. In fact, epoxy can be, and is, used in this way for some FRP applications and results in a highly water-resistant surface, but it has problems that affect its use in marine mouldings. The basic problem common to all epoxy resins and paint systems is that of their susceptibility to ultra-violet radiation. Thus strong sunlight will degrade the surface of an epoxy gel-coat and cause it to yellow and lose its gloss in a relatively short time.

It should be realized that polyester gel-coats are not immune to this problem and will also become dull and chalky over a period of time and will eventually (after five to ten years on average) need to be repainted if their appearance is to be maintained. The loss of gloss and the change of colour is most noticeable when dark colours are used, and if a repair to the gel-coat is needed after only a year or two it will be seen that it is virtually impossible to match the colour of the repaired area to the rest of the surface.

There has been some discussion recently about the effects of the use of fillers to colour the resin on the water resistance of the gel-coat. In fact, many authorities recommend the use of a clear gel-coat for underwater areas, arguing that the use of any filler will reduce the water resistance of the resin. It seems, however, that the use of pigment in the resin is quite acceptable as long as only enough is used to give the required colour depth and stability. While the use of a clear gel-coat may or may not help reduce possible osmosis problems (see Chapter 11), it certainly does allow examination of the laminate for voids and other defects that would otherwise be hidden.

A product similar to gel-coat is topcoat resin. This is used on the inside of a laminate to protect it from moisture and chemicals and to help improve the appearance. Polyester topcoat resin contains wax additive to prevent air inhibition of the curing process and so allows the laminate to cure fully. Before any bonding of bulkheads or interior mouldings can take place, this waxy surface must be removed or a satisfactory bond will not be achieved.

Topcoat resins can be pigmented to improve the appearance of the interior of the moulding, but if this is done the laminate should be carefully inspected beforehand, since when the topcoat is on any defects will be hidden forever more.

Gel-coat and topcoat resins use the same catalysts and accelerators as laminating resins and can be applied by brush, roller or spray methods, the last being the most common, at least for gel-coats, in production boatbuilding.

Resins for use with wood

Before leaving the subject of thermosetting resins, the use of resins in modern wooden boatbuilding should be considered. The use of adhesives is essential to modern techniques for building with wood, which rely heavily on the laminating of several thin pieces of this material into the required shape. Of the classes of thermosetting resins discussed in this chapter, only epoxies possess the properties of adhesion that make them suitable for this purpose, and it will be seen in Chapter 5, where the subject is more fully discussed, that this class of resin is finding increasing use in wooden boatbuilding. Polyester resins do not have the adhesive properties required for laminating with wood, but have been used on occasion to bond internal reinforcements to a wooden hull and to sheath the outside of a wooden hull with glass cloth. Neither use is really satisfactory as the many failures will testify: the bond between polyester and wood can be unreliable, especially if the wood is not perfectly dry.

Chapter 4 deals with the re-emergence of wood as a competitive building material and it will be seen that this is largely due to the use of epoxy resin as a coating to seal the wood. Because of its high resistance to moisture absorption, an epoxy coating on dry wood will prevent the material from changing its moisture content and hence its physical and mechanical properties. The other resins covered by this chapter are not used for wood coating because they cannot compete with epoxy for toughness, flexibility, adhesion and water resistance.

Two types of epoxy can be used for wood coating: solvent-free and solvent-based. The solvent-free epoxy coating resins can be compared with an epoxy laminating resin for FRP applications, since they are chemically similar, but the coating resin should be slightly cheaper because it uses cheaper raw materials as the required properties are less exacting. A coating resin for wood must have low viscosity in order to penetrate the surface wood cells, and it must be flexible to avoid cracking from movement of the wood, but it need not have the same high mechanical strength as an FRP laminating resin. Naturally, it must have as high a resistance to moisture as possible, and if the surface is to have a clear varnish finish the epoxy sensitivity to ultra-violet degradation should be as low as possible.

Solvent-based epoxies differ from the solvent-free variety by using a solution of resin and hardener in a solvent which evaporates when the coating has been applied to the surface. Solvent-free epoxy coatings have the advantage that thick films can be applied in one coating, but against this must be balanced the problem of a very short working time. Solvent-based epoxies are limited in the film thickness that can be built up with each coat, but have a much longer pot-life because of the inclusion of the solvents which retard the cure in the pot. Solvent-based epoxies are also less critically dependent on the accuracy of mixing resin and hardener and produce a film that can be more flexible. While the solvent-free systems can be susceptible to moisture pick-up during their curing time, causing a blooming of the surface, the solvent-based systems are much less sensitive to moisture, which can be an advantage when working in less-than-perfect conditions.

When epoxy gel-coats were discussed earlier, the problem of ultra-violet degradation was raised. This is also a problem with epoxy coatings on wood where it is intended to use a clear finish. Epoxy coatings are normally used as undercoats to seal and protect the wood and to provide a hard and stable surface for the application of a topcoat of paint and varnish. Under varnish an epoxy coating can turn yellow after exposure to sunlight, but the solvent-free epoxies are more susceptible to this problem than the solvent-based systems. If a paint topcoat is used over an epoxy coating there is, of course, no problem with ultra-violet degradation of the undercoat since it is protected by the topcoat. While the epoxy coatings can be pigmented and can be used as topcoats, their properties make them much more suitable, at least in marine applications, for use as a primer and undercoat under a high-quality polyurethane topcoat. The subject of paints and varnishes is more fully considered in Chapter 10.

Thermoplastic resins

While the vast majority of 'plastic' boats make use of thermosetting resins such as polyester, vinylester and epoxy resins reinforced with a fibre reinforcement, some sailboards and small dinghies are built using unreinforced thermoplastic resins.

Thermoplastic resins differ from the thermosetting variety in that they can be softened and hardened by the application of heat, time after time, without requiring a chemical reaction to create the finished product. This means that they are available in a variety of forms that are easy to store and transport and are clean to handle. These resins are obtainable in pellet, powder and sheet forms and are suitable for a variety of production processes using heat and/or vacuum at pressure to create the final product.

Three thermoplastics that are already being used in the building of small boats are acrylonitrile-butadiene-styrene (ABS), polypropylene and polyethylene. Of these, polyethylene is the most common and finds it way into a whole variety of small plastic products ranging from bottles to packaging material. Polyethylene can be in a rotomoulding process to produce sailboards as hollow, one-piece units which are then injected with urethane foam. Early versions suffered from low heat resistance to the extent that owners were able to alter the shape of their boards by wrapping them in black plastic and leaving them in the sun to heat to the required temperature. Later versions use a cross-linked polyethylene that has a higher heat resistance.

Polypropylene is used to manufacture the Topper dinghy which was first produced in conventional FRP. Polypropylene is not particularly stiff but has high impact resistance and excellent fatigue characteristics. It is easy to weld, is not damaged by ultra-violet light and is also cheap. Using an injection process, one Topper dinghy can be turned out every seven minutes, and so as long as sufficient demand for the product exists the process is extremely cost-effective, despite high tooling and initial development costs.

ABS is a stiffer material than the others and is very tough. It is now being used by the automotive industry and has many other uses for the production of virtually indestructible plastic goods. It is used quite extensively for production sailboards but has also been utilized to mould boats of up to 21ft (7m). While unreinforced themoplastics can be used successfully for smaller dinghies and sailboards where high strength and stiffness are not required, their use for larger boats is more doubtful unless they are reinforced in the same way as thermosetting resins.

Their use does, however, allow a very quick and clean production process that turns out identical items with high quality control. The cost of the materials roughly equates with conventional FRP materials, but the cost in labour is considerably less. Obviously this sort of production technique relies on high-volume sales, and while that may be achievable with sailboards and small dinghies it is far less certain in the case of larger boats.

3 CORE MATERIALS

The first two chapters took an extensive look at the range of resin systems and fibre reinforcements that can be used in the building of an FRP boat. Many boats are built using these materials to form a solid laminate, the properties of which will vary with the specific materials chosen to make it up.

Despite the many advantages that FRP laminates exhibit over other materials, the property of laminate stiffness (resistance to bending) is not one of FRP's strong points. Although this statement must be qualified with the information that the use of high-modulus materials, such as carbon fibres, and sophisticated production methods will give an improvement in stiffness, FRP laminates are nevertheless inferior to a low-density material such as wood, when the ability of a panel of a given weight to resist bending is considered.

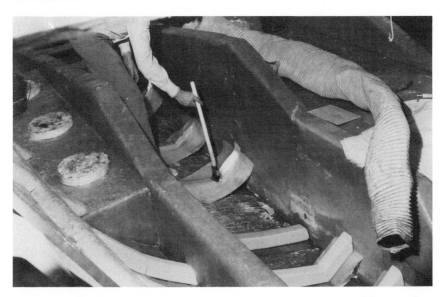

Fig. 3.1(a) Moulded frames or stringers can be used to stiffen a single skin. Here tailored foam pieces are used an non-structural formers for moulding floors.

Fig. 3.1(b) Sandwich construction utilizes a lightweight core with thin skins. The resulting sandwich is thicker than a single skin but stiffer and often lighter.

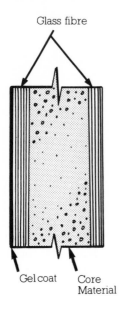

Glass fibre

Gel coat   Core Material

Fig. 3.2 A typical sandwich laminate with two GRP skins.

Fig. 3.2(a) The forces acting in a sandwich panel under bending loads. The upper skin is in compression, the lower in tension, and there are shear forces acting in the core. Compression strength of the skin can be important if thin skins are used.

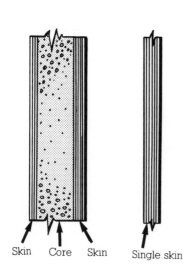

Skin   Core   Skin   Single skin

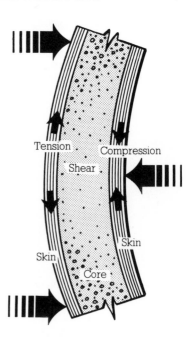

Tension   Compression
Shear
Skin
Skin   Core

There are several ways in which the stiffness of an FRP panel can be improved, such as the common method of using frames and/or longitudinal stringers to reduce unsupported panel area, but a method which has particular attractions for FRP applications is the use of sandwich construction.

The principles behind sandwich construction can be traced back to the nineteenth century and the development of the principle of the I-beam. It was realized that a beam could be stiffened and made lighter by cutting away superfluous material to leave two flanges separated by a web which holds them parallel and rigidly apart. That discovery was a major break-through and much of modern engineering is based upon it.

The use of sandwich construction in a laminate offers the same advantages as an I-beam configuration in a metal structure, but instead of the web and flanges, sandwich construction makes use of a light-weight core material which is faced on both sides by skins of wood, metal or, more usually, FRP.

Because the stiffness of a panel is dependent not only on the material's flexural modulus (the measure of the stiffness of the material) but also on the cube of the thickness of the panel, the thickness has to be increased by only a small amount to increase the stiffness considerably. This is the reason why low-density, high-volume materials like wood exhibit such outstanding properties of stiffness when compared with denser but stronger materials like metals and FRP.

One solution to stiffening an FRP panel would obviously be to make it thicker so that further support from frames and stringers is not required, but the result of this would be to make a very heavy laminate with unnecessary strength that was also very expensive and posed practical building problems. By making use of sandwich construction, extra thickness can be had for little, if any, weight increase and at a price and ease of construction that often compares very favourably with a conventionally-framed structure.

A sandwich laminate consists of two separate but complementary parts: the two skins and the core. The role of the skins in the structure is to withstand the bending moments on the panel or beam by resisting the compressive and tensile loadings set up in the opposite skins when the panel is under a bending load. In addition to having the required tensile and compessive strengths, the skins must also be thick enough to resist compressive skin buckling, tensile failure and localized impact damage, the last also being dependent on the impact resistance of the skin material and the impact absorption properties of the core.

For the skins to be able to resist the bending moments they must be held rigidly from the neutral axis of the sandwich (the centre-line) and prevented from moving relative to each other. It is the job of the chosen core material to fulfil these requirements, the first depending on the compressive strength and modulus of the core and the second on its shear strength and modulus. If the compressive strength of the core is too low, the two skins will be able to move towards each other as the beam or panel is bent, so reducing their distance from the neutral axis of the sandwich and, with it, their ability to resist the bending moment. If the core's shear strength is insufficient, the two skins will be able to slide relative to one another and will cease to work together to resist bending, with the result that the properties of the sandwich will depend on the individual properties of the skins.

In most design equations for sandwich structures using light-weight core materials, the flexural stiffness of the core is ignored, but it is true that a stiffer core material will contribute to the stiffness of the sandwich. The stiffer light-weight cores are, however, generally harder to shape around moulds and are also often somewhat brittle and more susceptible to impact damage.

In most sandwich applications the boatbuilder is interested in a reasonably strong but light-weight core to allow the laminate to be thickened to give increased stiffness without the penalty of extra weight. With this type of core, as we have seen, as long as the compressive and shear strengths are adequate for the task of supporting the skins, the strength of the core is not considered effective in assessing the total properties of the laminate.

Another approach, which may become more common, is to use a higher-density core such as wood or syntactic foam (see page 71) which can contribute considerable strength properties to the sandwich while still being lighter than a solid laminate. With this method, of course, the core would not be as thick as when using a light-weight one, because the weight of the sandwich would be too high.

There are a great many types of sandwich-core materials now available to the boatbuilder ranging from balsa and other types of wood through a variety of foam materials to the more recently developed honeycomb materials. Each class of core material – wood, foam or honeycomb – has advantages and disadvantages that can only be evaluated in terms of a particular application, and each class contains a number of products that may vary significantly from each other or be essentially the same product from a different manufacturer.

While the properties of the core materials will vary with the class, it is true to say that within any class the strength properties of the material generally vary with density – the higher the density of the wood, foam or honeycomb, the stronger is the material. For light-weight applications, therefore, the aim is usually to achieve satisfactory properties at as low a core density as possible. Because the cost of the cores that develop good strength at low density is usually high, cost is likely to have an influence on the choice of core in many applications when it may be inappropriate to choose the highest-performance material.

While the perfect core material would be cheap, light-weight, and have good strength properties, there are a number of other requirements that must always be considered. The core should not be friable (crumble easily), and it should not be too brittle or it may suffer delamination from the skins under impact. It must have the ability to bond well with the laminating resin or adhesive; have a good fatigue life; be able to resist deterioration from corrosion, fungi or water; and, very importantly, it should not absorb moisture.

The ease with which the material can be worked is also likely to influence the choice of core. There is little point in choosing a high-performance core if the material is not suited to the production method, since not only will time and money be wasted but the finished sandwich is likely to have lower properties than expected if it is not possible to realize the full potential benefits of that material.

Although this chapter isolates core materials and attempts to give some comparisons, the choice of core for a sandwich must be made as part of the design of the whole, with the skins, laminating resin or adhesive and core all being chosen together to suit the performance/cost specification.

For boatbuilding applications the obvious choice for a skin material is FRP, but it must be remembered that skins of wood or aluminium may be preferable in some circumstances. When FRP skins are used, the choice, as has been noted, is vast, ranging from cheaper skins of mat or woven E glass to thin skins of carbon or Kevlar fibres.

Equally important to the overall sandwich is the choice of laminating resin or adhesive for bonding the skins and the core. In boatbuilding, where the skins are usually of FRP, the sandwich is normally laminated in one piece with the core and skins being bonded by the laminating resin. In other applications, the skins are laminated separately and bonded to the core using an adhesive. This technique is not often used in boatbuilding but may become more common in the construction of light-weight interiors where plywood or FRP skins could be bonded to a light-weight core material, such as a honeycomb, to produce panels far lighter than solid plywood.

Whichever technique is used, the properties of the adhesive must match the properties of the skins and the core. In particular, the adhesion between skins and core must be the best possible and the adhesive must have good shear strength to transmit the shear loads and prevent delamination. Care should be taken to ensure that the adhesive or laminating resin does not soften the core or otherwise affect it during laminating.

Although we have highlighted the high-stiffness-at-low-weight advantages of sandwich construction, it must be noted that there are several other significant benefits to be obtained from this method of construction. These include thermal and acoustic insulation, an interior free of stringers and frames, high resistance to impact penetration, positive buoyancy and relatively low labour costs.

The development of sandwich construction in boatbuilding started soon after the first production FRP boats were built but, although many production builders have realized the production advantages, it has been left to the professional and amateur builders of one-off boats to develop and publicize the techniques. It has been the one-off builders who have also done much of the experimenting with the increasing number of core materials that have become available in the last few years, but now some production builders are starting to find uses for these newer materials. Without doubt, the use of sandwich construction will continue to grow, as will the choice of cores. Although most sandwich-built boats currently built make use of only one type of core, we may expect that, in the near future, it will become common to use two or more different core materials where their individual properties suggest their use for particular areas of the moulding.

Wood cores

Balsa

By far the most commonly used wood core is balsa, which has been employed as a core material for over twenty-five years in a variety of applications including boatbuilding. Although classified as a hardwood, balsa is the lightest commercially available wood and comes almost exclusively from Central America. Balsa is one of the cheapest core materials available for sandwich construction and has a number of advantages. The normal form of the balsa used for sandwich cores is the end-grain type, where the grain of the wood runs at right angles to the facing skins, and in this form it has very high compression strengths. Where flexural strength is more important in long, flat members, such as stringers, long-grain balsa may be more appropriate, even though its compression strength is a fraction of that of the end-grain variety, but it is rarely used in this form in boatbuilding.

As well as high compression strength, end-grain balsa has good shear strength and impact absorption and bonds well using the normal laminating resins, although its absorbency may soak up quite a lot of resin. Its properties vary with density and, while end-grain balsa can be had in a range of densities from 6 lb/ft^3 (96kg/m^3) to 20lb/ft^3 (320kg/m^3), it can be difficult to obtain sheets of consistent density. In sheet form, balsa is stiff and difficult to bend without breaking, so for laminating on curved surfaces it is used in either a semi-rigid or fully flexible form. Semi-rigid sheets are produced by cutting regular slits into but not quite through the balsa, along the length and

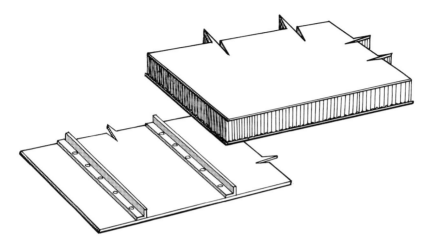

Fig. 3.3 A sandwich panel – in this case using a honeycomb core – is thicker than a stringer-reinforced single skin but exhibits better thermal and acoustic insulation, has two smooth skins and is often lighter.

Fig. 3.4 End-grain balsa being used in a female mould for a large motor cruiser.

across the width of small sheets. This allows the wood to take up some curve, but for easy use on curved surfaces it is best to use flexible panels formed by gluing small blocks of balsa to a glass-fibre scrim.

Balsa provides good buoyancy for a sandwich hull, supporting $50lb/ft^3$ ($800kg/m^3$), and also gives good sound and thermal insulation and vibration damping properties. It is also temperature stable and, in particular, does not soften at high temperature, unlike some foam cores.

Although balsa is popular and has the previously mentioned properties, it does have some disadvantages. First, it is a relatively heavy core material, and although it has excellent compression strength, its lower shear strength makes it difficult to use to its full potential. More importantly, perhaps, is its porous nature which can lead to the absorption of resin during laminating and an unnecessary increase in weight and the danger of resin-starved areas next to the core. This resin absorption is, of course, increased in semi-rigid or flexible sheets where the resin, or a filler, is used to fill the gaps between the individual balsa blocks.

There is also the danger of the core absorbing water during the life of the boat, leading to an increase in weight and possible rot and delamination. Although it may appear that this could only happen in the event of puncture damage of the outer skin, in fact small amounts of water vapour will penetrate even an undamaged polyester laminate and, over a period of time, result in a damp or saturated core. Some builders reduce the chance of this occurring by using balsa only in decks and topsides, but another approach is to use an epoxy resin which is far more resistant to the passage of water vapour than is polyester.

Balsa is supplied kiln-dried at a temperature above 195°F (90°C) which both stabilizes and sterilizes the wood. After kiln drying, the moisture content of the wood will be in the region of 10 per cent, which means that further shrinking is unlikely in normal conditions of humidity but expansion can occur if the moisture content is allowed to increase. At the 10 per cent level of moisture content the properties of the wood are near maximum (see Chapter 4) and the balsa should be stored in dry and warm conditions to avoid the danger of a significant increase in water content. Kiln drying also kills any bacteria and fungi spores present and the balsa will only become subject to such damage if the moisture content is allowed to increase and spores get to the wood from outside sources.

Considering the properties of balsa and its relatively low cost, one can see why the wood is popular. Because of its high compression strength it is often used in highly stressed areas, such as in the area deck fittings, while other lighter cores are used for the rest of the structure. If the relatively high density of balsa is acceptable and if an epoxy resin is used in the laminate to protect the balsa from water absorption, the wood can be a satisfactory, low-cost core.

Balsa can also be used effectively with skins other than those made of FRP, such as between skins of plywood for use as light-weight structural bulkheads, and it can also be used as the core of a strip-planked wooden boat, perhaps with stringers and ribs incorporated into the core between the skins, so leaving a very clear interior.

Other woods for core applications

Although balsa is the only wood used as a light-weight core in sandwich construction it is possible to use other woods as cores carrying some of the structural load with the rest being taken by thin skins. An example of this is the use of strip-planked western red cedar, giving fore-and-aft strength and stiffness properties, with inside and outside skins of E glass or S glass unidirectional or woven fibres laid ±45° and 90° to the fore-and-aft line to provide strength and stiffness in these directions. Although the core used in this case is not light-weight, having a density in the region of 20lb/ft³ (320kg/m³), the core has very significant strength properties parallel to the grain and can thus accept the loads that act in that direction. The total laminate can be quite light and like other sandwich hulls will have a minimum of inside stiffening.

An alternative to FRP skins would be the use of cold-moulded veneers laid up in the ±45° and 90° directions both inside and out or FRP outside skins with veneer skins inside. The latter approach would give the aesthetic appeal of wood inside the boat with an increase in insulation, with the greater impact and abrasion resistance of the FRP skins on the outside of the hull.

Foam cores

Foam-plastic cores, of one type or another, are probably the most commonly used boatbuilding core material at the present time. Among the different foams that are used in boatbuilding are polyurethane, polystyrene, flexibilized polyurethanes, tough-rigid polyvinyl chloride (PVC), cross-linked PVC, acrylic and the many varieties of syntactic resin cores.

Polystyrene and polyurethane foams have little place in boatbuilding as structural cores because they are quite weak compared with the other foams, but they are commonly used in sailboards and also as formers for laminating ribs and stringers in an FRP hull. They are also sometimes used for built-in buoyancy in dinghies and between the double skins of some larger boats. In the latter case they are not used as a core material in the way described in this book, but are solely used to fill unused space and provide inherent buoyancy.

Polyurethane is a brittle and friable foam, weak in both compression and shear and very weak in impact. It is not easy to bend but is easy to work with wood tools and can be used with any of the boatbuilding resins. The polyurethanes containing tertiary di-isocyanate (TDI) are very toxic when being blown and safety regulations on their production are tight. In densities of 2–3lb/ft³ (30–45kg/m³) they are popular for sailboards and are often foamed in place in production boards, but they are expensive, weak, and some types are not completely closed-cell so can absorb water.

Polystyrene is another light-weight foam sometimes used for formers and buoyancy which is now finding a place in the sailboard market. It is generally familiar for its use as a packaging material and in insulation tiles. Polystyrene is available in two forms: expanded and extruded. The former is cheaper and available in larger sheets than the extruded version. Both types do not have the properties required of sandwich construction but are more flexible than polyurethane and have better impact resistance. Expanded polystyrene has no weight advantage over a polyurethane since a density of 3lb/ft³ (45kg/m³) is required for reasonable properties, but the expanded type can be lighter, being used in densities of 1.75–2lb/ft³ (28–35kg/m³). Both are cheaper than polyurethanes. Polystyrenes are now being used for sailboard building, especially for one-offs and home-built boards. The foam is cheaper and lighter than polyurethane and so helps in the building of light-weight boards; but it cannot be used with polyester resins, which dissolve the foam, and an epoxy laminating resin must therefore be used to lay-up the skins. Polystyrene is quite easy to shape in the higher densities and can be worked with power tools or hot-wire shaped.

Two modified forms of urethane foam can be used as cores in the sandwich construction of larger boats. The first is a flexibilized polyurethane modified with methylene isocyanate which is 100 per cent closed-cell, has reasonably good compression and shear properties and is more flexible and less brittle than normal urethane foams. This type of foam is non-friable, has elastic recovery under shock loading and can be bonded or laminated with any of the boatbuilding resins. It can be worked by hand or machine tools and is available in rigid sheet form or a more flexible form with parallel slits machined into the foam to allow it to accommodate tight curves. It can also be heat-formed at temperatures above 130°F (55°C). It is, however, quite heavy, having a density, for most boatbuilding applications, of 6.5lb/ft³ (105kg/m³) with a 12lb/ft³ (210kg/m³) version used in highly stressed areas.

A new core material now on the market uses polyurethane foam in a different way from conventional cores. This material consists of strips of moulded polyurethane with convex and concave faces on the two long sides of each one, and the core is made up of mating strips with skins of 1¾oz/ft² (525g/m²) chopped-strand mat already bonded to the foam and with webs of glass fibre running between the foam strips to tie the outer skins together.

Because the foam strips are shaped for a hinging action, the core will conform to tight curves when bent at right angles to the strips and can also be bent in line with the strips since they are partly slit at intervals along their length. Because the strips are moulded, they have a non-porous surface which helps avoid the problem of air trapped under the core and reduces the resin absorption while still allowing a good bond.

In use the foam is cut to shape – it can be easily cut with a knife – and one side is wetted-out with resin and the foam is positioned in the mould. The remaining skin is wetted-out and more skin material added as required. Capillary action draws the resin from the surface mat into and along the webs connecting the two skins and it is these webs that contribute considerably to the strength of the core. In particular, the glass webs act as shear webs and are responsible for the good shear strength and modulus of the core. In fact, the core's shear properties are better than its compression strength, although the latter is still acceptable in many applications. It should be noted that the shear properties of this core are in the direction of the webs and will be less in the perpendicular direction, but this can be allowed for by altering the direction of lay-up of the core.

Because the material is so conformable it can be moulded in very tight curves, even being used as a core material for tubes and piping. Unlike conventional foam sheets, which are scored to make them flexible, the shaped polyurethane foam strips do not open up when bent but continue to mate, thus reducing air entrapment and heavy, resin-rich areas.

At the moment, this material is only produced in one thickness, $\frac{9}{16}$in (14mm), and with one type of skin material, chopped-strand mat, but this may soon change. This type of core has a density of 4lb/ft^3 (63kg/m^3), costs about the same as balsa and is not affected by temperatures under 210°F (100°C).

Further up the price scale come two types of PVC foam that are probably now the most used of the sandwich-core materials. These two foams are the so-called 'rigid-elastic' PVC, a pure compound of PVC and the cross-linked PVC foams which are a blend of PVC and polyurethane. Both types have their proponents, depending on the importance the designer/builder places on flexibility or stiffness. The cross-linked PVC foams have good compressive and shear properties and are stiff but brittle. The rigid-elastic PVC foam, on the other hand, is considerably weaker in compression, slightly weaker in shear but is not brittle, can be bent relatively easily and has good impact properties as it will yield and then recover. Both types are fully closed-cell and both can be heat-formed at temperatures around 210°F (100°C). Although the use of the rigid-elastic type in decks exposed to high temperatures was suspect, newer versions of the foam have acceptable heat-deformation properties.

Heat-forming works best in thin sheets of foam but thicker sheets are

Fig. 3.5 An Airex 'rigid-elastic' PVC
core being fitted over a male mould
for a 38-ft catamaran.

available with slits machined partly through them, or in a fully contoured
version (in the case of the cross-linked foam) which consists of small blocks
of foam bonded to a glass scrim. These contoured forms do, however, suffer
the disadvantage that the resin needed to fill the gaps in the foam adds to the
weight of the core. A typical density of the rigid-elastic type for boatbuilding
is 5lb/ft³ (80kg/m³) while the most usual density of the cross-linked variety is
4.7lb/ft³ (75kg/m³), but a range of densities and thicknesses are available.
Although the cross-linked PVC foam is not affected by boatbuilding resins,
the rigid-elastic foam can suffer from styrene migration from polyesters.
Styrene absorbed into the core can act as a plasticizer, and lack of styrene in
the resin can cause an incomplete cure unless the resin is catalysed to gel
quickly.

In order to prevent styrene migration, the foam can be pre-treated with an
accelerator which causes the first coat of laminating resin to cure quickly, or
a sealing coat of fast-curing resin can be applied and allowed to cure before
laminating. Two more alternatives are to use a very fast-curing resin for the
first laminating coat, which may cause difficulties in working, or an epoxy
resin which has no effect on the core.

One rigid, closed-cell foam that has only just appeared on the boatbuilding market is polymethacrylic imide rigid expanded plastic foam (PMI). This foam promises to find many applications in the building of light-weight, high-performance boats since it has similar strength properties to cross-linked PVC foams but at a lower density, and indeed its strength properties are better than any other foam at the same density. It is, however, stiff, and since it has such a high heat-distortion temperature – it must be heated to 355°F (180°C) for heat-forming – it is most likely to be used in areas of flat panels such as decks or topsides. In another way, though, this high-temperature performance is an advantage since it means that the foam can be used with pre-preg skins cured at about 315°F (160°C). Since no other foam can be used with pre-pregs, this advantage is likely to lead to PMI becoming popular for use in high-performance mouldings. One problem with PMI foam that may affect its use in boat hulls is the fact that it is not resistant to weak alkaline solutions – conditions that may exist in some harbours and estuaries. Normally, of course, the foam would be protected by the skins, but in the event of skin damage the foam could lose strength if it came into contact with even a weak alkaline solution. In practice, of course, PMI foam is not likely to be used in underwater areas because of the difficulty of shaping the panels to the necessary degree of curvature, so this problem will not arise.

Syntactic resin cores

Another technique that is quite new to boatbuilding is the use of syntactic resins as a core material. Syntactic resins are made by adding hollow microspheres of glass, carbon, or a resin such as phenolic, to a thermosetting resin such as epoxy or polyester, and are commonly used as fairing compounds, fillers and for pattern making and casting. They can also be used as set-in-mould core material, although there can be difficulties in achieving a constant thickness. Syntactic resins are relatively heavy in core terms, having a density about the same as a light wood such as cedar – 19lb/ft³ (300kg/m³) – but they do have excellent compression and shear strength. Given these properties, a syntactic resin could well be used as a core to reduce the amount of CSM in a normal single-skin lay-up and add thickness, thus giving a stronger and lighter laminate.

Syntactic resin cores may be used in the future – if the problems of laying a regular thickness can be solved, perhaps by laying the resin on to an open-weave scrim – for moulding small- and medium-size workboats as well as production pleasure craft. They could also be used in thin, light-weight skins, such as that of a canoe, where the skin could be considerably thickened by a thin core of syntactic resin and hence made much stiffer at minimum weight.

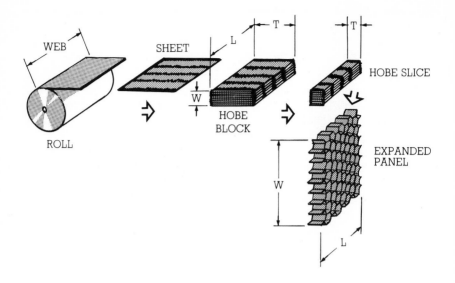

A core material that is similar in principle to a syntactic resin is a non-woven mat product based on polyester fibres and microspheres. The mat is easily cut and can be laid in the mould before being wetted-out with resin. This approach of mixing the microspheres with a fibre mat overcomes the problem of laying an even core of wet syntactic resin but the result is somewhat heavier because of the presence of the fibres. The mat is available in a range of thicknesses and has a density of 40lb/ft^3 (650kg/m^3).

Honeycomb cores

The latest type of core material to arrive on the boatbuilding scene is the honeycomb core of which several versions are now available. Several materials are used to make honeycombs, including woven cloths of glass, carbon and nylon fibres; they may also be made from kraft paper, cardboard or aramid paper; or from metals such as aluminium.

Honeycombs are generally made by a process of expansion in which sheets of the web material are printed with lines of adhesive and stacked until the adhesive cures. Metal honeycombs using sheets of aluminium can then be expanded and cut to size or, alternatively, they can be cut to size before expansion. Aluminium honeycombs will remain expanded, but cloth and paper ones need to be dipped in a thermosetting resin, squeezed to remove the excess and then expanded and the resin allowed to cure. This process is completed by the manufacturer in the case of paper honeycombs,

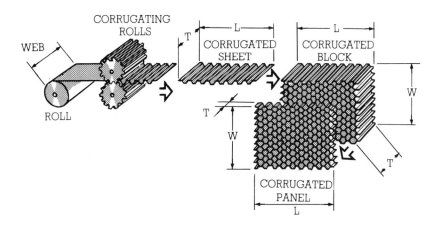

Fig. 3.6 & 3.7 The expansion method is the most common method for honeycomb manufacture although the corrugation technique (Fig. 7) is also used.

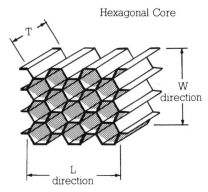

Fig. 3.8 The normal hexagonal-shaped honeycomb.

but some types of cloth honeycomb are available unexpanded and unimpregnated, so can be dipped in resin and expanded immediately before use. The impregnated honeycomb must be fully expanded and held securely while the resin cures but, used in this way, it is possible to shape the material to suit compound and difficult curves while it is still wet.

Honeycomb cores, generally, have the highest compression, shear and stiffness properties of any core material of equivalent density, which is the reason for their use in all manner of light-weight applications where strength is important. The boatbuilding applications in which honeycomb cores have

Ox-Core

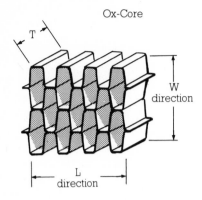

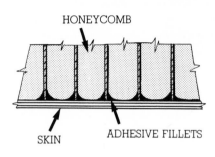

Fig. 3.9 An over-expanded core is used for heavily curved areas. By over-expanding in the width direction the core bends more easily in the length.

Fig. 3.10 An adhesive used to bond a skin to a honeycomb core must be able to form fillets along the individual cell walls in order to provide an adequate bond.

so far been used have been mainly racing power and sailing boats where the extra expense of these materials can be justified, but they have also proved themselves in many commercial marine applications and their use in a wider variety of pleasure craft may soon become more common.

The most commonly used honeycombs for sandwich construction of light-weight racing craft are the honeycombs made of aramid fibre paper. This type of honeycomb exhibits excellent strength properties at low densities, as well as excellent impact resistance, fatigue strength and moisture resistance. In addition it is fire-resistant, provides sound and thermal insulation and has a top operating temperature of 300°F (150°C). Many of these properties are common to the other types of honeycomb material, but the aramid paper honeycomb is generally thought to have the best combination of properties for boatbuilding. Aluminium, for instance, has excellent compression and shear strength and is stiffer than aramid paper, but it is heavier and not as good in impact or fatigue. Also, of course, it can be susceptible to corrosion in a marine environment. It is most used, at the time of writing, as a core for light-weight bulkheads and interior panelling.

Kraft paper honeycombs are cheaper than those of aramid fibre but are less strong and only available in low densities. They also suffer from low impact and fatigue properties, yet are popular in the USA for use in decks and can also be used for interior panels.

Woven-cloth honeycombs are available in a wide range of cloths and densities and can be had with excellent all-round properties but they are generally heavier than aramid fibre honeycomb. Woven honeycombs are available with the cloth cut on the bias so that the fibres in the webs run at ±45° to the surface, giving very strong shear properties. Cloth honeycombs incorporating carbon fibres are, of course, light and very strong, but they are also very expensive and hence have a very specialized use.

Most honeycombs can be fitted to shallow curves; however, when more heavily curved surfaces are involved it is usual to choose a larger cell size or use an overexpanded form. This type is made by overexpanding the regular hexagonal honeycomb in the width direction, thus making the material more easy to curve in the length direction. Overexpanding also slightly increases the shear properties across the width, at the same time reducing them somewhat in the length. While a honeycomb can be held in place on a curved mould by weights, it is much better to use vacuum techniques to ensure that the core bonds well to each skin.

In most commercial applications honeycombs that are to have FRP skins use either pre-pregs cured under heat and pressure directly on to the core, or the skins are cured separately and later bonded to the core with an adhesive. The wet lay-up method can, however, be employed with honeycombs and is the one that has been so far favoured for boatbuilding.

Whichever technique is used, it is most important that the adhesive or laminating resin is suitable for bonding to the honeycomb structure with its open cells. In particular, the resin must be able to wet-out the cell walls quickly but have a controlled flow so that resin does not run down the walls, leaving a low-strength bond with all the resin at the bottom of the cell. For use with a honeycomb, an adhesive or laminating resin should have as high a viscosity as is practicable and consistent with the need to wet-out the skin fibres, and it should have a fast gelling time.

When an FRP skin has been correctly bonded to a honeycomb core, the edges of the honeycomb will show through the transparent skins and will appear thicker than before their application as a result of the correctly formed fillet between the resin and the edges of each honeycomb cell.

As well as being available in a wide range of materials, honeycombs come in a range of web thicknesses, cell size and density, all of which affect the properties of the honeycomb. Manufacturers will supply a comprehensive list of the different sorts of honeycombs and their properties so that the designer can readily choose the types suitable for particular applications. At the time of writing, the use of this type of core is mainly limited to racing craft, but it is to be expected that its use will spread since it offers the best specific properties of any of the core materials, allowing the designer not only to save weight but also to increase core thickness which provides further gains in terms of stiffness.

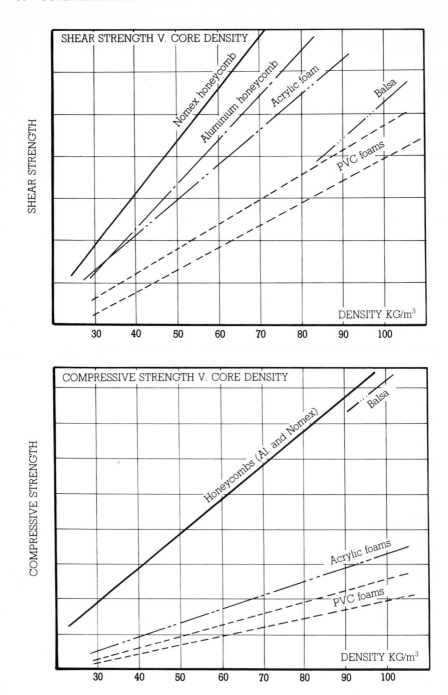

Skinned panels

Honeycombs are commercially available in skinned panels and can be used to replace plywood where stiffness and light weight are important requirements. These are now being used for applications such as bulkheads and interior furniture for high-performance craft. Panel sizes of 8ft x 4ft (2.44m x 1.22m) – the same as plywood – are standard, and common thicknesses cover a range of ½ in to 2in (12.5mm to 50mm). The first of these products used aluminium honeycomb skinned with either FRP or aluminium, but other products are likely to become available soon, using the other types of honeycomb cores. While standard panels are flat, it is possible to produce a range of curved panels which could then be suitable for hull construction. Another possibility is the use of skinned honeycomb panels sliced into thin strips which could be employed for fast strip-planking.

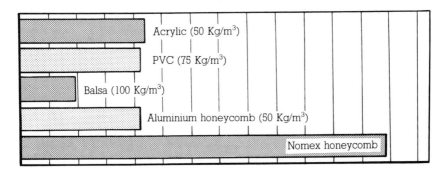

Fig. 3.11 A comparison of the range of core materials with shear strength and compressive strength set against density of core.

Fig. 3.12 A comparison of the prices of the common core materials.

4 WOOD

It may appear strange to some readers that a book dealing with modern materials and techniques should include the oldest building material known to man. While there is nothing new about wood, it still remains one of the best materials for many boatbuilding applications and, with the relatively recent development of some new techniques for using it, wood promises to remain extremely popular.

The use of wood for boatbuilding has suffered a steady decline in the last forty years as FRP has taken over the production market and the use of high-performance fibres for one-off construction has become commonplace. The reason for this move away from wood has been largely due to the predictable and reproducible nature of FRP composites and the reduced labour costs associated with them. Wood, on the other hand, has not been regarded as a stable engineering material and its use in boatbuilding has always required highly skilled labour.

Despite this move away from the use of wood, the material has much to commend it and exhibits properties that are extremely competitive in certain circumstances, even when compared with the most recently developed fibre reinforcements. As has already been mentioned, one of the most important considerations in boat design is skin flexural stiffness. While structural strength is relatively easy to provide for, the stiffness of the structure is much more of a problem, and it is often necessary to overbuild the structure in strength terms in order to satisfy the stiffness requirements. This requirement for stiffness is one of the main reasons why wood can be such a competitive boatbuilding material. Weight-for-weight, wood has a natural advantage in stiffness since it is a low-density material with excellent mechanical properties. In applications where minimum weight is important and where a thick skin is acceptable – such as in a boat hull – wood scores well against higher-density materials such as FRP, or metals where extra thickness cannot be used to generate stiffness (unless a sandwich construction is used) without greatly increasing the weight of the structure.

Wood also has good strength-to-weight properties – although the compression strength of this material is considerably less than its tensile strength and is thus a limiting factor; is very resistant to fatigue and stress concentrations; is a good sound and heat insulator; and, when it fails, it does so gradually by transferring the load from the compression side of the member to the side in tension. Wood is also a very pleasing material to work with and to look at – hence the substantial amounts of timber used in the interiors of many production boats. It is easy to work with hand or power tools, is readily available and relatively cheap.

Although the advantages of wood are unfortunately often forgotten, its disadvantages rarely are, and they are frequently quoted as reasons for the use of FRP. The basic problem with wood is that it is susceptible to rot, can be damaged by marine borers and, most importantly, it can absorb moisture with the result that its physical dimensions and properties are subject to change. It is this tendency of wood to shrink and swell with moisture and temperature changes that has always caused problems in the construction of wooden boats and for which the design and engineering of the structure has had to make allowances.

The cause of wood as a true, stable engineering material is not, however, lost. In the last fifteen years there has been a major development in the use of this material that has already encouraged many builders to return to wooden boatbuilding. But before examining how the disadvantages of wood have been overcome, the basic structure of the material itself should be considered.

The structure of wood

It is the fibrous nature of wood that gives it its excellent properties but at the same time causes its susceptibility to moisture absorption. Wood is composed mostly of long, hollow cells called fibres that are aligned parallel to each other along the trunk of the tree. The direction of these fibres is seen as the grain of the wood in cut timber. Another type of cells, called 'wood rays' or simply 'rays', run horizontally in the tree from the centre outwards. The number of these rays in the wood varies from species to species, but it is important in determining the resistance of the material to splitting. The greater the number of rays, the greater is the wood's cross-grain strength.

A cross-section of a tree reveals a series of well-defined features: first is the bark which is made up of an inner and outer layer, then comes the sapwood, the heartwood and finally the central core known as the pith. Between the bark and the sapwood is a layer, invisible without a microscope, made up of thin-walled living cells in which the growth takes place by cell division. As the diameter of the trunk increases, the bark is pushed outwards, resulting in the typical cracked and ridged patterns of the trunk.

The well-known growth rings often seen in a cut log are produced, especially in trees grown in temperate climates, by differences between new wood formed early and that formed late in each growing season. The inner part of each growth ring, called 'spring wood' or 'early wood', is formed first in the growing season, while the outer part, formed later, is known as 'late wood' or 'summer wood'. Early wood has cells with relatively thin walls and large cavities while late wood cells have thicker walls and smaller cavities. When growth rings are very noticeable, the early wood and late wood differ in their properties: the early is lighter, softer and weaker than the late.

Further in towards the centre of the tree from the bark and the layer of living cells is the sapwood which contains only a few living cells and is mainly an area of food storage and a passage for the transport of sap. The heartwood is made up of inactive cells often containing various desposits which may give it a darker colour and which usually make it more durable than sapwood.

Cut timber

There are two main ways of cutting logs into usable timber which endow it with different properties. Plain-sawn timber is cut tangentially to the growth rings, without rotating the log as it is cut, and the grain of the wood then runs roughly parallel to the cut planks. Quarter-sawn timber, on the other hand, is cut radially to the growth rings (parallel to the rays) and results in the grain being at right angles to the width of the plank. Plain sawing gives the greatest amount of usable timber from the log, but quarter-sawn timber is often chosen for boatbuilding since it has better dimensional stability and also tends to be slightly stronger and easier to work.

Moisture content

Living trees contain moisture in their cell walls and cavities and have a moisture content (weight of water in the wood as a percentage of the weight of oven-dry wood) that can range from 30 per cent to 200 per cent or more. A cut tree immediately begins to lose moisture, the first to be dispelled coming from its cell cavities. The moisture content of the wood at the point when there is no more moisture left in the cell cavities but the cell walls are still completely saturated is known as the 'fibre-saturation point' and is typically about 30 per cent.

The moisture content of wood below the fibre-saturation point depends on the relative humidity and temperature of the surrounding atmosphere. As its moisture content falls below the fibre-saturation point, the wood's properties, both mechanical and physical, change as a function of the moisture content.

Above the saturation point, wood is dimensionally stable, but below that

Fig. 4.1 The moisture content of wood
below the fibre-saturation point
depends on relative humidity and
temperature.

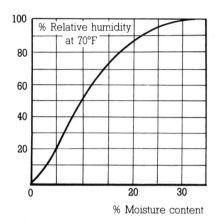

% Moisture content

point it shrinks on losing moisture from the cell walls and swells on gaining it.
As the cell walls dry out, they shrink and stiffen and cause the wood to
become stronger – especially in crushing and bending strength – and this is,
of course, an advantage, except that the strength will again be reduced if the
moisture content is allowed to rise.

The moisture content also has an effect on wood's susceptibility to rot: if it
rises above 20 per cent, it can support the fungi that cause rot. In addition to
moisture, these fungi also require oxygen (which is why wood fully sub-
merged in water is resistant to rot), and adequate warmth. Changes in
moisture content are much more dependent on changes in the amount of
water vapour present in the atmosphere than on the presence of water in its
liquid form. Water is a relative constant and has, in fact, a stabilizing
influence on wood, but the water vapour in the atmosphere varies constantly
and wood is much more susceptible to its presence. Wood cell walls are
naturally resistant to liquids and absorption of water via them takes place
relatively slowly compared to the speed at which water vapour from the
atmosphere is absorbed. When the relative humidity of the atmosphere
changes, the moisture content of the wood tries to change to stay in
equilibrium. For every temperature and relative humidity level, there is an
equilibrium level of moisture content that the wood will try to reach with the
consequent dimensional changes and variations in strength associated with
such changes.

The use of a wood/epoxy composite

At the beginning of the chapter it was stated that wood is a very versatile material with many attractive properties for boat construction but it suffers because of the aforementioned disadvantages which stem from changes in the level of moisture within it. It should also be obvious that if the moisture content can be reduced to a low level and, most importantly of all, held at this low level irrespective of changes in relative humidity, the properties of the wood can be maximized and maintained, and the shrinkage, expansion and danger of rot can be eliminated.

Throughout the history of wooden boatbuilding, continuous efforts have been made to overcome the limitations of the material. Various surface finishes, paints, sheathing systems and the like have been tried, all with the aim of preventing dry wood re-absorbing moisture. At the same time the construction methods using wood have still had to allow for changes in shape and strength since none of these finishes has eliminated the problem. The latest technique – and one that has shown itself to be highly successful in the ten or more years since its introduction – is the use of epoxy resin as a coating as well as a glue for all wooden parts.

The surface coatings used over the years have all proved themselves as more or less successful at keeping water away from wood but the real enemy, water vapour, is much harder to combat since it can easily penetrate small pores in the coating that would not be passable to a liquid. Of all the coatings currently available to the boatbuilder, epoxy resin offers the most vapour-resistant barrier, although even this type of coating will not completely eliminate the passage of vapour. Rather, it succeeds because the passage of water vapour is slowed down to such an extent that the moisture content of the wood remains in equilibrium with the long-term average humidity and is not affected by short-term changes. Thus wood treated with epoxy resin does not suffer from the usual changes resulting from shrinkage or expansion, is not susceptible to rot, and its mechanical properties are stabilized.

Obviously if the properties of the wood are to be as high as possible, its moisture content must be low – it is of little use to seal the wood at a moisture-content level of 20 per cent or so since the mechanical properties will not then be at their maximum. Wood that is to be used with an epoxy resin should be well dried – a moisture content of about 10 per cent is ideal – and it must be stored in warm and dry conditions until it is coated with the resin.

In order for the coating to provide an efficient water-vapour barrier, at least two coats of resin should be applied, or a minimum of three if the surface is to be sanded before painting or varnishing. Since epoxy cures to a very hard finish that is difficult to sand, it is best if as much finishing and sanding as possible is done to the wood surface before application of the resin. The only sanding that will then be required is a light abrasion of the surface to provide a key for the paint or varnish.

Since the resin provides a hard and stable finish, it is an ideal undercoat on which to apply any of the conventional finishes and helps to prevent cracks and crazes in the topcoat caused by movement of the surface. Because of this, epoxy-coated wood is a suitable surface on which to use the hard and inflexible polyurethanes which cannot normally withstand the small movements of uncoated, unstabilized wood.

Besides sealing the wood and acting as a good surface for the application of paints and varnishes, the epoxy coating can provide another, perhaps unexpected, advantage. As has already been observed, wood is much stronger in tension than in compression, but a typical epoxy for use with this material possesses the opposite property, having a compressive strength of the same order as wood's tensile strength. When the two materials are used in composite, the overall strength can be increased, usually at a greater rate than the increase in weight. This increase in strength does, however, depend on the thickness of the wood part, thin parts (as typically used in modern wooden construction) showing a far greater gain in strength than thick parts.

As will be seen in Chapter 5, epoxy resins are also extremely good adhesives and most boats built using epoxy as a coating also use the resin as the prime adhesive. In fact some of the resins on the market for use with wood are intended to be used as a coating and an adhesive, various fillers being added to the basic resin and hardener to suit the particular adhesive application. Thus the boatbuilder has only to buy one resin system which will then cover all his various requirements. This only applies, however, when the coating resin is a solvent-free system, as a solvent-based epoxy is not suitable for use as an adhesive. The comments on the two systems in Chapter 2 should be taken into consideration. In many cases of modern wooden construction, glass or other fibres are used as additional reinforcement or as an outer layer to provide increased abrasion resistance to the hull or deck. When such cloths are to be used, the same epoxy resin will act as the laminating resin for laying-up the cloth on to the wood. Thus the new ways of using wood in light-weight construction can truly be thought of as wood/epoxy composite construction.

Plywood and veneers

While conventional wooden boatbuilding can be characterized as the use of many parts of solid timber joined together by fasteners and glues to form a wooden structure, modern use of wood for light-weight construction is much more akin to the techniques used in FRP moulding. There is far less use of large pieces of solid timber these days, the emphasis now being on building up what thick parts are required by laminating together several pieces of thinner stock and by creating the hulls of boats as one-piece monocoque structures by the use of plywood or laminated veneers.

Indeed, it was the introduction of plywood to the domestic boatbuilding market in the early 1950s that was responsible for the boom in the building of small dinghies and yachts and the development of the DIY market. Although wood has excellent properties, it develops its strength in the direction of the grain as do unidirectional synthetic fibres, and its properties in other directions are considerably lower. That is why conventional wooden construction had to resort to the use of a considerable amount of framing, stringers and ribs in order to provide strength in all the required directions.

The development of techniques for slicing wood into thin sheets or veneers, and then bonding these veneers together so that their grain ran at 90° to the preceding veneer, allowed wood to become far more useful by increasing its strength and stiffness-to-weight properties. Furthermore, it enables the designer and builder to achieve much more consistent and accurate results since the properties of the resulting panels are easily determined. The use of plywood or individual veneers also reduces the labour required to build a wooden boat and makes it possible for the amateur builder to tackle quite ambitious projects that would be out of the question using more conventional methods.

Veneers can be cut in a variety of thicknesses from many different woods and with a great range of quality, depending on their intended application.

Fig. 4.2 The slicing process for veneer manufacture.

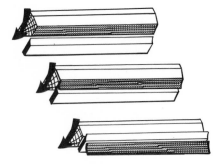

They are cut directly from the log by rotary or slice cutting. In rotary cutting the log is rotated between spindles and a knife moved so as to cut off a continuous sheet. In slice cutting the log is first cut into quarters and then cut by a straight knife that makes repeated cuts through the cut log. In both methods the log is first soaked to aid cutting, so the cut veneers have to be thoroughly dried before use. Because rotary-cut veneers are more susceptible to expansion and contraction than sliced veneers, the latter are usually preferred for low-pressure laminating.

Plywood is made by laying-up several sheets of veneers with the grain of each running perpendicular to the ones next to it – although some specialized types of plywood lay-up the internal veneers with the grain running in the same direction. In most plywood the lamination is made up of odd numbers of veneers so that the grain of the two outer faces runs in the same direction. For plywood intended for marine applications it is essential that only best-quality veneers are used and that the adhesive used for laminating the assembly of veneers is what is known as "water- and boil-proof".

Marine plywood is now the most commonly used form of wood in boatbuilding, thanks to its versatility. Not only is it strong and stiff but it is also much less likely to warp than solid timber and is easily available in a wide range of thicknesses from ⅛in to 1in (3.2mm to 25mm). Sheets are sold in standard sizes of 8ft x 4ft (2.4m x 1.2m), although special large sizes can sometimes be obtained or standard sheets scarfed together.

Plywood is used in many different areas in boat construction including hull planking, decks, frames, bulkheads, doors and most interior joinery. When it is used in conjunction with an epoxy resin, all the advantages of wood can be enjoyed without the disadvantages of conventional timber construction. One limitation of plywood is the difficulty of bending a panel to more than a gentle curve in one plane. In most of the applications for plywood this is not a problem, but when it comes to hull panels it is necessary that the design of the hull takes this restriction into consideration. In practice this means that hulls using plywood for panels use single, double or multiple chines to achieve the required shape without contorting the plywood into difficult curves. Although the use of plywood has been somewhat overshadowed in recent years by the development of other materials and methods of construction, it still remains a viable alternative, especially when price and speed of completion are important considerations.

For the builder whose design is for a round bilge hull for which plywood would be unsuitable, the alternative is to use veneers laminated directly over a male mould. Veneers are easily bent and held to the mould using staples while the adhesive cures. In effect the builder is laminating his own plywood in place and an additional advantage of this technique is that he can choose the direction of lay-up of each succeeding layer of veneers to cater precisely for the expected loads on the structure in the same way as a builder of an FRP hull would use undirectional fibre reinforcement.

Sliced veneers can be had in a range of lengths up to about 16ft (5m) with widths that are often random but are generally up to about 2ft (0.6m). A range of thicknesses are available but boatbuilders usually prefer to use the thickest possible – about ⅛in (3mm) – unless very tight curves have to be accommodated. Without doubt the use of laminated veneers can, if a clear finish is used, provide the best-looking boat, with excellent stiffness and strength at a low weight. If an epoxy resin is used for both laminating and coating, the useful life of the boat can be as good as any competitive material.

5 ADHESIVES

Adhesives are not a recent development but have been in use throughout recorded history. The Romans caulked their ships using a mixture of pine-wood tar and beeswax, while even earlier the Egyptians used gum arabic from the acacia tree, egg glue, resins from trees and semi-liquid balsams. Papyrus was an early laminated material made from beaten slices of reeds laid at right angles to each other and coated with flour paste. Apart from the introduction of rubber cements in the late nineteenth century, there was little development in adhesive technology until well into the present century.

In the period since the Second World War there has been a steady development of various types of synthetic adhesives. This rapid growth has resulted from the many advantages enjoyed by adhesives over other methods of joining materials. In many instances, thin films, fibres and small particles cannot be joined at all by alternative methods, while in other cases adhesives make it possible to build stronger, lighter assemblies than could previously be achieved. This is because the stresses involved can be distributed over a much larger area than if mechanical fastenings are used.

The greatest development of adhesives has taken place in the aerospace, automotive and construction industries, with natural spin-offs for boatbuilding. The strength-to-weight ratios and dimensional stability of many materials can be improved by laminating with the correct adhesive. Wood is a good example of such a material, being inherently water-sensitive and liable to dimensional change as well as variation in physical properties. Bonding thin wood veneers to form water- and warp-resistant plywood sheet was a major breakthrough in wooden boatbuilding made possible by the development of synthetic adhesives. Later developments of, in particular, epoxy resins have made possible even greater use of wood as a true engineering material.

The use of adhesives in boatbuilding is generally confined to the gluing of wood to other wood parts or, on occasions, to an FRP moulding, although the trend now is towards the use of adhesives for more varied applications. This move has begun with the bonding of FRP hull and decks solely by adhesives, although the majority of builders who use an adhesive in this area still employ mechanical fastenings as well. In the future we may see more use of true adhesive technology, particularly in the bonding of hull and decks but also to bond separately laminated FRP skins to a core material to make bulkheads, interior partitioning and even hulls and decks.

Although laminating resins may, in some ways, be considered to be adhesives, their roles are quite different and only the epoxy class of resin has the range of properties to be used in boatbuilding in a variety of applications. Although some builders, and particularly DIY builders, do make use of polyester resin to bond wood to an FRP laminate, this practice is not to be recommended where structural strength is important because of the poor adhesive properties of polyester, both to wood and to a curved polyester laminate.

Requirements of wood adhesives

Although the needs of gluing wood to itself or other materials will be considered here, the necessary properties of the adhesive differ little if the materials are FRP, wood or foam.

When any two materials are bonded together, the resulting composite has at least five elements that may cause bond failure: material 1/interface/

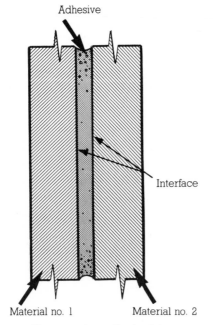

Adhesive

Fig. 5.1 The parts of an adhesive joint.

Fig. 5.2 Four forms of failure in an adhesive joint.

Interface

Material no. 1   Material no. 2

The parts of an adhesive joint

adhesive/interface/material 2. With the glues available to the boatbuilder it is, ideally, possible to create a bond where any failure would occur in the adherent rather than the adhesive or at any interface. To achieve this ideal, the adhesive must be able to fulfil several different and often contradictory requirements. In order to effect an optimum bond when gluing wood, for example, the adhesive must penetrate the wood surface to the level of solidly attached fibres without too much of it leaving the surface and thus causing a glue-starved joint. Once the adhesive has penetrated, it must also be able to wet the fibres. Both penetrating and wetting ability will be affected by the variations in permeability and chemistry of the wood surface. Variations in both occur between different species, between heartwood and sapwood, spring wood and summer wood and between timber with differing grain orientation. Other variables that directly affect both penetration and wetting are the moisture content of the wood and its surface condition, although these factors can be controlled by the user.

Given good penetration and wetting by the adhesive, the next requirement is that sufficient strength should be developed in the cured adhesive so that failure will not occur due to lack of cohesive strength within it or through lack of adhesion at the interface. To satisfy these requirements, the adhesive

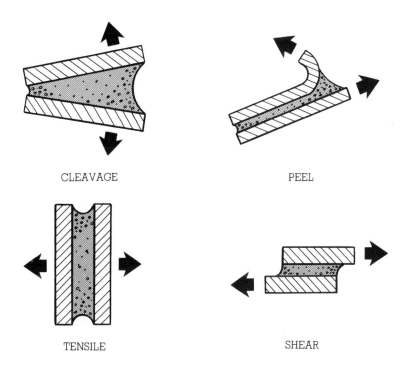

CLEAVAGE   PEEL

TENSILE   SHEAR

must have good mechanical strength properties as well as good flexibility. The two most likely modes of failure for the adhesive in wood gluing are shear or peel failure. To achieve adhesive properties to prevent these failures demands careful formulation since there is a trade-off between mechanical properties and flexibility. Although flexibility is important, the adhesive should not be too flexible, especially for use in pre-stressed structures, since otherwise it will creep over a period of time, leading to eventual failure.

Shrinkage is another problem associated with many adhesives. When an adhesive shrinks substantially on curing, strains are set up within the glue line that tend to pull the adhesive away from the adherends and so weaken the bond. This problem will be compounded if the joint is flexed and may lead to peel failure. When an adhesive shrinks on curing, it becomes necessary to apply pressure to the joint during cure to minimize the possible built-in stresses. Some adhesives may also require pressure as an aid to penetration, especially those carried in an aqueous/alcohol solution that must displace moisture from the surface cells before penetration can occur.

Although many adhesives may be found to fulfil the necessary requirements to one degree or another, there are further considerations that need to be taken into account when choosing adhesives for boatbuilding. The adhesive must be capable of continuing to provide a first-class bond over a long period of time, even when exposed to moisture, temperature extremes and biological attack. In boatbuilding terms, an adhesive for interior use must be at least cold-waterproof and able to withstand reasonable temperatures as experienced in the conditions in which the boat will be used. For structural interior use, and all other applications, more rigorous criteria must be applied, and adhesives must only be considered if they are fully weatherproof and not subject to biological attack. In this country British Standard 1204 lays down standards for moisture-resistant adhesives and for those that are weather- and boil-proof as well as defining gap-filling standards.

Other aspects of adhesives that are of concern to the boatbuilder include ease of application, the need for control of temperature, pressure and wood moisture content, versatility, toxicity and, of course, cost. We can now consider the most commonly used boatbuilding adhesives and compare them in terms of the above requirements. It must be realized that, within the classes of adhesives considered here, individual manufacturers' products may vary considerably because of different formulations. When in doubt over a choice between adhesives of the same class from different manufacturers, it makes sense to choose one offered by a company with detailed experience and a history of research and development with that particular type of adhesive in the boatbuilding industry.

Urea-formaldehyde resins

Urea resin adhesives are products of the condensation reaction between urea and formaldehyde. Hot-press ureas are used in the manufacture of hardwood plywood and particleboard for interior use. Such hot-press ureas are capable of producing a joint as strong as the wood itself. Room-temperature setting ureas are also used and are useful for small-scale bonding applications. These too can result in bonds as strong as the wood but they require the use of stronger acid catalysts than the hot-press varieties. The most convenient form of such a room-temperature setting urea is a ready-mix adhesive in which the spray-dried resin powder is mixed by the formulator with solid catalyst, buffer and filler. This combination is sold in powder form and needs only to be mixed with water in the recommended amount to be ready for use. Alternatively the resin part of the adhesive may be supplied in powder form – with a shelf-life of up to three years – and the hardener as a separate liquid. To use, the powder is mixed with water and applied to one surface while the hardener is applied to the other surface. The resin powder and water mix has a usable life of about three months so there is none of the wastage with this type that occurs with a ready-mixed powder resin and hardener. The other advantage is that the resin does not begin to harden until the two pieces to be joined are brought together.

Ureas have the advantage of being cheap but they are only suitable for limited uses since they are resistant only to cold-water immersion, are not weatherproof and are of limited durability. Hence they should be used only for interior finishing, preferably in non-structural applications. The two-part ureas can also be used for the construction of small dinghies that will be well protected by paint or varnish. However, because other building materials can be expensive, the small extra cost of a fully weatherproof adhesive would be well justified in terms of strength and durability of the finished craft.

Like all the adhesives formed by a condensation process, ureas shrink on curing and require pressure to achieve a satisfactory bond. Pressures in the region of 50–100psi (3.5–7.0kg/cm^3) are commonly required and this may be applied by clamping, nailing, screwing or bolting or by a combination of these methods. Along with all wood adhesives, urea resins are sensitive to the moisture content of the wood. As a general guide, a moisture content of between 12 and 15 per cent is suitable for these adhesives. At higher moisture contents the resin may not achieve sufficient penetration and wetting, while at levels lower than 12 per cent, resin-starved joints may occur as a result of the wood absorbing too much adhesive from the glue line. Temperature is also important: ureas in general need a minimum glue-line temperature of 50°F (10°C), although individual manufacturer's recommendations should always be followed.

Phenol-formaldehyde resins

Phenolic resins are the oldest of the synthetic resin adhesives. Originally used for hot-pressing of softwood plywood, cold-setting phenolics were developed during the Second World War. However, these adhesives require high concentrations of acid catalyst, and while hot-press phenolics are capable of producing bonds of 100 per cent wood strength, and will withstand harsh conditions, the cold-setting phenolics with highly acidic glue lines tend to lose strength quite rapidly. Furthermore, they may cause acid staining of the wood and, as well as having a short storage life, they have a very critical mixing ratio. They also have high toxicity and users may be more prone to dermatitis than with the other adhesives discussed here. For these reasons, phenolics are no longer used on their own but are quite commonly mixed with resorcinol adhesives to lower the latters' cost.

Resorcinol-formaldehyde resins

Resorcinolic adhesives, formed by condensation reactions between resorcinol and formaldehyde or phenol-formaldehyde, were used during the Second World War for the construction of plywood aircraft, fast patrol boats and minesweepers. These adhesives provide high-strength bonds, are usually durable, cure rapidly and can be used with a wide variety of adherends other than wood. Since their introduction they have been used in many industries, including boatbuilding, as important structural adhesives.

Resorcinolic adhesives can be most efficiently cured under neutral conditions, although some formulations are cured under mildly alkaline conditions to shorten clamping time and lower the minimum working temperature. However, these formulations may become more brittle with time and in general more neutral formulations show better stability. Resorcinolic adhesives for boatbuilding conform to BS 1204 WBP/GF (water- and boil-proof and gap-filling) and are capable of providing high-strength joints, usually stronger than the wood itself, given correct bonding techniques. They are resistant to virtually any of the conditions to which the wood may be exposed and will retain their original strength over a long period of time. They are capable of bearing heavy loads without creep and although they do, in general, have low flexibility, this can be varied with formulation and by the addition of certain modifiers and fillers.

As with the other condensation-formed adhesive resins, the resorcinols do require relatively high clamping pressures of between 50 and 200psi (3.5 and 14kg/cm³), depending on wood species, surface quality and moisture content. Although they are termed 'gap-filling', to BS 1204, this requires a gap of only 0.05in (approximately 1.25mm) to be filled. In practical boatbuilding terms this is very small, and in everyday use the adhesive will often be called upon to fill larger gaps. Although fillers can be added to achieve this, the strength of the glue line will be much reduced. The full strength of a resorcinol can only be achieved with a fully contact joint.

Resorcinolic adhesives shrink on cure since they have a solids content in the region of 50 to 60 per cent. In general they shrink less than the ureas, but this shrinkage is another reason why pressure must be applied if stresses (or total failure) in the glue line are to be avoided. The resorcinolics are more critical to the condition of use than the ureas, and one of the biggest problems of the manufacturers involved in the DIY market is the education of the users. The moisture content of the wood used should be between 12 and 18 per cent for most formulations and the minimum temperature generally recommended is 61°F (16°C) unless a fast grade of hardener is being used. In the case of high-specification work, a higher temperature of about 77°F+ (25°C+) may be called for with a cramping time of at least twenty-four hours and a curing period at the same temperature of about eight days.

Since resorcinolics cured at high temperature will have better mechanical properties, good working conditions are important. If gluing has to be done in poor conditions, it may be better to use a urea glue and accept the loss in performance due to the less efficient adhesive rather than have a doubtful bond with resorcinol.

Resorcinolic adhesives can suffer from temperature shock, which means that if the mixed adhesive is subjected to a temperature drop below a critical temperature, it will not cure properly even if the temperature is later raised. This is important when gluing out of doors and especially if the adhesive is left to cure overnight. In such conditions some form of heating must be provided to keep the temperature of the glue line at its correct level.

Dense timbers such as oak often cause gluing problems, and temperatures of 104°F+ (40°C+) with pressures of up to 200psi (14kg/cm^2) may well be needed to achieve consistently reliable results. These temperatures and pressures can be difficult to attain by both amateur and professional alike, and if difficulties are experienced the adhesive manufacturer should be consulted.

Epoxy resins

As the various urea, phenol and resorcinol-formaldehyde adhesives caused a revolution in wood boatbuilding in the 1940s and 1950s, so epoxy resin adhesives are likely to do now and in the future. While epoxy resins are more expensive than the adhesives so far described, they are superior to those adhesives in several important ways.

Epoxy adhesives are composed of 100 per cent solids and thus shrink only fractionally on curing. The shrinkage that does occur is caused not by solvent evaporation but by molecular cross-linkage and can be reduced to less than 1 per cent by the use of appropriate fillers. The practical effect of this is that only contact pressure, or even no pressure at all, is needed to create a high-strength bond. Unlike the ureas or resorcinols, epoxies cure without releasing water or other condensation by-products, and therefore they do not increase the moisture content of the wood at the glue line. Epoxies are also superior in mechanical strength, with the result that a thick glue line does not detract from the strength of the joint. While manufacturers of ureas and resorcinols talk in gap-filling terms of up to 0.05in (1.25mm), epoxies can fill gaps of ¼in (6mm) and more with ease. They also have far superior flexural strength, which results in joints with greatly increased peel strength.

Epoxies were first developed some forty years ago and have been used extensively in the aerospace, automotive and building industries for many high-strength applications. Because of the great cohesive strength of the cured adhesive and its excellent adhesion to so many materials, failure under load often occurs within one of the adherends rather than within the adhesive or at the interface. This happens with glass and aluminium in some applications as well as weaker materials such as concrete and wood. Epoxies are, for all practical purposes, impervious to water when cured and also have an outstanding resistance to solvents and heat. Early epoxy formulations were not, however, good wood adhesives since most were of high viscosity and did not spread, penetrate or wet-out well. Much work has been done to develop epoxies for use with wood, and suitable formulations are now well established which have excellent wetting properties.

Epoxies, unlike the other adhesives, can be easily modified to suit different applications by the selection of the base resin and hardener and by compounding with various fillers. When choosing an epoxy for a particular job, the boatbuilder may have the choice between a pre-mix; a two-pot resin and hardener with fillers already added; or a self-mix resin, hardener and fillers. The great advantage of the last type is that a good system of resin, hardeners and fillers enables the user to formulate his own mix on site to suit the particular application. Since a virtually infinite number of mixes can be obtained, a manufacturer formulating a pre-mix has to decide on the properties needed without seeing the application. With a little practice to develop a feel for the material, the user can quickly become expert at making up his own mixes, with the advantage that it is cheaper and involves less wastage than a pre-mix.

Epoxies have not only given boatbuilders an excellent adhesive that is capable of being used in all the traditional ways, but they have also enabled new construction techniques to be developed. One of these is the fillet technique of bonding. This was first used in the aerospace industry for bonding sheet and honeycomb materials and is made possible by the negligible shrink properties of the epoxy. The fillet joint is now being used in boatbuilding and can be an extremely useful technique, being strong, quick to carry out and cheap when compared with conventional methods. Since the density and strength properties of the adhesive can be varied at will by the use of the appropriate fillers, different types of fillets can be used for differing applications. Using this method, interior structures can be quickly bonded in place to create structural reinforcements very simply. This technique is by no means limited to wooden boats and is now commonly employed for the bonding of interior joinery and bulkheads to FRP hulls. Epoxies are also being used to bond glass-fibre decks and hulls to provide a strong but flexible joint that eliminates the chance of leaks from this sometimes problem area.

The curing temperatures required by epoxies vary considerably with the formulation, but for a boatbuilding epoxy adhesive a temperature of about 61–68°F (16–20°C) would be ideal. Unlike the resorcinols mentioned earlier, epoxies do not suffer from temperature shock and a batch of mixed resin and hardener can be frozen and later thawed, when it will still cure.

The moisture content of the wood should be no higher than 18 per cent, but there is no lower limit. The drier the wood, the better its mechanical properties and, if an epoxy coating is being used to encapsulate the wood (see also Chapters 2 and 4) the moisture content will be unable to vary significantly. Glue-starved joints can be avoided by the use of non-thixotropic fillers that prevent excess resin being drawn away from the surface, while still releasing enough resin to ensure thorough penetration. Epoxies do, generally, have a shorter pot-life than ureas or resorcinols since the latters' solvents help prevent a large mass of adhesive from curing too quickly. In practice this means that only enough adhesive should be mixed as can be applied in the gel time of the resin at the working temperature.

Using adhesives

When faced with a bonding problem, the boatbuilder has first to choose the adhesive for the job. Unfortunately, many builders select an adhesive purely on a cost basis without taking the other considerations fully into account. In any building situation the cost of even an expensive adhesive is a tiny proportion of the total cost of the structure. The importance of the adhesive, however, cannot be overstated: after all, the integrity of the entire structure may easily depend on the strength and durability of the adhesive which, if it fails, is unlikely to be easily repaired. While it may make economic sense to use an adhesive such as a urea for interior, non-structural use, for all other applications the best adhesive available must be chosen. It is likely that epoxies will come to be used more and more in the near future which will, of course, have some effect on lowering an already falling price. At the moment resorcinols are two or three times more expensive than ureas, while an epoxy is perhaps twice the price of a resorcinol, although it must be remembered that an epoxy, being 100 per cent solids, is less expensive than it might at first appear.

The working conditions in which the adhesive will be used must also be considered. Where possible, the choice of adhesive should be made first, then the working conditions adjusted to suit it. If, however, the builder has no control over his working conditions, he should consult the supplier of the adhesive for advice on his particular problem. Although the modern glues are very good indeed, they all need to be used in reasonable conditions and it is illogical for the user to pay for the best and to then expect it to perform to its full potential in conditions for which it was never designed.

The timber to be used should be carefully selected and stored so that its moisture content is in the range recommended by the adhesive manufacturer. Air-dried timber stored under cover outside will seldom have a moisture content of less than 16–18 per cent, and even timber stored in a centrally heated house is unlikely to have less than 10 per cent moisture. To achieve a moisture content of less than 18 per cent, which is needed for all adhesives, the wood must be artificially dried, then stored in warm and dry conditions. It is no use to bring a bit of wood in from outside and then expect the adhesive to perform as it is meant to do. Where possible, very dense timbers should be avoided since none of the adhesives works well on them because of the difficulty of penetrating and wetting the surface fibres. If such woods must be used, an epoxy is probably the best adhesive for the job, although the supplier should be consulted to ensure reliable results.

Whatever wood is used, the surface should be clean and roughened before the adhesive is applied. After a piece of timber has been worked, and then left, its surface becomes case-hardened, the fibres close up and it becomes more difficult for the adhesive to penetrate. Always roughen the surface with a coarse sandpaper immediately before bonding. Wood that is to be treated with a preservative should not be treated prior to bonding since the preservative may affect the adhesive penetration. Once the bond has cured, most adhesives will not be affected by the application of preservative; but check first with the adhesive manufacturer.

Whichever adhesive is used, it should be mixed carefully and exactly to the manufacturer's instructions. When the two parts have been brought together in the correct proportions, they should be thoroughly stirred for at least a minute to ensure even mixing. Fast mixing, especially with mechanical mixers, may cause aeration and the adhesive should be allowed to stand for a short while to allow the air to escape.

If the working temperatures are such that the adhesive is likely to cure too quickly, the mixing pot can be stood in a bowl of cold water to reduce its temperature. Always mix only that amount that can be applied before it begins to gel, otherwise wastage will occur. Usually the adhesive should be applied evenly to both surfaces and any areas that look dry, due to glue starvation, should be given another coat before the two surfaces are brought into contact. Enough adhesive should be spread so that, when pressure is applied (if needed), a small amount of glue is forced out of the joint. This indicates that enough glue is present in the joint, but minimizes wastage. If high pressure must be applied, as will be the case if a urea or resorcinol adhesive is used, this should be done immediately and the joint then left under pressure for the length of time recommended for that temperature.

The use of mechanical fasteners as well as the adhesive is only required to provide any necessary pressure while the glue hardens, or to increase the cross-grain strength of the wood, or as a belt-and-braces safety factor. Since the joint can only be as strong as the grain strength of the wood, woods weak in this respect may need additional fasteners. Rather than use conventional fasteners, the best method (where extra pressure is not required) is to use a dowel that is glued into a drilled hole into which it fits snugly. The advantage of this over screws, bolts or nails is that it has a much greater surface area and does not damage the wood fibres or internally stress the wood.

Whenever a synthetic resin adhesive is used, the user should endeavour to work clean, since all the synthetic glues are, to some degree, toxic. The hardener element is usually the most toxic, but every effort should be made to avoid skin contact with either part of the mixed adhesive. This can be best achieved by wearing disposable gloves and/or by using a good barrier cream recommended by the adhesive supplier. Given these simple precautions, the user should run little risk of becoming sensitized to the product.

6 PAINTS AND VARNISHES

The range of surface coatings on the market today is a bewildering one and so, despite the efforts of some manufacturers to educate the public, it is no surprise that many boat owners (and some professional builders) are confused as to the properties, advantages and disadvantages of the different systems. Modern paint technology is so advanced that it is no real problem for the paint formulator to develop a paint system with specific properties for particular applications, although since there is a trade-off between the different properties it is possible to optimize only some of them. Within the marine pleasure market the number of these possible applications is almost infinite and coatings now exist that are designed to suit most requirements.

As the level of technology has risen and the range of products expanded, it has become increasingly important for the user to know about and use the correct product for the job as well as the correct methods of preparation, application, thinning and brush cleaning. Many people criticize high-performance products unfairly when the cause for complaint is usually one of application. If the best finish is required, it must be accepted that more time and effort must be spent by the user if the performance possibilities of the materials are to be realized. Limited space does not allow discussion of specialized finishes or procedures in detail here, and this information can, in any case, be obtained from your chosen paint manufacturer or supplier. Of more importance is to understand the broad types of coatings that are available for common marine use and their particular attributes.

The range of commonly used marine coatings includes the conventional paints and varnishes composed of a mixture of natural and synthetic oils and resins, the one-pot polyurethanes, two-pot polyurethanes and the increasingly popular two-pot epoxy resins. All these systems have their advocates, but the choice between them should be made on the basis of performance and their ability to meet the requirements of a particular application.

In general, any surface coating has two functions: to protect the surface and to provide an aesthetically pleasing appearance. In the case of a working vessel, the latter requirement may be of minimum importance, and in certain instances some protective ability may also be sacrificed in favour of simple application and low cost. The marine environment is a harsh and demanding one, and to provide as complete a protection as possible the coating must be capable of resisting water and vapour absorption, chemical attack, ultra-violet breakdown, abrasion and other mechanical damage. Equally important, the coating must also have excellent adhesive properties if it is to remain on the surface it is intended to protect.

For cosmetic purposes the coating should provide a deep, high gloss (except when eggshell or matt finishes are used for interior surfaces) and should retain this finish for as long as possible without chalking, yellowing or cracking. In the case of a varnish the coating should not darken the wood (this can be achieved, if desired, by adding an appropriate stain) and should itself not darken with age. As well as providing good protection and an attractive appearance, other requirements of a coating system are ease of application, lasting ability and value for money. Although modern painting systems have, in many areas, an unquestionably superior performance over conventional systems, these advantages have to be balanced against the increased cost and the greater care needed in their application. There is little point in spending more on a high-performance system if slapdash application nullifies its performance potential and causes a repaint to be necessary a season later.

Fig. 6.1 The modern paint job not only protects the surface but can add greatly to aesthetic appeal and create a very individual boat.

Types of coatings

Early paints and varnishes were based on natural oils and early yachting books and magazines sometimes included recipes for the preparation of one's own paint. Nowadays, with the exception of a few tung oil varnishes, the cheapest marine paint systems are the synthetic, long oil base, alkyd finishes. Many types of oils can be used in their formulation but the common ones are soya, cotton seed and sunflower oils. These alkyd finishes are cheap and moderately durable, although their initial appearance will not last very long, especially if used on exterior surfaces, and yearly repainting will be necessary.

On the next step up the ladder of paint technology lie the one-pot polyurethane products. It is at this stage that misunderstanding often begins. The one-pot polyurethane range can be split into two distinct types. In the first group are the urethane modified oils and urethane modified alkyds. Both types are commonly used in the general DIY market but really only the modified alkyds should be considered for marine use. Neither type is a true high-performance, catalyst-cured system, both drying in the same way as conventional finishes by oxidation when in contact with air. The advantage of the alkyd modified with urethane is its excellent resistance to abrasion and its improved resistance to chemicals. The resistance to abrasion of this type is, in fact, often better than that of the more advanced, catalyst-cured systems.

The second type of one-pot polyurethane is the true isocyanate that cures by chemically reacting with atmospheric humidity. This type of finish is more expensive than previously described coatings and requires more care in its application, but it offers increased performance in gloss retention, durability, chemical resistance and moisture protection. Properly applied, this sort of coating is capable of lasting two seasons before needing recoating. Some moisture-cured, one-pot finishes can provide a finish to rival two-pot products, although they are not as controllable in formulation as the two-pot materials.

Two types of two-pot polyurethane finish are generally available, a point which is not often realized by the paint-buying public. The first-category finishes use what is called an aromatic hardening system, while the second – and superior – system uses an aliphatic hardener. The two can be distinguished in a paint manufacturer's brochure where the type of system is normally specified. The first type provides a first-class finish with an improvement in performance over conventional finishes and most one-pot polyurethanes. Ideal for interior use, it will, however, eventually chalk and yellow when applied to exterior surfaces, although it should be two or three years before recoating is necessary.

Fig. 6.2 One-off FRP hulls from male moulds rely on their paint system for protection and usually use an aliphatic or aromatic two-pot polyurethane system.

The aliphatic polyurethanes provide the best finish of all the types discussed, the resultant film giving excellent protection from abrasion, chemicals and heat. It is also very stable and makes a good water- and vapour-proof barrier. This type of finish usually provides a film that is slightly more flexible than the aromatic polyurethanes and so is less liable to cracking if the substrate flexes. It is ideal for exterior use since the film does not yellow or chalk and has very good gloss retention. Given correct surface preparation, application methods and conditions, this paint finish should last at least five years between recoating and may last considerably longer. It has been commonly used in the aerospace industry for a number of years and was also chosen for the coating of the superstructure on the *QE2*.

The aromatic polyurethanes should be considerably cheaper than the aliphatic, aromatic type, but in practice this often seems not to be the case. Naturally both types are more expensive than alkyd and one-pot finishes, but better results and a longer life can be expected. In future we may see aliphatic one-pot polyurethanes becoming commonly available with performances to rival existing two-pot finishes.

Some manufacturers of two-pot polyurethanes claim that their products need no undercoats, unlike conventional paint finishes. Although the use of an undercoat is certainly not vital, a better finish can usually be achieved by its use. This is because an undercoat will normally increase intercoat adhesion and will also increase the depth of gloss because of the higher pigment loading of the undercoat.

Another area in which confusion often arises is the possibility of overcoating conventional or one-pot finishes with two-pot polyurethanes. Most manufacturers say that this is impossible, and indeed the solvents incorporated in these products do often attack the existing coating. However, if the existing coating is old and stable, it is often possible to overcoat with a two-component product, although adhesion will be only as good as that provided by the existing coat. Before attempting to overcoat an existing finish, a small sample area should be tried to check the result.

Relatively recently two-pot epoxy finishes have become available to the marine pleasure market and they can be expected to take an increasing share in the future. They offer outstanding resistance to abrasion, water and vapour absorption and chemical attack as well as excellent adhesion, high build and durability. Their use as a topcoat is, however, limited by their susceptibility to ultra-violet attack. Ultra-violet light will cause the film to yellow and also chalk if not overcoated. Their performance characteristics make them ideal for use as a primer and undercoat under a topcoat of an aliphatic polyurethane. Epoxies are now available that are specifically designed for this purpose, in either clear or pigmented forms, which can be applied by roller, brush or spray methods.

Paint v varnish

When wood is to be coated, a choice exists between using a clear varnish or a paint finish. In general the comments made previously about the different types of finishes available apply equally to varnish and paint, but there are other important considerations that affect the choice between the two. Although varnish allows the beauty of the wood to be displayed and adds to the aesthetic appeal of any boat, it is undoubtedly true that no clear finish can offer the same degree of protection as a pigmented finish when used on exterior surfaces.

All varnishes provide a thinner film than the equivalent paint finish, and one- and two-pot polyurethanes give thinner films than conventional alkyd and modified alkyd products. Therefore, to provide the same degree of mechanical protection as a paint, the number of coats must be increased. If sufficient protection is not provided, and the film is damaged, moisture can get under the film. At best this will simply discolour the wood, while at worst it may lift the varnish film. When one- and two-pot polyurethane finishes are used, their excellent impermeability to water vapour causes any that finds its way under the film to build up a vapour pressure that can lift the film in places or in its entirety. This can also occur without mechanical damage if edges are present that are difficult to seal with the varnish.

The other serious cause of deterioration is the effect of ultra-violet light. This penetrates the varnish film and indeed is magnified by refraction through the film and by any salt crystals present on the surface. The ultra-violet attacks the wood surface, bleaches it and causes a breakdown of the surface wood fibres. As these fibres degrade, the adhesion of the film is seriously weakened, causing eventual failure at the wood surface. To reduce this effect, deep penetration of the wood fibres by the varnish is necessary.

When exterior wood surfaces are to be varnished for aesthetic reasons, there are different approaches that can be used, depending on the amount of wood surface to be covered. If there is only a small amount of wood trim, a cheap conventional varnish can be used and would provide a satisfactory coating, provided regular maintenance is carried out. In fact there is probably no better solution than to use a traditional tung oil varnish, which gives a high build and good gloss retention and seems to provide some protection to the wood from ultra-violet attack. Regular rubbing down and recoating must be carried out to maintain the finish.

If a larger surface area is to be coated, such as the topsides, a different approach can be recommended, especially in the case of a new boat. This alternative is to use an epoxy and aliphatic polyurethane combination. The bare wood is coated with three or four coats of a clear epoxy before being overcoated with at least two coats of the polyurethane. Ideally the polyurethane should have an ultra-violet barrier incorporated to help reduce its absorption. The epoxy coats will provide excellent adhesion to the wood fibre, a high build and will seal it nearly completely from water absorption. The polyurethane topcoats will add to the high gloss and protect the epoxy from the ultra-violet. Since epoxy is sensitive to this type of light, it will eventually begin to yellow, although such a finish could be expected to last up to eight or ten years in Northern European conditions before needing attention. Because the epoxy is used under the polyurethane, the yellowing that does occur is purely cosmetic and results in no other deterioration of its properties.

Choosing a paint system

The decision as to which type of system to use will always depend to some extent on the type of boat and its construction. In the case of an older, conventionally built wooden boat, the problem is one of protecting the surface as much as possible from mechanical and chemical damage as well as providing an attractive finish. Waterproofing the surface to the extent normally possible with high-performance systems is usually not possible, given the movements in this type of structure, and is often undesirable. Most conventionally built wooden boats have some movement and many need to be able to absorb moisture if the hull or deck is to remain tight. Therefore the use of a highly impermeable two-pot polyurethane would be inappropriate. A conventional alkyd or urethane modified alkyd system will provide the necessary protection while also being relatively cheap and easy to apply.

On surfaces such as plywood, moulded wood, wood/epoxy composite, GRP, ferro-cement, steel and aluminium a different system can be used. These types of surfaces are generally stable and should not move to any important degree. Here the most important requirement is to prevent moisture penetration through the coating, to maximize surface protection from mechanical, chemical and corrosion damage, and to provide a pleasing, long-lasting appearance. The high-performance systems are best able to do this and for exterior use the best choice really lies between an aliphatic polyurethane system or a combination of epoxy undercoat with aliphatic polyurethane topcoats. The latter combination is probably the best system currently available.

Many people still seem dismayed at the thought of painting GRP yachts. The fact is that GRP is not an impermeable material but very slowly absorbs moisture. This permeability can and should be reduced on new boats by the use of a gel coat on underwater surfaces that is clear or only lightly pigmented. In the case of one-off GRP boats or other such male-moulded craft built without a gel-coat, painting will always be necessary to protect the glass fibre from water absorption and to provide a good appearance. Two-pot polyurethanes and epoxies provide a more impermeable barrier to moisture than does gel-coat; hence there are advantages to the painting of even new boats with such a system. In any case, there will come a time when the gel-coat has deteriorated to such an extent that painting is required to restore the appearance. The use of a primer over the degreased gel-coat is usually recommended. When used on newish craft, this primer will be able to bond chemically with the gel-coat, but in older craft this is unlikely to happen, with consequent risk to all subsequent coats of paint. A more secure solution is to abrade the gel-coat firmly to remove all gloss and then apply two or three coats of epoxy before overcoating with an aliphatic polyurethane.

Aluminium alloy does not, of course, require painting above the waterline, although most people prefer the appearance of a painted surface to that of bare aluminium. Before painting either aluminium and steel, the surface will need a thorough degreasing, etching and priming. The paint manufacturer should always be consulted and his recommendation accurately followed.

In the case of boats that are kept ashore when not in use, the same paint system that is used for the above-water surfaces should be used for the bottom. Boats kept afloat, however, will need antifouling to prevent underwater growth. Many types and strengths of antifouling are available and if in doubt as to which to use or which type is already on your boat, you should consult a paint manufacturer. Epoxy or two-pot polyurethanes will provide a good base for use under antifouling and even gel-coated GRP yachts will benefit by their use to reduce the risk of moisture absorption and the possibility of osmosis.

Interior surfaces are not generally subjected to the same amount of abuse as exterior ones, so less expensive paints or varnishes are generally acceptable. The one- or two-pot aromatic polyurethanes are very acceptable for such uses and will provide an attractive, long-lasting finish. In the case of plywood, moulded wood and wood/epoxy craft, care must be taken to prevent the absorption of moisture by interior surfaces. If any moisture change can occur in the wood, physical changes such as shrinkage and expansion may occur. If the outer surfaces are painted with a high-

Fig. 6.3 Modern paint systems can be toxic so full precautions should be taken to avoid inhaling fumes, especially when spraying. Cover as much exposed skin as possible to prevent skin-contamination.

performance system, water absorption from the inside can easily affect the adhesion of the outer film. Due to the often high humidity levels inside boats, the inside surfaces of wooden craft should receive similar attention to the outer surfaces. An ideal treatment is to coat all wood surfaces both inside and out with two or three coats of an epoxy to ensure a stable surface before overcoating with a polyurethane finish. For interior use an aromatic one- or two-pot polyurethane would be satisfactory.

Whatever type of finish is eventually chosen, it is critical to good results that the manufacturer's recommendations are followed exactly, both for surface preparation and application. With all types of finish the preparation of the surface should take far longer than the application of the coating, and unless this is done thoroughly the resulting film cannot be truly satisfactory. One of the common criticisms made about high-performance systems in general concerns their application. Many users naturally use the same technique as they would for conventional paints and run into problems with brushmarks. The reason for these complaints is usually a lack of understanding of the products. The one- and two-pot catalyst systems differ markedly in flow properties, and while the conventional paints and varnishes require quite a lot of brush work, the catalysts do not. These catalytic-cured finishes have self-levelling properties, but this attribute can be ruined by over zealous brushing. The paint or varnish should be applied to the surface, brushed out quickly and then left. Do not try to brush it out further, or to work a new area into a drying one, or brushmarks on the cured coating will result. Once the different techniques for using catalytic coatings are learnt, they should be found to be no more difficult to apply than conventional finishes. If the best possible surface finish is required, the catalyst-cured, one- and two-pot polyurethanes have the advantage of being able to be burnished. This is done to the final coat when cured by rubbing with an abrasive compound followed by the compatible polish. Because of the very hard surface and deep gloss of these finishes, this treatment will remove minor surface imperfections to give a very smooth and glossy finish. If after a period of hard use the finish is showing some signs of wear, it can be restored to its former appearance by the same procedure.

Modern paint technology certainly has a lot to offer to all types of craft and it is worth spending some time reading manufacturers' brochures and consulting them to find the best solutions for your particular painting problems. Do not, though, expect something for nothing. If you choose a high-performance paint system, you must be prepared to follow the correct procedure for surface preparation and the application of the coating.

SECTION II
METHODS

7 DESIGN CONSIDERATIONS

In the previous six chapters a variety of materials have been considered which between them account for the majority used in modern boatbuilding. Although an understanding of the separate materials is important if the properties of the finished laminate are to be understood, it is equally vital to consider how the different, sometimes complementary, materials affect each other and how the method of construction has an effect on the finished product.

While the person intending to have a one-off yacht built, especially a high-performance craft, will usually take an interest in the materials and the method of construction chosen by the designer, the owner of a production craft is often woefully ignorant of what has gone into his pride and joy, the way in which it was built, and the effect that both have on the performance and life expectancy of the finished product. The new generation of boat owners tends to treat boats like any other consumer product, such as a car, and takes little interest in the way the product is produced. This is a very short-sighted view since a boat is such an expensive item – even a small dinghy costs a not insignificant sum – and is expected to have a long life-span, retain its value and be safe to use in a hostile environment. Given these unique requirements, it is obviously sensible for the boat user, owner or potential buyer, to have sufficient understanding to be able to choose a good product from an experienced and efficient builder.

One of the most obvious requirements of a designer is to ensure that any new design, be it a small family cruiser, a round-the-world maxi racing yacht or a fast powerboat, is strong enough to cope with the variety of loads to which it will be subject throughout its life. In practice it is not usually ultimate strength that creates design problems – except in some specialist designs – but rather it is the need for stiffness which is sometimes difficult to achieve.

Fig. 7.1 The designer and builder of performance yachts, like this main hull for an 80-ft. trimaran, will go to a lot of trouble to optimize the materials and construction method used, to give a light, stiff and strong hull.

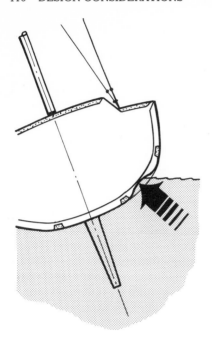

Fig. 7.2 Flexural stiffness of hull panels is important if the hull is not to deform under wave pressure.

Fig. 7.3 Panel stiffness can be increased by using regularly spaced stringers laminated to the moulding.

The word 'stiffness' has, unfortunately, rather a vague meaning for most of us and so it should be defined exactly. There are two types of stiffness of interest to the boat designer: one is the stiffness of hull or deck panels – that is, the ability of the panel to resist bending – and the other is the stiffness of the hull or deck material when loaded in tension or compression. The measure of a material's stiffness is called its modulus – flexural modulus is concerned with bending resistance and tensile or compressive moduli are concerned with the ability of the material to resist being stretched or compressed.

The flexural stiffness of hull panels is important in any boat, since if the hull cannot withstand water pressure without flexing the boat will change shape with every wave that passes, the interior reinforcement and any sub-mouldings and joinery will be subject to changeable and unfair stress, fatigue damage is likely, and forward, driving energy will be wasted, with the result that the boat will be slower than it should be.

Panel stiffness is dependent on the area of unsupported panel, the panel thickness and the flexural modulus of the panel material, so changes in panel stiffness can be caused by changes in any of these factors. Obviously the faster the boat travels, the higher will be the impact energy from each wave that passes, as designers of fast multihull yachts or offshore powerboats know well. In fact, fast offshore powerboats are often subject to enormous deceleration forces and impact loads on hull panels are measured in tons.

While the designers and builders of high-performance craft will usually be well aware of the need for panel stiffness and will design and build accordingly, the builders of less performance-oriented boats do not always seem to give sufficient attention to this problem. Even a relatively small cruising yacht can be subject to considerable impact from waves, especially in the forward sections when beating to windward in a strong wind and large sea. It is not unusual for owners of production boats to complain of interior furniture pulling away from the hull, of doors and drawers no longer fitting and even bulkheads cracking or pulling away from the hull. Such damage is often put down to the swelling of interior woodwork, but the real reason is often the flexing of the hull panels and in many cases this will be shown by the ultimate cracking or crazing of the gel-coat or exterior paint or varnish and/or the delamination of whatever internal ribs or stringers might be fitted.

It is often the skimping of internal reinforcement that is the root cause of panel flexing. The reason that ribs and stringers are fitted is to reduce the area of unsupported panel and so control flexing. Unfortunately, the laminating of such reinforcement is very time-consuming when compared to the relatively quick process of laminating the hull itself and consequently adds to the labour costs. For this reason the amount fitted is often cut down to the detriment of the finished boat, and with consequences that often do not become apparent for some time.

The answer to panel flexibility in production boats would usually be an increase in the amount of internal stiffening, although an increase in panel thickness could also be a solution. Increasing the thickness of a solid lay-up would, however, increase the weight of the hull considerably and would often result in an over-strong, heavy boat. The answer here would be to use a sandwich construction to give extra thickness without a weight penalty, but the cost effectiveness of this approach would have to be assessed according to the individual application, as would the cost and difficulty of adapting the production process of a design already in production. For a new design the advantages of sandwich construction outlined in Chapter 3 should be considered at an early stage. The use of an alternative fibre reinforcement or a production technique to give a panel with higher flexural modulus could also be considered, but is the most unlikely course of action for the production builder who must always consider the cost effectiveness of any changes he may make.

The designer of one-off boats, especially high-performance sail or power craft, will be most concerned to achieve maximum panel stiffness and is likely to use a combination of sandwich construction and high-modulus fibre reinforcement together, probably, with a production process that allows for tighter control of the laminate, although the final choice will still be determined by any financial constraints. This is not to say that a thin skin over a rigid framework of internal reinforcement cannot achieve high panel stiffness, but this method of construction, although sometimes used with wood (and, of course, with aluminium), is complicated to build, expensive, and does not give the impact resistance or clean interior, thermal or acoustic insulation, offered by a sandwich hull.

When high-modulus fibres first appeared on the boatbuilding scene, some designers and builders tried to use them on existing designs to reinforce panels that had proved to be lacking in flexural stiffness. The temptation was to laminate limited amounts of these fibres on to the inside panel faces to add stiffness without extra design work and with minimum extra cost. Unfortunately, this approach of adding a high-modulus fibre to a low-modulus laminate simply meant that the carbon fibres were now taking, or trying to take, the full bending stress on the panel with the result that the carbon reinforcement either failed or delaminated from the rest of the

Fig. 7.4 An alternative approach to increase panel stiffness is to use sandwich construction.

laminate. It must be emphasized that there can be no short cut in design work and the whole laminate must be designed to withstand the loads to which it will be subject.

The other type of stiffness of the structure – the resistance of the hull and deck to being stretched and compressed – is also of importance to the success of the design, especially when performance boats are being considered. Any boat suffers a variety of stresses throughout its life and at times these can be substantial. In a sailing yacht, for instance, the mast presses down into the middle of the boat while the shrouds pull up at the sides and the forestay and backstay attempt to pull up the ends of the vessel. In addition, passage through waves imposes wringing strains on the structure, as does the righting moment of the keel of a monohull.

A multihull does not, of course, have the problems associated with keel-imposed strains; instead it has to cope with the righting moment and associated strains of the floats and crossbeams. A fast powerboat does not

Fig. 7.5 A comparative graph shows the amount the various materials stretch under load – the elongation – and their resistance to stretching. The steeper the line on the graph, the higher the tensile modules of the material.

Fig. 7.6 The specific stiffness and specific strength of fibres is important when a lightweight hull is required.

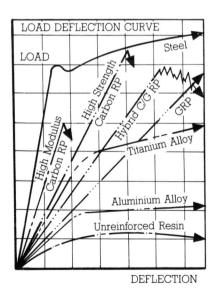

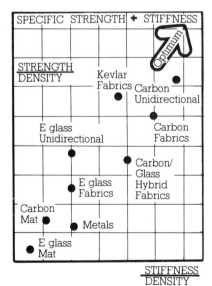

suffer these problems, but it too has a variety of forces acting on it as it becomes partly airborne off the top of waves before crashing back down at speed.

Whatever material is used for a boat's structure, it will have to stretch, to some extent, to resist tensile loads and compress under compressive loads. The tensile and compressive moduli are the measures of the resistance of the material to such stretching or compressing, but no matter how high the moduli some movement will always occur.

The tensile modulus should not be confused with the elongation of the material under load. While the modulus is the measure of the resistance of the material to stretching, the elongation, expressed as a percentage of original length, is the amount the material will stretch under load up to its ultimate tensile strength (UTS) or point of failure. As will be seen later, the relationship between the elongation of the fibre under load and the elongation capacity of the resin matrix has a significant effect on the ultimate strength of a laminate and the way in which it fails under high loads.

The stiffness of the hull and deck material is especially important for a sailing yacht if full performance is to be realized. Any distortion in hull shape under load will result in a reduction in rig tension, increased forestay sag and a resulting loss in pointing ability and overall performance. The sophisticated rigs used on modern racing yachts can, in fact, be put in jeopardy by even small deflections in the hull shape under rig tension, so small is the margin for error with these rigs. Consequently, if a high-performance rig is to be tuned to peak efficiency and kept tuned, the hull must deflect as little as possible under rigging loads that can often be measured in thousands of pounds.

Under fore-and-aft rigging tension, the bottom of the hull is under tension as the ends of the hull are pulled upwards, while the deck is under compression. The sideways rigging loads have a similar effect, creating tensile strains in the hull and compressive strains in the deck, both in an athwartships direction.

The magnitude and direction of such forces can be identified by the designer whose job then is to decide on the allowable deflections under such loads and to specify a lay-up to cope with these requirements. In order to resist such stresses, the designer has the choice of the range of fibre reinforcements with different moduli as well as strength properties. One technique used in the building of high-performance craft is the use of limited quantities of high-modulus fibres in areas of the laminate where they are needed to resist deflection under high loadings. Thus the fore-and-aft centre-line of the hull, athwartships between the shrouds and around the keel/hull joint, along the length of the deck and across it in the area of the mast, are all areas where the use of such reinforcement is very beneficial.

The designer does, however, have to be careful when increasing the stiffness of parts of the structure to avoid causing problems in other areas through the transfer of loads in what can be quite unexpected ways.

Another technique used to isolate these rigging and keel loads is the incorporation of a space-frame, usually of aluminium or carbon-fibre tubing. Such a space-frame is used to tie in all the high-stress areas such as rigging points, mast step, keel and rudder, to resist the deflections that the stresses in these areas can cause and to isolate these stresses from the rest of the structure.

Multihull yachts also have problems resisting the deflections caused by large stresses in their structure. With righting moments created by the use of high-buoyancy floats on the end of long, slim crossbeams, the potential for deflection in the structure is high. In the last few years the stiffness of multihulls has increased enormously, even though the rigs carried by these yachts have also increased in size. High-modulus fibre reinforcement has found extensive use, especially in the crossbeam areas of both trimarans and catamarans. Shrouds have been moved inboard from the floats to the main hull on trimarans and close to the mast of catamarans with the result that large headsails can be sheeted closer and fore-and-aft stiffness has been increased to the extent that forestays can now be kept tight under load.

Although the examples above have concentrated on high-performance craft where the stiffness of the structure is vital to performance, stiffness is also of importance for cruising boats if to a somewhat lesser degree. If a cruising boat lacks stiffness, it will not only suffer a reduced efficiency from the rig but will also suffer distortions in hull shape that could become permanent, thus affecting the fit of interior joinery, doors, drawers, hatches and even the engine installation.

Dinghies, too, should have a structure that is stiff enough for the purpose for which they are designed. While general purpose, knock-about dinghies can achieve satisfactory stiffness without the use of anything more than a general-purpose laminate, racing dinghies fall into the same category as the larger racing yachts and many now make use of the highest-modulus fibres to resist in-plane deflections, and of sandwich construction to achieve panel stiffness. Indeed, many of the techniques now used in larger offshore craft were first tried out on high-performance racing dinghies.

Weight

Uffa Fox hit the nail on the head when he said that the only useful place for weight is in a steamroller. Designers of modern performance boats know this well and, like the designers of aircraft, most work on the principle of 'adding lightness'. Reducing the weight of any boat can reduce the energy costs of production as well as the energy required to drive the craft, whether power or sail.

The beauty of reducing weight in a boat's structure is that it has a cumulative beneficial effect. A lighter sailing yacht requires less sail area to drive it than does her heavier sister, with the result that more weight is saved through the smaller rig and loads on gear decrease allowing lighter fittings. The reduced forces now acting on the structure because of the smaller rig in turn allow further weight savings in the hull and deck. By resulting in the use of smaller, lighter equipment, the reductions in weight of the structure can, as long as they are not achieved at enormous expense, reduce the cost of the whole boat.

An alternative to reducing the overall weight of the boat is to keep the displacement the same by adding weight saved in other areas to the keel to increase the ballast ratio and hence the sail-carrying power. Multihulls, of course, do not use the weight of a keel to give righting power, and with this type of boat weight saved translates directly into extra speed through an increase in the power-to-weight ratio.

Power craft can use weight savings to reduce the required engine size for a given top speed and hence further reduce the overall weight of the craft and increase the fuel economy and the range. Alternatively, the same size engine may be retained to increase the maximum speed.

Du Pont, the manufacturers of Kevlar aramid fibres, quote an example of weight savings achieved in a fast, commercial and sports fishing boat. By substituting a lay-up of Kevlar for the conventional glass-fibre laminate, the total all-up weight of the boat was reduced by 12 per cent. Using identical engines, as in the conventional glass-fibre version, the Kevlar hull was 10 per cent faster under a light load and 15 per cent faster with a heavy load. The cruising range was increased by 50 per cent, as was the fuel economy. Alternatively, the Kevlar boat could carry a payload of 2425lb (1100kg) heavier than the standard hull and although the Kevlar version cost more to produce the reduced fuel consumption or increased payload could soon pay for the difference in cost.

Another good example of the benefits of weight saving, this time from outside the boating world, is the use by Formula One racing teams of FRP sandwich construction for the chassis of racing cars. A typical light-weight monocoque chassis uses Kevlar and carbon fibres over an aramid honeycomb core. The carbon fibres provide maximum stiffness while the Kevlar increases the impact strength. When compared with an aluminium alloy chassis, weight savings of between 30 and 50 per cent have been achieved and the FRP chassis are capable of lasting a full season whereas the aluminium versions would normally be replaced during the season because of fatigue. Impact resistance has also been shown to be excellent following several high-speed crashes.

Boat designers have naturally concentrated on reducing the weight of performance craft since the benefits here are quickly seen in the racing results, but it should not be thought that weight saving has no place in cruising craft. Of course, it must not take place at the expense of structural integrity, fatigue resistance or longevity of the product, but the fact is that reduction in weight can bring many of the above-mentioned benefits to cruisers as well as racers. In particular, the attraction of having a smaller rig or engine, lighter gear and easier handling must appeal to many cruising people, with the added benefits of easier and cheaper maintenance and reduced all-round running costs.

Weight distribution

It is not only the total weight of the boat that is of interest to designers: the position of that weight within the structure is equally critical to performance. Any boat, power or sail, will pitch when sailing in waves, but energy absorbed through pitching is energy lost from driving the boat forwards. In order to reduce pitching, the weight of the whole structure should be concentrated as much as possible near to the centre of gyration of the boat – about amidships – and the ends of the craft kept as light as possible. The designer of a performance boat of any type will always strive to reduce the weight of the structure at the ends as much as possible, adding weight if that is required by a rating rule, minimum weight requirement or desired displacement, at the centre of the craft.

The owner should, however, be aware that non-structural weight, i.e. interior fittings, deck gear, etc., amounts to a significant proportion of the total weight and this too should be kept out of the ends if the designer's efforts are not to be nullified. The same also applies to the weight of the rig and keel since weight distributed away from the centre of gyration, even in a vertical direction, still affects pitching. In practice this means that yachts with lighter masts, rigging and sails, and with ballast carried internally or near the top of the keel, will pitch less than other yachts in which less attention has been given to this problem.

Weight cannot, obviously, be reduced at the expense of the minimum requirements of strength and stiffness, although where a boat is over-designed in these areas simple reductions of the amount of material may be possible. Normally, however, weight reductions are achieved by specifying a lighter, more efficient material instead of the more customary production lay-up which provides a relatively heavy, low-performance but cheap laminate. In fact, boats with the highest priority for minimum weight are invariably racing craft which also have a need for maximum strength and stiffness, so the designer cannot afford any reduction in these properties in order to achieve weight reductions. This usually results in a need for the use of the more expensive materials, together with sophisticated building methods in order to satisfy the two requirements.

Cruising boats, on the other hand, can usually achieve satisfactory and worthwhile weight savings without going to the expense of using 'exotic' materials or building methods. Not only is the need for light weight less urgent in this type of craft, but the designed safety margins will usually be greater and the importance of cost more critical. It is usually possible to reduce the weight of such designs simply by altering the materials specification slightly and using a more controlled building method or by changing the specification from single-skin to sandwich construction.

When considering a specification for any boat, the designer will be most interested in the specific properties of the various materials. Specific strength and specific modulus are simply and respectively the strength and modulus of the material divided by its specific gravity, and are thus a measure of strength and stiffness in relation to weight. The higher the specific strength and modulus of a material, the better it is suited to building a low-weight but strong and stiff structure.

Many light-weight, high-performance boats are built with sandwich construction to give maximum panel stiffness at low weight, and in this case the designer will consider the specific properties not only of the skin material but also of the core. For performance boats where cost is a secondary consideration, a core material will be chosen that has the highest possible compression and shear properties at the lightest achievable weight and this will be allied with a skin material that shows high specific strength and stiffness. Throughout the design of any boat it must be borne in mind that there is usually little point in mixing high- and low-performance materials. Thus the use of a cheaper, lower-performance core with high-performance skin materials will waste the potential of the latter which will never be able to achieve their full potential because of the limitations imposed by the performance of the core.

It is not, of course, only the specific properties of the chosen materials that will affect the weight, strength and stiffness of the structure. Many other variables have considerable affect and these will be considered in the next section.

Matching materials to requirements

Once the design requirements of the yacht or boat have been decided upon, the building specification can be considered. Using either FRP or wood, the specific choice of materials and lay-up specification can then be tailored to give exactly the properties required by the designer.

Material stiffness

When considering the in-plane stiffness of an FRP laminate – that is, the tensile or compressive modulus or resistance of the material to being stretched or compressed – a quantitative estimate of the dependence of the stiffness on the materials used in the laminate can be found by using the so-called 'rule of mixtures'. Although this does not give an exact result, it is supported by practical tests and allows a good understanding of the effect of altering the type and quantity of the reinforcement.

If 'E' represents the modulus of the laminate, 'Ef' and 'Er' the moduli of the fibre and resin respectively, and 'Vf' and 'Vr' the volume fractions of the fibre and resin, then, by the rule of mixtures:

$$E = Er \, Vr + \propto Ef \, Vf$$

The variable $\propto$ is a factor that depends on the efficiency of the fibre reinforcement. If a continuous unidirectional (UD) fibre is used in which all the fibres are neatly arranged in one direction, the efficiency factor = 1. In

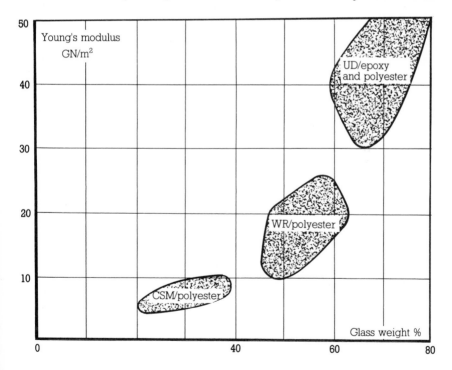

Fig. 7.7 Typical stiffness data for unidirectional, woven roving and CSM E glass. The envelopes refer to a scatter caused by variations in the resin system used for laminating.

this case, however, the modulus of the laminate, E, refers only to the modulus in the direction of the fibres. The modulus in any other direction will be much lower and cannot be determined from this formula.

If a balanced bidirectional (biD) fibre reinforcement such as woven rovings or woven or knitted fabric is used, the efficiency factor will be in the region of 0.5, since half the fibre in a given volume runs in any one of two directions. Loosely woven rovings or knitted fabrics in which the strands are not tightly crimped will produce a slightly higher efficiency factor than tightly woven fabrics made from twisted yarns in which the twisting and crimping of weft and warp do not allow the fibres to lie flat and straight.

The modulus of a laminate containing balanced bi-directional reinforcement is true for the two directions of the fibres, usually but not always arranged in perpendicular directions, but for other directions the modulus will be less.

In a chopped-strand mat (CSM) or other random-fibre laminate there is, in theory, no preferred fibre direction in the plane of the laminate and the efficiency factor is approximately equal to 0.3 and the modulus given by the rule of mixtures applies for all directions in the plane of the laminate. In practice the production process of CSM tends to impart a slight bias of fibres

Fig. 7.8 The stiffness and strength of a hybrid laminate depend on the proportion of the fibres used. The diagram above shows the increase in stiffness and strength as the percentage of carbon fibre is increased in a CF/glass laminate.

Fig. 7.9 Typical tensile-strength data for unidirectional, woven roving and CSM E glass. The envelope scatter is caused by differences in the resins used for laminating.

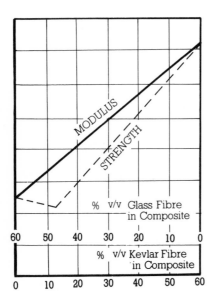

in the direction of the roll and this should be allowed for when laminating by varying the direction of alternate layers of the mat.

Because the moduli of any of the possible fibre reinforcements are far higher than that of the resin matrix, the dominant part of the above equation is the second, and the modulus of the laminate is thus dependent on the fibre type, its volume fraction and the amount of fibre oriented in a particular direction.

Taking E glass as an example, we can find the following figures for the moduli of laminates comprising CSM, WR and UD reinforcements.

If Ef = 71 GPa (E glass fibre)
  Er = 3.5 GPa (typical polyester resin)

For CSM:
  $\propto$ = 0.3
  Vf = 0.2
  Vr = 0.8

Then E (CSM) = 7.06 GPa

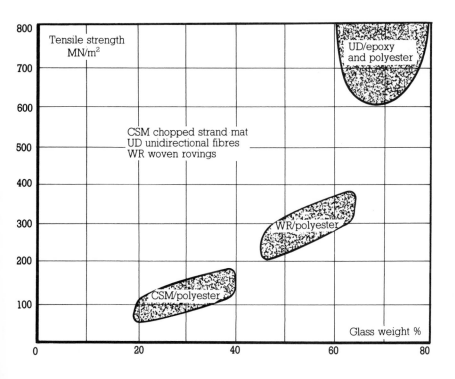

For WR:
  $\propto$ = 0.5
  Vf = 0.35
  Vr = 0.65

Then E (WR) = 14.7 GPa

For UD:
  $\propto$ = 1.0
  Vf = 0.5
  Vr = 0.5

Then E (UD) = 37.25 GPa

(NB These figures give the modulus of the laminate in the direction of fibre orientation and figures for UD and WR reinforcements will be considerably lower in other directions.)

If an S glass fibre reinforcement were to be substituted for the E glass used in the above example, the higher modulus of S glass (85 GPa) would translate into improved laminate properties. For instance, E (S glass WR) would equal 17.15 GPa and E (S glass UD) would equal 44.25 GPa. Further improvements would be found by the use of Kevlar or carbon fibres, with the latter in high-modulus unidirectional form, giving a laminate modulus in the region of 200 GPa.

The above formula for the stiffness of a laminate gives an indication of the short-term properties only. Reinforced plastics are subject, like most other materials, to fatigue failure under long-term repeated loads and also have a tendency to creep under sustained loads. Both affect the long-term properties of a laminate and will be limiting factors in the design of a laminate for marine purposes.

For the designer of a wooden structure there is a wealth of published information on the properties of the whole range of wood species, but he may use a similar procedure to the above if more than one type or density of wood is used in a structure. As with FRP laminates, the properties of wood vary according to grain orientation and, indeed, wood can be considered in a similar way to unidirectional fibre reinforcements used in FRP laminating.

In an FRP laminate it is not, of course, necessary to use only one type of fibre. Laminates in which more than one fibre is used are known as 'hybrids'. They may be made from a hybrid cloth (see Chapter 1) in which the two fibres are woven together, or one which is composed of separate layers of the different fibres. In either case the stiffness of the laminate will depend on the volume content of each fibre and their orientation in the laminate. For a hybrid, the rule of mixtures can be extended to handle more than one fibre by splitting the fibre part of the formula so that each fibre is dealt with separately.

Strength

Since the fibre part of an FRP structure also strengthens the resin matrix as well as stiffening it, the strength properties of a laminate can also be determined by the proportion of fibres oriented in a particular direction. Thus the rule of mixtures can be used to provide an estimate of the strength properties of a laminate with varying types and amounts of fibre reinforcement. However, the use of this rule will not give as reliable a prediction of strength as it does of stiffness, since while the modulus of a FRP material defines an average property of a volume of material containing a large number of fibres, the strength of the material is dependent on the failure mechanism of the fibre/resin relationship. Thus the strength characteristics are less predictable because of the presence of voids and variations in fibre and resin strengths, as well as the strength of the bond between the two, but the formula can still be used as a guide for our purposes.

If 'X' stands for the tensile strength of the laminate, 'Xf' is the ultimate tensile strength of the fibres and 'Xr' is the tensile strength of the resin at the fibre failure strain. As before, 'Vf' and 'Vr' are the respective fibre and resin volume fractions and $\propto$ is an efficiency factor which is approximately equal to 1 for UD reinforcement, 0.5 for woven rovings or cloth, and 0.3 for CSM. The rule of mixtures is therefore:

$$X = Xr\ Vr + \propto Xf\ Vf$$

Using E glass as an example as before, the following figures can be found for the ultimate tensile strengths of laminates comprising CSM, WR and UD reinforcements.

If Xf = 2400 MPa (E glass fibre)
Xr =   40 MPa (polyester)

For CSM:
$\propto$ = 0.3
Vf = 0.2
Vr = 0.8

Then X (CSM) = 176 MPa

For WR:
$\propto$ = 0.5
Vf = 0.35
Vr = 0.65

Then X (WR) = 446 MPa

For UD:
$\alpha = 1.0$
$Vf = 0.5$
$Vr = 0.5$

Fig. 7.10 The two sets of bar graphs show the difference in tensile properties between single-fibre data and that for resin/fibre laminates.

Then X (UD) = 1220 MPa

(NB These figures for ultimate tensile strength refer to the property in the direction of the fibre orientation. For WR and UD fibres, strength values measured in directions other than along the fibres will be far lower, often below that figure given for CSM.)

If an S glass-fibre reinforcement were to be used, the UTS of a UD laminate would increase to 1970 MPa, while Kevlar would give 1830 MPa and VHS carbon fibre 1470 MPa. From this it can be seen that S glass, in terms of UTS, scores over both Kevlar and carbon fibres.

As with the figures derived for the stiffness of an FRP laminate, the figures for strength provided by the rule of mixtures refer to the short-term strength only and long-term strength will be less owing to the effects of fatigue and creep under load. The use of a hybrid laminate will affect the UTS as it does the stiffness, and a guide to the UTS of a hybrid laminate can be had from this rule although the way in which the two or more fibres are mixed in the laminate can cause a 'hybrid effect' which may alter the results obtained by the formula.

Fibre-to-resin ratio

From the foregoing it will be clear that the fibre-to-resin ratio plays a very important part in the strength and stiffness of an FRP laminate. Since it is the fibre part of the laminate that provides strength and stiffness, the more fibre that can be got into a given volume, the higher will be the properties of that laminate.

Unfortunately, the quantity of resin that can be used with any particular type of reinforcement is not in the hands of the designer or builder. Each type of reinforcement is associated with a particular range of resin volume fractions since there is a minimum quantity of resin that is necessary to wet-out that particular type of reinforcement. When the correct amount of resin has wetted-out the mat or fabric, the excess resin will flow off or be removable with a squeegee.

Of all the types of reinforcement available, CSM requires the most resin for saturation and wetting-out and thus results in the lowest fibre-to-resin ratio with consequent effects on the strength and stiffness of the laminate. A typical volume fraction of fibre when CSM is used would be in the region of 10–25 per cent, depending on the production process. In practice it is easiest

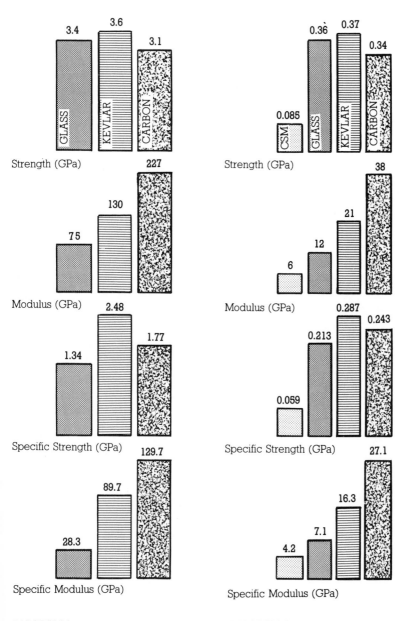

DIAGRAM 1
Comparative Fibre Properties (Tensile)

DIAGRAM 2
Comparative Laminate Properties (Tensile)

to determine the weight ratio of fibre or resin and for CSM the corresponding weight fraction is 20–40 per cent.

Bidirectional cloths made from woven rovings or yarns, or knitted bidirectional fabrics, need less resin for full wetting and have typical volume fractions of 30–50 per cent or weight fractions of 45–65 per cent. Within this class are many different types of weaves using different weights of yarns or rovings, but in general terms it is true that the looser the weave the easier the cloth is to wet-out and the higher the weight or volume fraction of the fibre. Cloths made from rovings rather than yarns will also be easier to wet-out and will again result in somewhat improved properties. Unidirectional fibres can achieve the best fibre-to-resin ratios, with typical volume fractions being in the range of 45–65 per cent or weight fractions in the region of 60–80.

Although each type of reinforcement is associated with a particular obtainable fibre-to-resin ratio, the actual weight or volume ratio that is achieved in practice is very much in the hands of the builder. The secret of laminating is to apply enough resin to wet-out the fibres fully but no more. Unfortunately, it is easier to wet-out the fibres by applying more resin than is needed, and unless the excess is removed from the laminate by careful work with a squeegee – and the use of this tool is difficult or impossible on reinforcements such as CSM or UD fibres – the resulting laminate will have more resin than it should and will be heavier than the designer intended. The best way of avoiding this problem is by careful quality control and by the determination of the builder to keep the fibre content as high as possible. The exact amount of resin needed for the particular job should be carefully measured and applied and the laminate must be thoroughly rolled to ensure complete and even wetting of the fibres without disturbing the way they have been laid.

The problem for the laminator, though, is that the dividing line between too much resin or an insufficient amount is very narrow. If too much is applied, the laminate will not have the fibre content that was intended and will be likely to have resin-rich areas which are weak and brittle. If, however, not enough resin is applied, the laminate will have voids or resin-free areas where the resin has not penetrated the fibres and they have been left dry and consequently weak. These voids will usually be deep within the laminate and difficult or impossible to spot. Hence the need for hard and thorough rolling to ensure that the resin penetrates the fibres completely. It should also be noted that part of the job of the resin is to protect the surface of the fibres from weather or other damage, and a high fibre content will naturally reduce the amount of resin that can provide this protection.

However carefully the hand laminator measures and applies the resin, the restrictions of this production method mean that it is never possible to achieve the optimum fibre-to-resin ratios for each type of reinforcement, and

Fig. 7.11 Variations in fibre-resin ratio affect tensile modulus and flexural modulus of a laminate of CSM/polyester.

Resin:glass ratio	3:1	2.5:1	2:1	1.75:1
% glass weight	25%	28.5%	33.3%	36.4%
Tensile modulus	7.1	7.5	8.1	8.5
(GN/m²)	6.4–8.2	6.8–8.7	7.3–9.3	7.9–9.1
Flexural modulus	5.8	6.1	6.7	7.0
(GN/m²)	4.9–6.7	5.1–7.1	5.7–7.7	6.0–7.9

Fig. 7.12 The effect of angle of load, relative to the principal fibre direction, on the tensile modulus of UD glass/epoxy, WR glass/polyester and CSM/polyester.

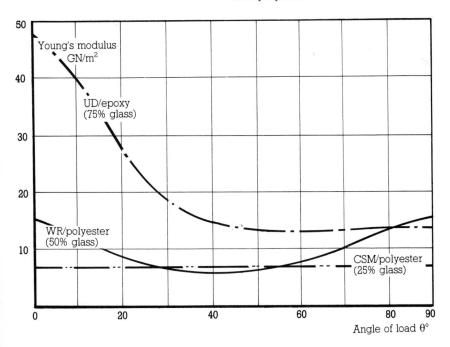

laminates moulded in this way will almost certainly be heavier and/or weaker than those produced by other methods such as pressure or vacuum moulding, or by using pre-pregs.

It should always be remembered that the fibre-to-resin ratio is critical to the performance of the laminate, and the more specialized and performance-orientated the reinforcement being used, the more vital it is that the ideal resin ratio is achieved or the potential benefits of that reinforcement will be wasted.

Although this section is mostly concerned with the use of FRP, it should be noted that wood has much in common with FRP in that it can be regarded as a ready-made fibre and resinous material. When dealing with wood, one is primarily concerned with the density, since most of its properties are related to its density. Thus, in the same way that an FRP laminate with a higher proportion of fibres will give improved properties, a denser species of wood will, in general, also provide higher stiffness and strength properties.

Directional properties

In the sections dealing with the strength and stiffness of laminates, it was shown that bidirectional and unidirectional reinforcements are more efficient than random-oriented reinforcements because of the alignment of the fibres in one or two directions, but it was also shown that the improvement in properties associated with these materials only applies when the load is in line with the fibre orientation. Materials in which mechanical properties are strongly dependent on direction are known as 'anisotropic', in contrast to isotropic materials such as many metals, or a CSM laminate under in-plane loads, where stiffness and strength are normally independent of the direction of loading.

These directional properties should not be seen as a disadvantage; they allow the designer to maximize the properties of a laminate in a particular direction(s) to suit expected loadings and allow a very weight-efficient laminate to be designed. A good example of a clear use for unidirectional fibres is in the beams of a multihull which are subject to relatively easily defined loads. Another example is their use along the heavy load paths (already described) in the hull and deck of a racing yacht or powerboat.

Unidirectional and bidirectional fibres are often used, not necessarily to form a laminate possessing these respective qualities, but within a multilayer oriented quasi-isotropic laminate. Each individual laminae is made up of unidirectional or bidirectional fibres and is then stacked with the others to produce a laminate with tailored properties. Usually the laminate should be symmetrical, or balanced, with laminae of the same type, thickness and orientation placed at equal distances on either side of the central plane to avoid twisting or warping.

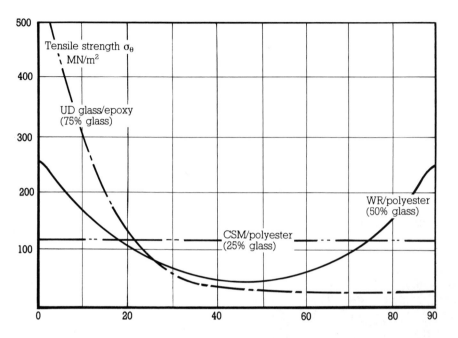

Fig. 7.13 The effect of angle of load on the tensile strength of UD glass/epoxy, WR glass/polyester and CSM/polyester.

Fig. 7.14 Typical values for tensile modulus and strength in the principal fibre direction for different laminating materials and methods.

Fabrication method	Glass weight %	Tensile modulus GN/m^2	Tensile strength MN/m^2
UD/epoxy prepreg	60–70	30–45	600–700
Fabric/epoxy prepreg	60–70	20–30	300–500
Filament winding, polyester or epoxy	70–80	30–55	700–1000
Pultrusion polyester	45–60	20–40	450–650

In data presented on high-performance fibre-reinforced laminates, the properties are normally given with respect to the fibre direction. Sometimes, however, transverse properties are also given. For unidirectional composites, such transverse properties are basically a guide to resin performance and the fibre/resin bond. For woven or knitted cloth or fabric composites, the quoted transverse properties relate to the weft fibres and will depend on the amount of fibres in that direction. A balanced weave, with equal amounts of fibre in each direction, will, if the same fibres are used for the weft and warp, give approximately equal properties in both warp and weft directions.

Wood can be considered in the same way as a unidirectional fibre and, indeed, should be so thought of when a wooden structure is being designed. Plywood is built in the manner described above for a stacked laminate with the grain (fibre) of each veneer, or ply, laid in a particular direction, and a balanced construction is also normally used to avoid warping or twisting. Whereas the traditional method of wooden construction used numerous frames, ribs and stringers to provide strength and stiffness in all directions, modern moulded hulls align layers of veneers, in the same manner as FRP, to form a monocoque structure that is capable of resisting the imposed in-plane and flexural loads, usually with little, if any, supplementary reinforcing.

The stress/strain relationship

The stress/strain relationship is vitally important to an understanding of the behaviour of any material under load. A tensile stress/strain diagram shows the behaviour of a material under tensile loading: how it stretches and how it fails. The stiffness or tensile modulus of FRP materials has already been discussed and this is shown in the stress/strain diagram by the slope of the line – the steeper the slope, the higher the modulus.

Most metals are ductile – that is, they yield at high stress levels to even out the stress distribution and provide a high-strain safety factor. FRP materials do not behave in this way (although Kevlar does exhibit ductile properties) but are elastic to failure. At high stress levels the fibres do not yield and failure is abrupt with delamination and fibre breakage.

The modulus (slope of the stress/strain curve), the UTS and the mode of failure of a laminate will, of course, depend on the fibre type, fibre volume and the nature of the reinforcement (UD, biD, random-fibre) in the laminate, but it will also depend on the resin properties, in particular its toughness and adhesion.

A typical CSM/polyester laminate with 30 per cent by weight glass content is linearly elastic for small strains up to the proportional limit when the slope of the curve changes to a lower amount. Above the proportional limit, the curve is again linear, but at these loadings the material is permanently

Fig. 7.15 A stress–strain curve for a typical CSM/polyester laminate under short-term loading.

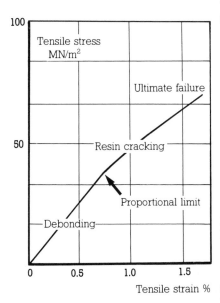

Fig. 7.16 Stress–strain curves for polyester, vinylester and epoxy resins postcured at 80°C for five hours to improve elongation performance.

Fig. 7.17 A comparison of the fatigue strength of carbon fibre, glass and various CF/glass hybrids.

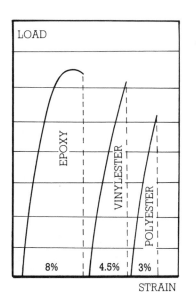

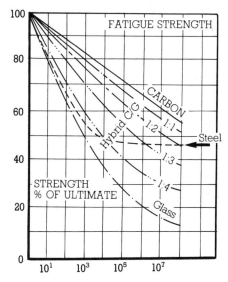

damaged and if unloaded it will not recover elastically but will show a permanent set.

When the CSM/polyester laminate is progressively loaded in a short-term test, the first stage of damage is the debonding of the resin from fibres at right angles to the load direction. This typically occurs at about 0.3 per cent strain and at stress levels of about 30 per cent UTS. As the load is increased, the debonding develops resin cracks which lead to the loss of bond between the resin and fibres parallel to the load direction. It is the start of resin debonding and cracking which causes the loss of modulus at the proportional limit and thus defines the point at which some permanent damage occurs to the laminate.

As the cracks in the resin spread, the laminate reaches its failure point as fibres fracture and pull out. Resin cracking occurs at about 50–70 per cent UTS and the cracking inside the laminate leads to gel-coat cracks which typically occur at about 60–80 per cent UTS.

The short-term stress/strain curves for cloth- or fabric-reinforced resins are similar to that for CSM. However, bidirectional and unidirectional fibres are anisotropic and the failure process depends on the orientation of the fibres to the load and there are thus different stress/strain curves for each loading direction. For loads in a fibre direction, the stress/strain curve is linear up to a limit of proportionality that corresponds with resin cracking after the debonding of resin and transverse fibres. Above this point is a second linear region with reduced slope, and in the case of a balanced 0°/±45°/90° laminate there is a second reduction in the slope of the curve associated with the debonding of the resin from the 45° fibres.

When UD fibre laminates are loaded parallel to the fibres, the stress/strain curve is linear to failure with no change of the slope before total failure. The stress/strain curves of UD, cloth and fabric, and random fibres, do, when compared, show clearly the differences in UTS and modulus obtained with the different types of reinforcement, and the stress/strain curves of UD-reinforced laminates are often used to compare the various types of fibres available to the designer.

From the above discussion it will be clear that, while the UTS is of interest to the designer, it will be rarely used as a design limit since serious damage will have occurred to the laminate in many cases long before the UTS is reached. It will also be clear that the performance of the resin matrix is vitally important to the behaviour of the laminate under loads and the reduction in modulus of the laminate caused by resin debonding and cracking. The two most important criteria when considering resin performance from this point of view are the adhesion and the elongation capability under load. In particular, if resin/fibre adhesion and elongation are poor, the resin will debond from fibres not in line with the loading direction at a low stress level.

The modulus of the material will then be reduced and resin cracks will spread, leading to total failure. Resin adhesion obviously has to be as high as possible, but the resin must also have the ability to stretch with the fibres if debonding and cracking are to be postponed as long as possible. Carbon fibres are the stiffest of those under consideration and they achieve their maximum strength at elongations up to about 1.3 per cent, depending on type. Kevlar, on the other hand, stretches more – up to about 2.4 per cent – while E glass, S glass and R glass have elongations that are respectively up to 3.5 per cent and 5.2 per cent.

Thus it is of less importance that the resin be able to accommodate high elongation if carbon fibres are used than it is if S glass or R glass fibres are the chosen reinforcement. If a low-elongation resin is used with a fibre that has a relatively high elongation under load, the laminate will fail as a result of resin debonding and cracking before the fibres can achieve their full potential strengths and the strength of the laminate will be limited. From Chapter 2 it will be remembered that a typical polyester resin has an elongation capability of only 2 per cent or less, while epoxies and vinylesters can be had with elongations of up to 5 per cent or even more, depending on the curing temperature. It will also be remembered, however, that the higher elongations are difficult to achieve without loss in other aspects of a resin's performance, and in any case cannot usually be obtained with room-temperature cure systems. Thus, if it is necessary to accommodate high elongation, it will almost certainly be essential to cure the moulding at elevated temperatures if optimum properties are to be obtained.

Interlaminar shear strength

Another property that is very dependent on the resin performance – and, again, toughness and adhesion – is the interlaminar shear of an FRP laminate, which is not an in-plane property and is not dependent on the type or quantity of reinforcement. The interlaminar shear strength is thus a measure of how well the resin bonds adjacent layers of reinforcement. The need to prevent delamination between layers is the primary reason why so much use is made of CSM in laminates which also make use of fabrics or cloths. The most common type of resin used in boatbuilding – polyester – does not have particularly good adhesive properties, and so to prevent delamination between layers of woven rovings it is normal to intersperse layers of resin-rich CSM between the WR. The layers of CSM give random orientation of fibres, some of which stick up and down and bond well with the layers of cloth or fabric on either side, although the overall properties of the laminate are necessarily reduced by the use of the inefficient CSM.

If a resin with better adhesive properties is used, the need to use a material like CSM to improve interlaminar shear strength is much reduced or eliminated. If it is still desired to use some random fibres between layers of cloth to improve interlaminar shear strength further, it is better to use a paste of milled fibres and resin since this mixture can be spread thinly, bonds well to the adjacent layers, and results in a lighter laminate than if CSM is used. Another alternative is to use a cloth which has random continuous fibres knitted on one side, which will again help to improve interlaminar shear properties, will provide some bulk to help increase laminate flexural stiffness and will provide more strength than CSM at lighter weight because of the use of continuous fibres.

Long-term properties

The strength and stiffness properties described above are short-term properties and while they are of importance to the designer he will also have to consider long-term properties if the boat is to have a useful life. Short-term properties are of particular interest in the design of FRP laminates which experience generally low stress levels but may be required to withstand the occasional short-term high loading. When designing a boat, however, one has to consider a structure that may be required to withstand sustained and repeated high loadings.

When an FRP material is subjected to sustained loads, creep deformation of the laminate occurs and the long-term properties are likely to be significantly lower than the short-term values. A boat structure will also experience repeated loadings and unloadings and in this case the fatigue strength of the laminate must be considered; again, this is likely to be well below the short-term strength.

Data on creep and fatigue properties for FRP materials is limited partly because such long-term testing is time-consuming and expensive and partly because creep and fatigue are not considered to be important at low stress levels with a sufficiently high built-in safety factor. From the data that is available, it seems that under long-term static and dynamic loads the failure process of an FRP laminate is generally similar to that described for short-term failure under previous headings, but failure occurs at significantly lower stress levels. Thus the stress that is needed to cause resin debonding or cracking under short-term loads may be close to the UTS for sustained or fatigue loads. However, the behaviour of the various types of fibre available may be significantly different; for instance, a carbon-fibre-reinforced laminate is much less fatigue-sensitive than is a GRP laminate.

The current practice in the design of FRP laminates is to specify an allowable stress or, alternatively, an allowable strain that is below the stress or strain at which mechanical damage – fibre/resin debonding or resin cracking (the latter the more serious condition) – occurs under short-term loads.

Finding strength and stiffness data for laminates

When designing a structure to be built of FRP (or wood, which has many similarities) it is necessary to use a design approach that takes into consideration the distinctive characteristics of these materials. Of course, there is a long history already of building in these materials and standard specifications and guidelines to quantity and types of materials are readily available to the designer, especially if the structure is to be built of GRP or wood. However, if the full potential of the many varied types of reinforcements now available is to be realized, and especially if a design is to be weight efficient, the specification needs to be carefully considered and designed specifically for the intended use.

There are several ways of approaching the design of an FRP (or wooden) laminate, but the most precise results can be obtained by using actual measured results of a single layer of laminate which is made in-house using exactly the same procedure as will be used for the moulding. It is possible to use a design technique that considers only fibre properties, but such a technique does not take into account failure criteria based on matrix properties and could thus lead to premature failure unless high safety factors are used. A method that uses actual measured properties of a single resin/ fibre layer allows a more accurate prediction and minimizes the effect of process variables. To be able to cover all the possible variations of fibre type, resin type, volume fractions, reinforcement type (i.e., UD, WR, random-fibre, etc.), hybrids and so on takes a lot of testing, but once the basic data is collected a computer program can check the difference in properties and cost effectiveness for a wide range of lay-ups and can determine the best lay-up and orientation of plies for any particular design application. This approach need not be limited to FRP materials – it could also be used in the design of a wooden structure using oriented layers of wood veneer or combinations of wood and FRP.

Such a computer program is now being used by one British company – SP Systems Ltd – which specializes in supplying high-performance fibres and resin systems specifically for boatbuilding and which also does much design consultancy work in the development of high-performance laminates. Using this company's program, designers and builders now have access to a design system based on data from physical tests on a wide range of lamimae and which allows as much experimentation with the laminate specification as is desired.

The effects of the building system

In order to be able to design and accurately predict the properties of an FRP laminate, the influence of the moulding system on the finished product must be understood. Because the moulding system will affect the achievable resin-to-fibre ratio, the consolidation, impregnation and void content of the laminate, the ease with which certain types of reinforcement can be used and the types of resins that are suitable, the choice of production system will have a great influence on the mechanical properties of the laminate as well as on its appearance.

The oldest production FRP moulding method, contact moulding using a female or male mould, still accounts for virtually all of FRP boatbuilding production. The most commonly used reinforcement in contact moulding is E glass in CSM or woven roving form. The mat or fabric is placed in the mould and wetted-out by resin by hand before being rollered to consolidate the laminate. Laminates are built up layer by layer and a core material can be included if desired. Female moulds are invariably used for production building where the cost of the mould can be spread over many units, but male moulds are usually used for one-off construction in FRP or wood or for very limited numbers of mouldings. From a production point of view, a female mould has the advantage of allowing a gel-coat finish on the exterior surface which reduces the work required to finish the moulding.

Any type of reinforcement fibre and any type of mat, cloth or UD tape can be used in contact moulding, but manual application of resin and its rolling-out does not allow the most efficient fibre-to-resin ratios to be achieved and also tends to disturb the orientation of bidirectional and unidirectional fibres with a resultant loss in properties. Contact moulding is also labour-intensive and is a messy process requiring good ventilation of the moulding shop.

The use of bidirectional and unidirectional fibres is somewhat easier with a male mould than a female one since the cloth or tape can be stretched slightly over the convex mould surface, whereas this cannot be done on a concave surface or the cloth would lift off the mould. It is also easier to bend the stiffer core materials over a male mould than it is to fit them into a female one. Furthermore, if excess resin is applied to the reinforcement in a female mould, it will tend to drain to the bottom of the hull where a resin-rich area is created from which it is difficult to remove the excess with a squeegee.

Many production boats are moulded in a female mould using a spray-up technique in which continuous glass strands are fed to a spray gun on which is mounted a chopping head. The gun sprays resin, catalyst and chopped strands into the mould where it is consolidated by hand rolling and the desired thickness is built up by spraying successive layers. Layers of woven roving can be incorporated into the laminate to improve the properties, but this is not usually done since it is time-consuming. The mechanical properties of such a laminate are low, yet this method is popular because the moulding operation is cheaper, quicker and cleaner than hand lay-up.

The mechanical properties of wet lay-up laminates using the more advanced fibres in cloth or UD form in male or female moulds can be improved by using a vacuum bag sealed over the mould and evacuated by an air pump. Resultant atmospheric pressure consolidates the laminate and forces the resin into any cavities, and also gives an improved surface finish to the off-mould side of the laminate.

In some applications of FRP moulding, matched moulds are used with resin injection, vacuum moulding or a combination of the two – vacuum injection moulding. The latter has been tried in boatbuilding and is used to produce the OOD 34. The advantage of these methods is that the fibre reinforcement can be positioned dry exactly where needed and in the correct orientation, and the achievable resin-to-fibre ratios should, in theory, be closer to the optimum than when wet lay-up is used. Core materials, too, can be positioned into the mould before the two parts of the mould are brought together. Because two matching moulds are used, the finished laminate has a smooth surface on both sides. Such methods are, however, quite slow and require expensive tooling.

Probably the most advanced technique so far available is the use of pre-pregs in either matched, heated moulds or a heated single mould with a vacuum bag. Pre-pregs are clean to lay-up and have the resin already on the fibres in the correct fibre-to-resin ratio. Heating is necessary to cure the resin, but this can be achieved by heating the mould directly or by inserting the mould into an oven or autoclave.

Several other techniques are used in general FRP moulding to create high-performance laminates using mainly UD fibres and these will be briefly mentioned in the next two chapters, which deal with the production processes in more detail. From the foregoing, however, it should be clear that the type of production process chosen for a moulding has a strong influence on the properties that can be obtained from that moulding. If high performance is required and high-performance materials are chosen to achieve it, the correct moulding must be matched to the materials if the desired properties of the laminate are to be realized.

8 MOULD CONSTRUCTION AND WORKING CONDITIONS

In previous chapters a variety of materials that can be used in the building of FRP or wooden boats has been examined, and it has been seen how design considerations will determine the choice of materials for a particular project. Intimately linked with the selection of materials, performance requirements and cost objectives is the method chosen for construction. Many methods exist to produce FRP mouldings and the choice must be governed by the type of materials being used and whether the production is of a series of mouldings or a one-off hull and deck.

The use of high-performance fibres, resin and core materials demands a more controlled moulding process than the production of mouldings using the cheaper and more common materials and this must always be considered when making a choice. If high-performance materials are used with a moulding process designed for standard production materials, the finished product will not exhibit the properties that are to be expected from the use of the more expensive materials and, where racing craft are concerned, the properties of the moulding may reduce the designed safety margin.

Ninety per cent or more of all FRP mouldings are still produced using contact moulding – a process in which layers of resin and fibre are laid-up and cured in or on a mould by hand, without the use of pressure and heat. From this basic and oldest of methods many others have been developed to give more controlled mouldings, faster production times or other benefits. Contact moulding will be described in some detail, as will other methods that are now being used in the production of marine mouldings.

Whenever FRP is moulded, some type of former or mould must be used to give the uncured resin and fibre shape and support. Moulds can be either female or male type, depending on which side of the moulding needs the finished smooth surface given by the face of the mould. In production boatbuilding female moulds are nearly always used for hulls and decks to give the finished surface where it is needed: on the outside. Other sub-mouldings such as a cockpit are produced on a male mould since a finished inside face is required. The use of female moulds for the construction of hulls and decks requires that a plug must first be built that is an exact replica of the finished product. The mould is then constructed over the plug and, once

Fig. 8.1 Production boatbuilders invariably use female moulds – usually with hand lay-up or spray lay-up techniques – to produce large numbers of identical craft like these Maxi 77s.

completed, can be used to produce a series of identical mouldings, thus spreading the cost of making the plug and mould.

For the amateur or professional builder involved in the construction of a one-off hull, the cost in terms of time and money of building a female mould is rarely justified and it is usual instead to build on a temporary male mould which can be broken up when the hull or deck has been removed, although sometimes the same mould can be used for another moulding. The use of male moulds was made popular by amateur builders of foam sandwich hulls. Originally it was normal for the core material to be attached to the mould and the outer skin to be moulded before removing the partly finished moulding from the mould and then laminating the inner skin. Lately it has become more common to work from the inside out, laminating the inner skin first, then the core and finally the outer skin. This means that the moulding is complete, and rigid, before removal from the mould, although it does require that the mould be more complicated.

While the use of a male mould makes the moulding of a one-off quicker

Fig. 8.2 Female moulds for boat hulls and decks are usually made of GRP.

Fig. 8.3 A split mould is used for large or complicated mouldings to ease withdrawal of the finished moulding.

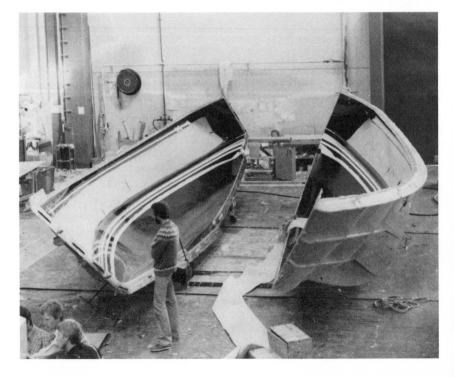

and cheaper to produce than if a female mould were used, it must be remembered that the mould must still be fair and smooth or defects will be reflected in the moulding. It will also be necessary to sand, fill and paint the hull's or deck's exterior surface, and when the time and cost of this operation is counted, the savings over the use of a female mould will not be as great as first imagined. The latest high-performance fibres in cloth or fabric form and the use of vacuum-bag techniques to consolidate the laminate can help reduce the amount of finishing time as the external surface will not be as rough as when normal contact moulding methods and materials are used.

This and the following chapters are not intended to give a step-by-step guide to boatbuilding, a subject well covered in other books. Rather, they are meant to describe in outline the variety of moulding methods that are available to the builder and the effect that each will have on the performance and cost of the finished moulding. It is also hoped to show how important are the techniques and methods of building in ensuring the quality of the finished product. There are many short cuts that can be taken in the choice of materials and the moulding process that can result in problems developing with the moulding at a later date. If attention is not given to every detail, a moulding may look perfect but still contain virtually undetectable faults such as resin-starved or resin-rich areas, voids in the laminate or variations in thickness.

Female moulds

It is not easy to build a mould directly because of the difficulty of visualizing the inside-out shape that is required. Therefore the mould is usually made on a pattern or plug unless it is small and simple or is a temporary construction such as may be used for moulding an interior part *in situ.*

Female moulds for boat hulls and decks are usually made of GRP to give strength, accuracy of shape, simplicity of construction and a reasonable working life. The use of GRP for the mould is a further reason for the necessity of first using a positive pattern, since without the pattern it would be impossible to mould the material.

The design of the mould is a very important consideration if later problems of damage or difficulty with release are not to occur. Any mould must allow the moulding to be withdrawn cleanly. There must be no undercuts and there will usually need to be some taper to the sides. A short draw can have nearly parallel sides, but a deep draw must have an outward taper of about 10°.

The areas that are most likely to give trouble on withdrawal are sharp corners, particularly right-angles, so these should be avoided and all corners should be well radiused. The easiest type of mould to work with is a simple one: the more complicated the shape, the more chance there is of jamming and damage to the moulding. One of the advantages of FRP construction is the ease with which complicated shapes can be produced, but elaborate mouldings are best introduced when a few prototypes have been made. Any problems will then be known and the location of all attachments and localized reinforcement can be finalized.

Complicated or large mouldings will need a split mould made in two or more pieces. This type allows more elaborate mouldings to be produced and removes the restrictions imposed on shape by the use of a one-piece mould. A split mould also allows the easy release of simple but large shapes like the hulls of larger craft. The usual way of using a split mould in boatbuilding is to use a two-piece mould, bolted together along the centre-line of the hull. This has the added advantage to the builder of allowing easier storage and manoeuvrability about the workshop.

The usual method of producing a female mould is first to build a pattern identical to the finished moulding. In the case of boat hulls it is possible to use an existing hull on which the mould may be laminated directly after preparation of the surface. This method has been seen as a short cut by some builders wishing to build an existing wooden design in FRP. The problem with the method is in achieving a satisfactory surface finish on the hull, especially when it is an older craft.

In the case of larger craft there is also the difficulty of working underneath an upright hull or, alternatively, of inverting it. Sometimes a builder will choose to build a prototype in wood before starting series FRP production, and the mould is then likely to be taken off the prototype hull, itself usually of cold-moulded wooden construction which will give a good surface for mould making if it is well prepared.

Most often, however, the builder will erect a temporary plug which may be dismantled once the mould has been built and proved successful. Since the finish of the plug will determine the finish of the mould and every subsequent moulding, great care and attention is required to ensure the most accurate, fair and smooth surface. The plug can be built of any suitable material, usually wood or plaster, with wooden plugs being by far the most usual in boatbuilding. Either material demands considerable time and effort in finishing since the shape and dimensions must be exact; mistakes made at this stage will be reproduced exactly in all later mouldings.

The most usual practice for a wooden plug is basically the same method as is used to make a male mould for FRP or cold-moulded wooden construction. Frames are set up at close spacings on a building grid with a central backbone, transom, and fore-and-aft, closely spaced battens. A skin of hardboard, plywood or thin veneers is then stapled to the frames and battens. Alternatively, the plug can be built of strip planking (Chapter 10).

Fig. 8.4 A strip-planked plug being constructed. Once the plug has been completed and prepared, the mould can be laminated over the plug using the same techniques.

Remember that, although the finished shape must be exact, the pattern is not a boat, does not have to be attractive, and needs only to be strong enough to bear the weight of the finished mould. The plug should not be stopped at the sheer strake but should continue down for a few inches so that the mould can be laminated at a constant thickness past the edge of the deck edge. When mouldings are produced in the mould, they too will be laminated up past the deck edge and later trimmed to shape. To aid picking out the line along which the hulls should be trimmed, a cove line can be cut in the plug around the sheer which will be reproduced in the mould as a slight ridge. When mouldings are removed from the mould it is then easy to cut along the shallow groove to trim the edge to the correct line.

Once the plug has been built, the surface must be made flawless. The first job is to fill and thoroughly sand it before painting with several coats of a two-pot polyurethane or epoxy which will give a hard surface unaffected by gel-coat or laminating resins. The surface must be rubbed down between the coats until it is quite smooth. A glossy surface shows up defects better than a matt one, especially if a light is shone on each part of the surface in turn. After

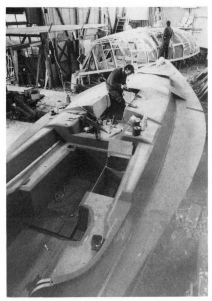

Fig. 8.5 A completed plug for a large GRP mould. The surface must be flawless.

Fig. 8.6 A plug is used to produce moulds for decks as well as hulls. In the foreground a deck plug is being finished while work has started on a plug for the hull in the background.

sanding with finer and finer wet-and-dry paper used wet, the final finish is obtained with a fine rubbing compound. Once the finish is satisfactory, the plug is treated with at least five coats of a non-silicon wax polish which must be thoroughly polished between each coat. It is best to complete the major part of the fairing and smoothing of the plug before adding any appendages such as blisters for rudder or propellor shafts, bilge or central keels. Such add-on parts can be made in any convenient material but must be as fair and smooth as the rest of the plug.

If a split mould is required, the plug is first built and finished as described above, but then a flange is fitted along the line of separation and is finished in the same way as the rest of the plug.

The mould itself is made by contact or spray moulding in the same way as subsequent mouldings and details of the lay-up procedure will be given later. There are, however, a few differences and points worth noting. Both the gel-coat and the laminating resin used for mould making differ from the types used for later mouldings. Because of the temperatures that can build up in the mould as each moulding cures, it must be laminated with heat-resistant resins. Tooling gel-coat, usually black in colour, produces a hard and heat-resistant finish but is more brittle than conventional gel-coat, as is the laminating resin used for moulds. Therefore the mould must be thick enough and have enough external support to prevent flexing, otherwise fatigue cracks in the surface are likely to occur. When producing later mouldings it will be possible to continue laminating wet-on-wet until the required thickness has been built up. With tooling resins, however, no more than two layers should be laid-up wet-on-wet or high temperatures produced by the curing of these high-reactive resins may cause stresses to build up in the laminate. As regards thickness of the mould lay-up, it is usual to laminate to a thickness that is about twice that of the mouldings to be produced in that mould. Moulded-in stiffeners are sometimes used, but really these should be avoided where possible because they can cause distortion ripples, especially if bonded in during lamination.

If a split mould is to be produced, one side should be built up against the flange which is then removed when the laminate has cured. After the laminated flange has been waxed and release agent applied, the other part of the mould can then be built up against the moulded flange. Always add extra thickness in the areas of flanges as they will take considerable strain when the mould is split to release each moulding.

The finished mould should be cured at as high a temperature as possible for some days (depending on temperature) before being removed from the plug. Before removal a strong and well-braced cradle should be constructed to support the mould. The amount of support needed obviously depends on the size and weight of the mould, but remember that a large mould will probably have to support the weight of several people working inside it during laminating. It is much easier to make a strong cradle than it is to repair a mould that has been inadequately supported. The cradle should be on wheels to allow easy movement around the workshop.

Split moulds can be supported on two separate cradles so that the parts can be moved individually and with ease. When a split mould has been removed from its plug, the parts should be brought together and carefully aligned. Bolt holes are then drilled through the flanges at close intervals and the mould checked to ensure that, when all the fastenings are tightened down, the separate parts are drawn snugly and tightly together.

Before the mould can be used, the surface should be inspected for flaws

which should be touched up immediately. The surface is then given a light sanding with fine wet-and-dry used wet, before drying and polishing to a high gloss with rubbing compound. Five or six coats of a non-silicon wax are then applied, each polished to obtain a high gloss before the next is put on. A new mould should be waxed between each moulding but once it has been used a few times it will be possible to take several mouldings out of the mould between each waxing, the number depending on the size and complexity of the mouldings.

Male moulds

Male moulds are mainly used, in FRP boatbuilding, by amateurs and professional builders involved in one-off projects using sandwich construction, the development of which, and the use of male moulds, was pioneered by amateur builders who wished to avoid spending the time and expense necessary to build a plug and a female mould. A male mould for sandwich construction can be quite a simple affair involving little of the difficulty of building a female mould. While it is perfectly possible to build a more elaborate male mould for use with a solid FRP lay-up, such an approach would have no advantages.

A male mould can, depending on how it is constructed, produce a good finish on the inside of the moulding, but the outer surface will need filling, sanding and painting if its appearance is important, as it is with a boat hull. In the case of sandwich construction, where thin skins are used, often of cloth rather than mat, the outer skin will be relatively smooth. A solid lay-up, especially one using CSM, will, however, be far rougher, requiring much finishing work if an acceptable outer surface is to be achieved.

As FRP sandwich construction has developed into the use of high-

Fig. 8.7 The outer surface of a hull moulded on a male mould needs filling, sanding and painting.

Fig. 8.8 A strongback ready to receive the mould frames.

Fig. 8.9 Once frames have been erected on the strongback, stringers are attached to the frames.

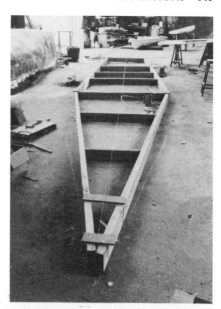

performance materials for highly specialized, one-off light-weight craft, professional builders have improved on the techniques pioneered by amateur builders. Whereas the standard method of construction of a sandwich composite on a male mould has been to attach the core material to the mould, laminate the outer skin, remove the hull from the mould and then laminate the inner skin, a different approach is now used by those builders who are concerned to achieve the best possible properties from the sophisticated materials used in the laminate. The latter approach starts by laminating the inner skin on the mould before applying the core material and the outer skin. Thus, when the hull is removed from the mould, it is complete, far stiffer than a hull without its inner skin, and thus less susceptible to alterations from the designed shape.

Whatever building technique is to be used, the basic details of mould construction are the same. On the building floor a strongback, usually of wood, is constructed which must be strong enough to take the weight of the building jig and the hull shell without distorting. The jig itself consists of frames or moulds mounted on the strongback, which are then connected by a stem and backbone before longitudinal battens are attached to the frames to give the shape of the hull. These fore-and-aft battens are usually simply nailed or screwed to the frames but may be notched into them if the mould is to be re-used and so needs to be as durable as possible. The shapes of the frames are taken from the lines plan but it must be remembered that their dimensions should be reduced by the thickness of the hull skins and core and of the fore-and-aft stringers if these are not to be slotted into the frame edges. If the inner skin is not to be laminated until after the hull has been removed from the mould, its thickness should not be allowed for when making the frames for the jig. It is not possible to subtract the required amount from the table of offsets and then draw the resultant curve since the deduction needs to be made at right angles to the hull's surface, not perpendicular to the centre-line.

The mould frames, which can be cut from any suitable timber and butt-jointed with scraps of ply, are mounted on the strongback. Care must be taken that all are true and vertical. With the frames in place and aligned, the stem piece and central backbone are fitted, and the fore-and-aft battening is run between the stem and the transom, being nailed or screwed to each frame. Batten spacing will depend on the flexibility of the core that will be used, and the radius of curvature of the hull. In areas of tight curves the battens should be close together but can be further apart on flat areas such as the sides of catamaran hulls. It will often be found that, if the battens are spaced close together at bow and stern where the curve is usually tightest, they will be correct on the flatter curves in between. The first battens to be attached are those at the sheerline, waterline and keel, and it is best to work on each side of the hull alternately so that the jig is not pulled out of shape. If the hull is to be lifted off the mould it is best to screw the battens to all the frames, but if the jig is to be broken out of the hull after it has been rolled over, it is common for the battens to be screwed only at the ends, with nails being used on the rest of the frames. Any areas that are to be of solid FRP, such as the keel, should have filler pieces added to the thickness of the foam.

When all the stringers and filler pieces are in place, the jig must be checked for fairness using a long flexible batten, and any discrepancies corrected. High spots can be planed down and hollows can be corrected by packing the frames under the appropriate stringers. If screws have been

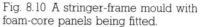

Fig. 8.10 A stringer-frame mould with foam-core panels being fitted.

used on all the frames, it is easy to insert small packing pieces as necessary. Once the jig has been faired and covered with plastic to avoid bonding should any resin seep between gaps in the core material, it is ready for the construction of a sandwich hull by the method in which the inner skin is not laminated until after removal from the mould.

To make a mould for a hull which is to be fully laminated from the inside out, a bit more work is required. In order to laminate the inner skin on the mould, the mould's surface must be solid, fair and smooth. The first stages of construction of the mould are the same as already described, but then the mould must be skinned, the thickness of this skin having been allowed for when the frames were made. The skin can be of hardboard, plywood or wood veneers laid-up in the manner described in the next chapter for cold-moulded construction, but usually using only one thin skin. Strips of hard-board, plywood or veneers are laid, in any convenient direction, over the frames and stringers to which they are attached by glue, nails, screws or staples as appropriate. With the jig skinned, the outer surface is faired and sanded until smooth. In order to avoid the inner skin sticking to the mould when the first skin is laminated, the surface of the jig can be treated in the same way as a female mould, i.e. painted, sanded and waxed; or it can be covered with a plastic sheet to which resin will not bond. This sheet is tailored to fit and stuck to the mould using plastic tape. As with a female mould, the best colour for the mould's surface is black, as this colour most easily allows defects to be spotted.

Fig. 8.11 When interior space is insufficient, an inflatable plastic bubble can provide an adequately controlled working environment and can be dismantled when the project has been completed.

Fig. 8.12 A plastic, inflatable covering is often the only answer when the hulls of a large multihull have to be bonded to the beams.

Simple moulds

While hulls and decks and some interior mouldings used in series production need to be built on fairly elaborate female or male moulds, there is often a need, when fitting out an FRP hull, for a simple and quick mould to allow *in situ* moulding. Such interior mouldings will often be covered by interior joinery or furnishings so the finish of the surface will be unimportant. In such cases the type of mould that can be used is limited only by one's imagination. Any convenient material such as cardboard, hardboard, plywood, Plasticine or other modelling clay can be used to form a simple mould for a part that will be usually moulded in place, using the boat's hull as part of the mould. In some cases the mould may remain as a permanent part of the moulding, such as in the case of a plywood former for built-in GRP watertanks. In this case the former would not be treated for release but would be bonded on both sides by several layers of GRP.

Large flat pieces, such as core construction bulkheads, can easily be constructed off the boat using a flat sheet of glass as the mould, or any other flat material covered with a peel ply of suitable plastic material. The first skin is laid-up, then the core material is placed on the still-wet skin and weights or a pressure bag used to ensure a close bond while the laminate cures. The second skin is laid-up directly on to the core, a second flat sheet covered in peel ply laid on top, and more pressure applied until cure is complete. When the laminate is removed from the flat moulds, both sides will be smooth and the light-weight moulding will be ready for bonding into the hull.

Working conditions

When building in FRP it is important to consider the working conditions and how they will affect the finished laminate and the health of the workforce. The conditions in which FRP can be moulded depend on the materials and the techniques being used and the extent to which it is important for the finished moulding to exhibit the optimum properties. The conditions in which materials are used in FRP boatbuilding are often a source of disagreement between builders and material suppliers. Suppliers, who naturally wish to see their products used to their full potential, specify optimum temperature, humidity and other conditions. Builders, on the other hand, are usually concerned with practical conditions – those in which they have to work – and are less interested in theoretical, optimum conditions and properties as specified by those who test materials under laboratory conditions.

The temperature of the moulding environment is the working condition to which most importance is usually attached. Ideally, all FRP mouldings should be produced under controlled conditions: unfortunately, however, boatyards are traditionally draughty places with building sheds that have little in the way of heating. When considering FRP boatbuilding, especially series production or the building of critical, high-performance, one-off mouldings, the builder should be thinking in terms of modern factory conditions rather than those found in the traditional boatyard. Unfortunately, such facilities are expensive and are to be found only in the more advanced yards, geared usually for large-scale production runs.

For most forms of FRP boatbuilding, high temperatures in the moulding shop are unnecessary as long as the temperature specified by the supplier for the materials and the particular process can be maintained at a constant level irrespective of normal external weather conditions. The temperature normally quoted for polyester laminating is 60–65°F (15–18°C), but it is quite possible to laminate at far lower temperatures by using extra catalyst and/or accelerator or by using a high-reactivity resin. The reason for not moulding important items in these conditions, however, is that the properties of the laminate will be reduced below their optimum level. While this may be of little importance in the construction of unsophisticated, heavy-duty craft which are designed with a very large factor of safety, a reduction in properties could be a serious matter in a moulding for a light-weight, high-performance boat, designed with a far lower safety factor for reasons of performance.

Temperatures above the average will, on the other hand, improve the degree of cure of the laminate and hence its physical properties. While some specialized resins need to be cured at high temperatures, those used for boatbuilding, both polyester and epoxy, are ideally cured at about 68°F (20°C). Once this has been done, however, there can be, with considerable benefit, a period of postcure at a higher temperature. This accelerates the maturing process during which the moulding hardens, and gives improved laminate properties. For standard production boats, using ordinary materials, this post-cure is usually dispensed with, but when a light-weight moulding is being built with higher-performance materials, the postcure is very important. To make sure that the moulding does not change shape, it should be left in the mould during the postcuring period.

It is usually impractical to consider raising the temperature of the whole building shed in order to postcure the laminate, but the necessary temperature can often be achieved by the use of a plastic tent over the moulding and localized heaters. Alternatively, heated moulds or a large oven may be used to heat the laminate. The difficulty is rarely insurmountable; the real problem lies in convincing the users that the benefits, although invisible, are worthwhile.

Humidity

Just as important as the temperature is the level of humidity in the moulding site. Any water, even in vapour form, that comes into contact with an unmatured laminate will affect the cure of the resin and the bond with the fibre reinforcement and so reduce the properties of the laminate. The levels to which the builder will go to reduce humidity will again depend on the degree of sophistication of the moulding but the use of dehumidifiers as well as heaters during the building of high-performance laminates is fully justified and will remove many gallons of water per day from the atmosphere, depending on the size of the building shed. All materials should be stored under warm and dry conditions, not brought into a warm moulding shop from a cold store. Moisture will quickly condense on a roll of cold glass fibre when .it is brought into a warmer environment and a small amount of condensation is enough to prevent the resin/fibre bond. Kevlar, too, seems to be particu-

Fig. 8.13 Ventilation of the working site is vital, especially when resins or paints are being sprayed.

larly susceptible to attracting water molecules and the builder must make sure that the inside as well as the outside of rolls of cloth are fully dry before use. When considering ways to reduce humidity levels, don't forget that the use of unventilated heaters burning oil, gas or solid fuels will add water to the air and the use of such heaters should be avoided.

Ventilation

Ventilation in the moulding shop is important, not only to help maintain the warm and dry environment, but also to remove the fumes given off by the resins being used. Many of these resins emit powerful fumes, close and continuous exposure to which can be harmful. For small mouldings and infrequent laminating normal ventilation is usually sufficient, but for serious moulding there should be forced ventilation of the moulding area with flexible exhaust hoses that can be directed about the moulding. Amateur builders working outside or under a simple lean-to will not normally need to worry about ventilation; heat and humidity will usually be their major problems, but fumes may still build up when they are laminating inside a large hull on a still day and a simple fan or blower may be necessary to ensure safe working conditions.

Light

Bad lighting is one of the worst handicaps under which a builder can work. In order to see defects as laminating proceeds there must be good, even lighting over the whole area. A wander-lead is invaluable, both for moulding inside the boat and for inspecting the surface of hull and mould for small flaws.

Space and equipment

When moulding FRP laminates there must be adequate room, not only around the mould but also close by, where an area for cloth shaping and cutting and resin mixing must be available. On a large moulding there may be a team of several people who must be able to work without getting in each other's way, and who must be able to get into the mould if necessary, carrying materials and equipment. If space is restricted, the work will not progress effectively and the likelihood is that resin and fibre will tend to get everywhere except into the mould. When considering space around the mould, remember also space above it. The moulding may have to be lifted out of the mould or a deck attached to a hull with the latter still in its mould. In such cases there must be plenty of clearance above.

The amount of equipment needed will, of course, depend on the type of moulding being undertaken, but certain things are basic to all moulding. Some form of balance for weighing materials is essential if you are to have any idea of the amount of resin and fibre going into the hull and the resin/fibre ratio. The more sophisticated the moulding, the more the builder will want to check that figure. Measuring out the correct amount of resin and hardener for each job requires experience and care, but once you have got used to the amount of hardener required for, say, half a bucket of resin there will be no need to weigh each batch.

When polyester resins are used, the amount of catalyst required in proportion to the resin is very small and this can cause problems with measurement, especially when small batches are being mixed. In such cases a calibrated measuring cup for the catalyst may be useful, or even an eye-dropper, with the amount of catalyst being counted in drops. This can be calibrated by measuring out a small, known amount of resin and counting the drops so that the weight of resin per drop can be worked out. Dispensing machines are available from resin suppliers and these should be used where their cost can be justified since they allow the simple measurement of resin and hardener in the correct ratios and so ensure consistent results.

Several polythene buckets should be available for the resin and thinners. If thin-wall buckets are used, it is easy to break out cured resin by bending the bucket. A large supply of solvent specified by the resin supplier should be available and should be used regularly to keep brushes and rollers clean. If this is not done, tools will quickly become useless under hardened resin.

While the fibre reinforcement can often be tailored on the floor, it is far better to have a proper cutting table with an axle at one end on which the rolls of material can be hung. This area should be kept as clean as possible since any dirt, grime or grease that gets on to the fibre will reduce the bond with the resin. If unidirectional fibres are being used, it is often best to wet them out on a separate table covered with plastic sheet before laying them into the mould and rolling the laminate. Several cheap paint brushes will be needed to apply the resin – 2in (50mm) wide is a good size – and they can be stiffened somewhat to make stipling easier by trimming off the ends with a pair of scissors. There should also be available a plentiful supply of barrier cream and an emulsion hand cleaner that will not dry the skin.

Cleanliness and safety

The difference between the inexperienced and the experienced moulder will always show up in the way that the latter seems able to keep himself and his surroundings clean, while the former inevitably gets covered in resin. In fact, keeping clean is only a matter of common sense and preparation. Before starting work, rub in a barrier cream such as Kerrocleanse on the hands and wrists, paying particular attention to the finger nails to which resin adheres particularly well. If working in a confined space, apply the cream to all exposed skin surfaces. Make sure that there is a plentiful supply of clean rags and wipe your hands regularly, applying more barrier cream every few hours. Wear overalls that will not leave fluff on a tacky surface and wear a hat if working in a confined space. Talcum powder dusted on the hands reduces stickiness and the build-up of resin.

At the end of the job use an emulsion hand cleaner, *not* a solvent, to clean off the resin. A solvent will dry up the natural oils, leaving the skin hard and dry, but the proper cleaner will act as a lubricant, easing the resin away without destroying the skin's natural protection. If resin does get stuck to the skin, it is best left alone as the natural oils and shedding of skin will remove it in a few days. Finger nails, however, bond well to resin and unless plenty of barrier cream is used, any resin on the nails will remain there until the nail grows out. It is possible to wear rubber gloves to protect the hands, but they soon become sticky and stiff with resin which also tends to find its way under the wrists.

The safety precautions to be taken when working with FRP materials are really quite simple and straightforward. Avoid skin, eye or mouth contact with all materials; work in a well-ventilated area; and do not smoke or use a naked flame in the moulding area. Many materials used in FRP moulding are corrosive or irritant and some can cause cases of dermatitis in sensitive people, especially the powerful grease solvents used to clean resin from tools. Following the rules for clean working given above should avoid any problems except in the case of extreme sensitivity. Many resins and their associated solvents are highly inflammable and so all forms of naked light must be kept away from the materials, both under store and in use. If a fire does break out, it should be fought with dry-powder extinguishers, not water, with the exception of the catalyst for polyester resin which must be extinguished with water. Do not throw waste resin away until it has cured. If catalysed but uncured resin is put with other waste materials, the heat build-up as the resin cures can be sufficient to ignite the other waste.

When finished FRP parts are machined, tiny particles of resin and fibre cun be inhaled or can irritate the eyes. Always wear a face mask and goggles when drilling, filing, cutting or sanding FRP laminates.

9 BUILDING IN FRP

Quantity of reinforcement

When the design of a laminate uses reinforcing fibres more sophisticated than simple CSM, the designer will usually specify all details of the laminate including thickness, weights of cloth in each layer, orientation of fibres and resin-to-fibre ratio. Many mouldings, however, use only the simplest and most common of reinforcements – CSM and, sometimes, woven rovings; and in these cases the designer may only specify the finished thickness of the laminate for each part of the moulding.

Given the resin-to-fibre ratio, it is possible to work out the amount of mat or woven roving that will be needed to give the desired thickness. Since mat and woven rovings are available in a range of weights, the total laminate thickness can be built up in a number of ways, the choice often being left to the builder.

Although the heavier mats build up thickness more quickly, they are harder to wet-out and will not conform to tight curves or indentations as well as the lighter mats. These practical difficulties can cause voids or resin-rich areas in the laminate, so the moulder should experiment to ensure that wetting-out can be completed well within the gel time of the resin, and that the mat will conform to all difficult parts of the mould. Whatever the weight of the mat used in the centre of the laminate, the layer next to the gel-coat should be of surfacing tissue backed up by a light mat that conforms easily to the mould's surface. If a heavy mat or cloth is used in this area, voids may occur under the gel-coat and the heavy stipling and rolling required to wet-out a heavy mat is likely to cause strands to be deeply embedded in the gel-coat. Either of these results will seriously reduce the effectiveness of the gel-coat and increase the risk of water absorption into the laminate.

Contact moulding in a female mould

This is the oldest and still most commonly used method of FRP production boatbuilding. In most production building the reinforcements used are the basic forms of E glass, namely CSM and woven rovings. It is perfectly

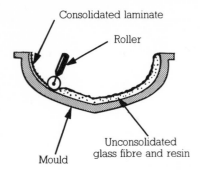

Consolidated laminate

Roller

Unconsolidated
glass fibre and resin

Mould

HAND LAY-UP MOULDING

Fig. 9.1 Hand lay-up is still the most commonly used production method.

Fig. 9.2 Before working on the moulding can begin, the mould must be cleaned and polished.

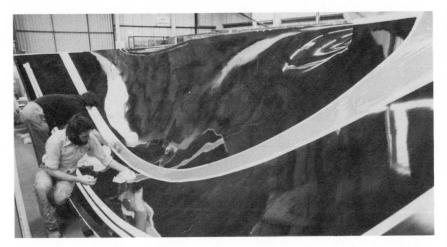

possible to use higher-performance fibre reinforcements, but a somewhat more advanced production process is better suited to such materials if their full potential is to be realized.

Although first used for moulding solid laminates, contact moulding in female moulds is also used to produce sandwich laminates. Because the cost of building a female mould is quite high, it is used, almost without exception, for series production where the cost of the female mould can be spread over a number of mouldings. Contact moulding on male moulds differs only in detail, as will be seen later, but the basic practices of hand lay-up remain the same.

Tailoring the reinforcement

With the mould well waxed and ready for moulding, the first task is to tailor

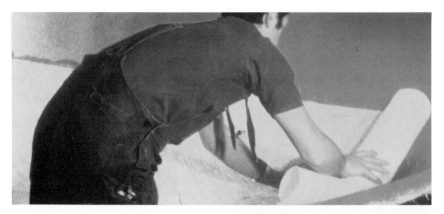

Fig. 9.3 The reinforcement should be tailored, dry, to fit the mould in manageable pieces.

Fig. 9.4 When expensive fibres are being used – such as this carbon-fibre unidirectional cloth – careful tailoring will save waste and allow accurate fibre-orientation.

the reinforcement using paper or cardboard templates. Production builders will often work with long runs of mat or cloth, carrying it to the mould rolled up, then unrolling it on to the mould. The inexperienced builder is, however, advised to design his template pattern to keep the largest pieces of cloth to manageable proportions – say 6.5ft (2m) – especially if working alone or with only one helper. As experience with the materials increases, so can the size of the pieces being worked. When deciding on a template pattern, start with the largest and simplest-shaped areas in the middle of the hull and work towards the ends. Mark the location of the first piece on the mould flange so that the correct starting point can be found when lay-up begins. The type of reinforcement and the stacking order of the laminate will have been specified by the designer, but both will determine the way the reinforcement must be tailored. When using surfacing mat and CSM, for instance, all joints should be roughly tailored with an overlap of about 2in (50mm).

Accurate tailoring is not important since the mat is easily persuaded into position, but in areas of tight curvature, such as at the bow and stern, it may be necessary to cut darts in the mat to allow it to lie flat on the mould. Since a CSM laminate has, in theory, equal properties in all directions in the plane of the laminate, it should not matter in which direction each layer is oriented. In practice, however, a slight longitudinal bias is given to the mat during manufacture, and so alternate layers of CSM should be laid at 90° to the previous layer. In hull production the first layer is usually laid athwartships with the second layer laid fore and aft. Following layers then alternate the direction of lay.

Templates for each layer should be designed so that joints in adjacent layers do not lie close to each other. Making templates for the second layer is best done with the templates for the first layer taped to the mould, so that the location of joins can easily be seen. When roven rovings, or other bidirectional fabrics are to be used, tailoring needs to be more accurate since all joints should be made to butt together. If overlapping joints are used with these thinner materials, the result will be an uneven thickness in areas of the laminate.

The direction of lay-up is important when using fabrics and should be clearly specified by the designer. Balance-weave fabrics of a single fibre have approximately equal properties in the weft and warp directions, but each layer should still be rotated through 90° relative to the preceding layer to allow for slightly increased properties in the weft direction. The laminate design may also call for some layers to be oriented in the ±45° directions, or for even more elaborate layer directions if unbalanced weaves, unidirectional or hybrid materials are used. Careful pre-planning and the making of templates for each layer, if necessary, will save much time and waste when it comes to the actual laminating. When making templates, number each one to denote the layer and position, and make a rough diagram to show the position of each template on the mould.

Templates should also be made for panels of the core material when sandwich construction is being used and when more than one hull is being made – the templates being taken off the panels for the first moulding which are tailored directly on the mould. Always dry-fit and tailor core panels in the mould before laminating begins. As before, start in the easier, shallow-curved or flat midships sections and work towards the ends. Use the largest size of panel that is manageable and stagger all joins. When using balsa or foam cores, use plain sheets wherever possible, resorting to contoured sheets only in highly curved areas where the radius of bend is too great for the thickness of the plain material. When a plain sheet will not take up the required curvature across the full curve, it may be possible to move the position of the join on to the curve and so still use plain sheet.

Fig. 9.5 Templates should be made for panels of any core material so that they can be fitted without wasting time during laminating.

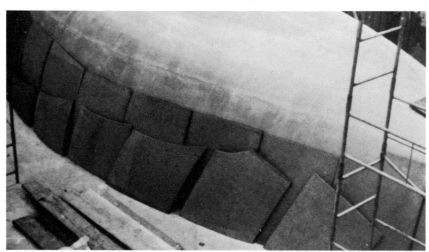

If inserts of a different core material are to be used, these should be marked on the templates, as should the position of any chamfered edges in areas where core construction gives way to solid lay-up; as at the sheerline, keel or other highly stressed areas. When tailoring sheets of the core material, use tape and weights to hold the panels on the mould.

The reason for using plain sheets of foam or balsa wherever possible is that these give the most weight-efficient laminate. Flexible, contoured sheets of kerfed panels or individual blocks bonded to a backing scrim conform easily to tight curves but leave gaps between each block which must be filled with resin, thus increasing the laminate weight and reducing its properties. And, since the gaps between the individual blocks will be largest on the convex, 'mould', side of the foam or balsa, it is difficult to avoid air pockets between the outer skin and the core. In high-performance laminates, vacuum techniques are often used to hold plain sheets under pressure while the bonding resin cures. This avoids the use of contoured panels, but when such techniques are not available it may be necessary to use contoured sheets in some tightly curved areas of the laminate.

Tailoring of any of the materials is best done on a large, clean table. Most of the materials used can be cut relatively easily with a sharp knife, scissors or shears. When cutting cloths or woven rovings, run a length of masking tape along the line of cut and cut down the middle of the tape. This prevents the material unravelling and is easily removed during wetting-out.

Gel-coat application

When all the reinforcement and any core material has been cut to shape and the mould has been prepared, the first step in the actual moulding process is the application of the gel-coat. If the mould has been broken in and is in regular use, it should be possible to use it for several mouldings in between waxing and without the use of a release agent, touching up any flaws in the mould after each demoulding. If there are any doubts as to the ease of release, or if the mould is large or complex, a layer of release agent should be thinly painted all over it and allowed to dry thoroughly. Check that all parts of the mould are dry since small, thicker patches of release agent may accumulate in places and will take far longer to dry than where the coat has been applied thinly. If the release agent is not totally dry, a skin will not form and the moulding could be damaged.

The gel-coat is the working surface and must protect the underlying laminate from the environment while retaining a good appearance. In order to do its job the gel-coat has to be relatively thick, and so the resin must be thixotropic to stop it draining off the vertical parts of the mould and so preventing the application of an even thickness. The gel-coat resin can be applied by brush, roller or spray. When spray application is used, the resin should be a lower-viscosity spraying type; alternatively the viscosity of a standard polyester resin may be reduced by the addition of 5–10 per cent styrene monomer.

When applying by the spray method, the desired thickness can be achieved in one operation, but when a brush or roller is used it is best if the full thickness is built up in two coats to prevent brush or roller marks in the thick, unflowing resin. A gel-coat applied by brush or roller will tend to be thicker than one that is sprayed, but whatever application method is used the total thickness of the gel-coat should be between 0.25 and 0.5mm ($300–500g/m^2$).

When two applications are used to build the full thickness, the first coat must be allowed to cure before the second is applied, otherwise the exterior surface may suffer from wrinkling due to its curing being affected by the second coat. It is important that great care be taken to ensure even gel-coat thickness. If it is too thin in places, its ability to protect the laminate will be reduced, it may not cure fully (because of styrene evaporation from the thin coating), the colour will be less dense than it should be, and a fibre-pattern may may be visible on the surface. If, on the other hand, the gel-coat is too thick, a problem which often occurs in sharp corners, it will be brittle and prone to impact damage. If the gel-coat is of uneven thickness, it will cure unevenly and this may lead to a crazing of the surface.

With the gel-coat applied all over the mould it is allowed to cure before laminating begins. The gel-coat resin is meant to stay tacky, even when cured, to provide a good bonding surface for the laminating resin. The correct stage of cure of the gel-coat can be checked by touching with a finger: if the surface feels tacky but the finger comes away clean, the gel-coat is cured and ready for laminating.

Surfacing tissue

Whatever material is being used as the fibre reinforcement in the underlying laminate, it is wise to use a surfacing tissue next to the gel-coat to increase the laminate's resistance to the environment and to provide the best possible surface appearance. The use of this extremely low-density mat which wets-out very easily prevents the fibres from the subsequent heavier layer embedding themselves in the gel-coat during rolling, and so prevents the possibility of fibre pattern on the surface and the risk of wicking.

To apply the surfacing tissue, some catalysed lay-up resin is applied to the gel-coat by brush, roller or spray. The tailored tissue is then laid into the resin and lightly stippled with a brush to bring the resin through to the surface and thoroughly wet-out the tissue. Any dry spots are dealt with by stippling on a small quantity of resin. If the tissue does not want to lie flat on some tightly curved areas of the mould, a few small cuts with scissors in the area of excess tissue will solve the problem.

Always use a stippling action to wet-out the reinforcement: do not use a painting action as this will disturb the fibres. When the whole mould has been covered with wet-out surfacing tissue, this is left to gel and begin to cure. Lay-up of the rest of the laminate can continue as soon as the first layer is sufficiently cured so that it will not be disturbed by further laminating.

Laminating

Laminating must be done in stages that can be completed conveniently within the gel-time of the resin system being used. Only mix enough resin for each operation as can be used, without rushing, before gelation begins. The actual amount that can be used depends not only on the gel-time of the resin, and therefore, of course, on the type of resin and the ambient temperature; but also on the size and complexity of the moulding being produced. Decide if the next layer can be laid-up completely within the working time of the resin or if it should be laminated in stages. Then calculate the amount of resin required for the type and weight of reinforcement being used. This can be done easily since the weight of the reinforcement should be known, as should the resin-to-fibre ratio (by weight) consistent with that type of reinforcement.

Fig. 9.6 Two people working together speed up the laminating process. One person wets the mould with resin and hangs the pre-tailored fabric or mat, while the other consolidates the laminate with more resin and a roller. It is much easier to work in a large mould if it is rotated on its side.

In perhaps 95 per cent of mouldings produced by hand lay-up in a female mould, all – or the majority – of the reinforcement is E glass CSM. Ideally the layer next to the gel-coat/surfacing-tissue surface should be a low-density mat which will conform easily to difficult shapes and ensure good contact with the gel-coat and so reduce the void content in this critical area.

Apply a portion of the total measured amount of resin on to the gel-coat/surfacing tissue, and place the tailored mat on to the mould, pressing it firmly into position. Stipple the mat with a brush to bring the resin up through the mat where it will dissolve the binder which keeps the fibres in position. Any areas which appear white instead of translucent after stippling should have a small amount of resin stippled on to complete the wetting-out. Once wet-out is achieved, the binder has dissolved and all the strands will have broken down into their individual filaments which are easy to mould to shape.

The laminate must now be rolled with a metal roller of the split-washer variety (or similar type), in order to consolidate the laminate and remove any air bubbles that may be trapped. Rollers must always be used 'wet' with resin, and should be used with short strokes, extending the area of working as the mat wets-out. Using long strokes on dry mat will result in a time-wasting mess of resin and mat stuck to the roller.

As soon as the resin starts to gel, all work on that area must stop or the laminate will be disturbed and voids created. Clean all tools before the resin gels and leave in solvent, using another set of brushes that have come straight from cleaning. If you have been working in stages along the mould, move on to the next area, measuring the correct quantity of resin and proceeding as before. If using mat, remember to overlap the edges at joins

Fig. 9.7 Use a brush to stipple resin into and through the mat or cloth. Do not brush resin as you would paint.

Fig. 9.8 Consolidation of the laminate should be done with a metal roller, wetted with resin.

by about 2in (50mm). If the edge being joined to has not cured no preparation is necessary, but if it has cured it will be necessary to sand the edge to remove loose fibres and nibs, and to feather the edge.

Where possible, laminating of successive layers should be carried on wet-on-wet, laminating two or three layers at one time. If the last layer has had time to cure, it will be necessary to sand down lightly to remove any protruding fibres, and if the laminate has been left for more than forty-eight hours, it will be necessary to sand the whole surface thoroughly to provide a good key for the next layer.

When applying a layer of reinforcement on to a wet layer, it will probably be unnecessary to apply more resin to the surface before placing the reinforcement in position. The wet layer will usually have sufficient surplus resin to help wet-out the next, unless extreme care has been taken to keep the resin-to-fibre ratio close to the optimum.

Instead of applying resin by brush or roller, the process may be speeded up by spraying resin on to the reinforcement, but consolidation by metal rollers must still take place in order to remove air pockets and ensure thorough wetting-out. One practice that is becoming far less common, however, is the use of a pigmented lay-up resin. Some builders using coloured resin claimed it was to give a better depth of colour to the gel-coat, but a good gel-coat resin will not need a coloured lay-up resin and the practice is to be avoided because it makes it impossible to check the finished laminate for flaws and renders it more difficult to spot entrapped air bubbles during laminating.

Once the full laminate thickness has been built up, the final layer should

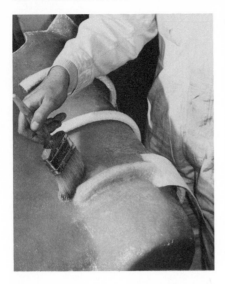

Fig. 9.9 Stringers and other stiffeners should be laminated, over a lightweight core, preferably before the final inner layers of the moulding are laminated.

Fig. 9.10 The correct way to bond a bulkhead to a hull.

Fig. 9.11 The moulded flange should cover a good area of both hull and bulkhead.

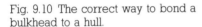

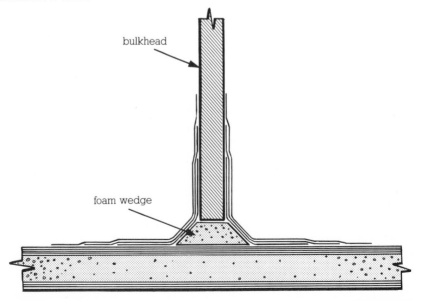

bulkhead

foam wedge

be of topcoat, preferably with a layer of surfacing tissue. Topcoat and surfacing tissue help to provide a smoother interior surface and increased protection to the laminate from moisture absorption, and, if a coloured topcoat is used (once the laminate has been inspected for voids), the appearance of the laminate is improved. Before topcoat and surfacing tissue are applied, the partly cured laminate must be lightly sanded to remove nibs and whiskers of fibres, to fair-out surface irregularities, and to provide a key for the topcoat resin.

Stiffeners

As we have already seen, thin-shelled, solid-laminate FRP needs internal support to provide the necessary stiffness and this is usually given by stringers internally bonded to the hull or deck laminate. Internal stiffening can be bonded-in during moulding, during the curing stage or later, prior to fitting out the hull. The best procedure is to laminate the stiffeners during hull or deck laminating, laying-up the stiffeners before the last layer or two of laminate, so that these layers and the topcoat/surfacing-tissue final layer pass over the stiffeners. This is the strongest procedure and gives the best finish as well as reducing the danger of distortion to the main laminate caused by curing stresses of the stiffeners. Stiffeners are usually laid-up over a light-weight former of foam, paper, rope or cardboard, which has no structural requirements but which acts simply as a former.

Stringers are not, of course, the only answer to providing stiffness in an FRP laminate. Curvature, decorative bumps or hollows, beading or flanges, or extra thickness can all be moulded in selected areas to add stiffness to a moulding. Frames, ribs, angles or webs can all be moulded in or added later. In most yachts there are a number of transverse bulkheads and it is these that often provide the majority of transverse stiffening.

Whatever type of stiffening is used, it must be moulded in so that the support given to the laminate does not result in any hard stress points which will cause local distortion and possibly failure of the laminate. Every stiffener, be it simple added thickness or a complicated web, must blend in smoothly with the laminate, and the moulding used to attach the stiffener must be smoothly tapered to spread the imposed stress over a large area of laminate.

The attachment of bulkheads to an FRP shell is a good example of this technique. If the bulkhead is cut to fit snugly against the hull and bonded in with strips of rovings or mat, the moulded angle fillets will have to be forced into a right-angle bend, with the strong likelihood of voids and poor bonding, and there will be considerable danger that the incompressible bulkhead will cause the hull to distort around the point of attachment when the boat is subjected to sailing stresses. Damage will be difficult to detect until it shows as cracks on the gel-coat, and by that time it will be difficult to repair.

The correct way to bond-in bulkheads is to avoid direct contact between the shell and the bulkhead and allow the moulded flanges to transfer the strain to the laminate. A wedge-shaped strip of foam or balsa can be used between the bulkhead edge and the hull to separate the two and to provide a smooth angle for the moulded flange to follow. On both sides of the bulkhead there should ideally be a moulded flange the thickness of which should be at least half the hull thickness. If it is not possible, for some reason, to mould webs on both sides of a bulkhead, it can be attached with only one flange, whose thickness in this case should be at least equal to that of the hull, and the area of hull covered by the single flange should be equal to that covered by two separate ones.

Another technique for bonding-in bulkheads is to use a filled epoxy resin, a syntactic foam, to both fill the gap between bulkhead and hull and to form a moulded fillet on both sides of the bulkhead. With the bulkhead simply tacked into position with a few pieces of cloth, or held by supports or wedges, the epoxy/microballoon mixture is simply trowelled into the gap and a fillet formed and radiused on each side of the bulkhead.

Using cloths and fabrics in a female mould

While the use of CSM is by far the most common production method in FRP boatbuilding, a more weight-efficient laminate can be obtained by using fabrics or cloth which are both stronger and allow a better fibre-to-resin ratio to be achieved. The basic process and rules of laminating remain the same, but the details of the working method will vary according to the type of fibre and the style of the reinforcement.

After the straight CSM laminate, the most common, most efficient type makes use of a mixture of CSM and woven rovings in alternate layers. Laying-up the fabrics and cloths commonly used in boatbuilding differs little from the use of CSM. In some ways fabrics are easier to work with than mats: many weaves drape easily and are more stable under hard rolling, not breaking up like mat. Fabrics are generally harder to wet-out and need thorough rolling to ensure complete wetting and to consolidate the laminate. The heavier fabrics and cloths made from twisted yarns are the hardest to wet-out thoroughly, and great care must be taken to avoid voids among the tightly packed fibres.

Because fabrics and cloths allow more efficient fibre-to-resin ratios, wetting-out is made more difficult since there is only the minimum amount of resin with which to work. The tendency of some builders using CSM is to let the mat virtually swim in a sea of resin. This certainly ensures thorough wetting but also results in a heavy, weak laminate. If the expense of the higher-performance fabrics is to be justified, the properties they offer must be realized, and this means keeping the amount of resin used under strict control. A squeegee is often used on these laminates, to help wet-out the reinforcement, to consolidate the laminate and, most importantly, to remove excess resin from wet-out areas before it begins to gel.

When CSM and woven rovings are used together in a laminate, the first layer, next to the gel-coat/surfacing-tissue layer, is usually CSM, with a layer of WR followed by another layer of CSM. Woven rovings are usually sandwiched between layers of CSM in production building, since with the use of a polyester resin the CSM is needed to improve the interlaminar shear strength of the laminate by providing a mechanical bond with the woven rovings, the random fibres of the CSM interlocking with the smooth-surfaced rovings and providing some degree of bond by tying the two layers together.

These weight-inefficient CSM layers are not necessary if an epoxy laminating resin is used since the adhesive properties of the epoxy are sufficient to ensure good interlaminar shear properties. For this, and other reasons, most high-performance FRP laminates use an epoxy as the laminating resin. While it is unnecessary to use CSM in an epoxy laminate, it can be helpful to employ a mixture of epoxy and milled fibres as an adhesive layer against a sandwich core. The filled epoxy gives an increase in interlaminar shear properties by providing the same 'tying' function at a fraction of the weight of CSM.

To ensure smooth laminates of even thickness, panels of cloth are usually edge-butted rather than overlapped, except in the final layer. This is easily done when the preceding panel is still 'wet', but if it has cured it will be difficult to marry up the new panel because of the inevitable resin runs and odd strands of cured resin and glass. In this case it is necessary to sand the join to a feather edge and overlap the new panel.

When cutting fabrics, do not forget to run a line of masking tape along the line to be cut, and cut down the middle of the tape. The tape prevents fraying at the edges of the cloth and is easily removed during wetting-out.

If you are planning to use one of the more expensive, less commonly used fabrics, check with the supplier to find the best way of handling and laying-up the reinforcement. Remember that a laminate designed to make use of unidirectional, bidirectional or tridirectional fabrics, especially those using the higher-performance fibres, will require accurate fibre orientation if the theoretical properties of the laminate are to be realized. Similarly, the fibre-to-resin ratio must be as close as possible to the optimum for that type of reinforcement. Hand lay-up can never achieve fibre-to-resin ratios comparable with those of more sophisticated and expensive processes, but the difference between careful and sloppy workmanship will have a considerable effect on the ratio actually achieved.

When working with UD fibres, it is often easier to wet them out on a sheet of polythene on the bench before transferring the strip to the mould. This procedure helps to avoid disturbing the fibres during wetting-out.

Core materials

The most commonly used core materials for the construction of boat hulls and decks by hand lay-up in a female mould are balsa and the PVC foams. Stiffer core materials, such as the acrylic foams, are less suitable for hulls but work well on flat panels, such as decks, while the more expensive honeycomb cores are generally used in one-off applications which usually make use of male moulds and vacuum techniques. The procedures for working with balsa or PVC foam are basically similar, with variations in building methods mainly depending on the specification of the fibre reinforcement and the resin system.

Unless vacuum techniques are to be used (see page 183), plain sheets of

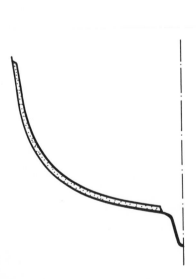

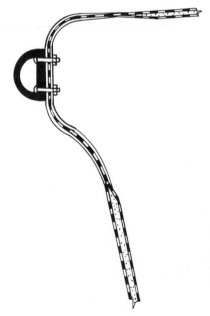

Fig. 9.12 The core material should be stopped short of the keel and the edge tapered to a slope of about 4:1. The inner skin is extended to join the outer skin to give a thick, single skin in this highly stressed region.

Fig. 9.13 A hull/deck joint is another area where core-construction should be replaced with a solid lay-up.

balsa or foam are not suitable for this method of construction except in flat areas. In curved areas it is necessary to use contoured foam or balsa – small blocks of the core material bonded on to a glass scrim to make up flexible panels – in order to ensure complete contact with the outer skin using the minimum of pressure.

In most production applications, where the skins will be laminated, as described earlier, using polyester resin, CSM or CSM/WR, the outer skin is laid-up, but stopped short of the last layer prior to the core. This will be applied with the core and is usually a resin-rich CSM layer.

With the inner skin in a partly cured state, and the core tailored to shape with the aid of templates, an especially resin-rich layer of CSM (the weight of which depends on the thickness of the core) is laid up with the minimum rolling required to ensure thorough wetting-out. Don't use all the resin that was measured for this operation on the CSM layer; lightly coat the face of the core with a portion of the resin before pressing the core into the CSM. When using balsa, do remember that it will absorb more resin into its surface than will foam, and this should be allowed for otherwise it is possible for dry areas to result from the absorption of resin into the core. The heavier the layer of CSM, the easier it will be to bed the core because of the extra 'cushioning', but the disadvantage is an increase in weight resulting from the inefficient resin-rich CSM layer. In most places in a female mould the flexible sheets of core are laid down with the block side to the mould, scrim side uppermost, to cater for the concave mould face. In any areas of reverse curve, however, the core is reversed. Press the core into the wet layer beneath, using hand pressure, and repeat the process after several minutes. On curved areas the gaps between blocks will open up and there must be enough resin in the underlying layer to be forced into, and fill, these gaps. If hand pressure is not enough to ensure complete contact, the use of weights may be necessary.

The resin should be catalysed to cure, at the ambient temperature, in between fifteen and thirty minutes, and care should be taken to ensure that final positioning of the core is done well within the gel-time of the resin. Once one panel is in position, move on to the next. If one or two people can be laying-up the CSM layer just ahead of you, the whole operation will be a continuous process and will proceed much more quickly, avoiding the problem of partly cured resin and whiskers of fibre interfering with the butt joints between panels. Your earlier work making the templates will also be well repaid at this stage.

Once the core/CSM layer has gelled, the core edges should be tapered to a slope of about 4:1, unless this was done when the panels were tailored. An alternative to tapering the core is the use of wedge-shaped inserts, cut from a plain sheet of the core, which are laid up along the panel edges, or the use of a tapered fillet of a syntactic resin mix. Check every inch of the core for a

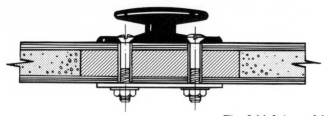

Fig. 9.14 It is useful to be able to insert compression-proof blocks of wood or high-density foam into the core before laminating the second skin.

good bond by tapping or scraping a coin along the surface. Areas which have not bonded will show up by a definite change in tone, and those which are suspect should be dealt with by cutting-out and the application of a new block. Alternatively, resin can be injected through the core, but the result of this method is uncertain in large patches and so should be limited to small, localized voids.

Once the core has been checked for integrity and with any large bumps or raised edges sanded flat and all gaps filled, lay-up of the inner skin can continue in the normal way with the layer next to the core again being of CSM. Neither so much resin nor so heavy a mat needs to be used for the inside adhesive layer as it does not have to act as a cushion, or provide excess resin to fill large gaps. Make sure that the core surface is thoroughly wetted with resin before laying-up the CSM, and beware of resin absorption into the core if balsa is being used. Coat the area to be worked on and then recheck the surface, adding resin to any dry spots. Any backing scrim that is on the core need not be removed before laying-up the inner skin. Once the first layer is in position, the rest of the inner skin can be laid-up, wet-on-wet.

The disadvantage of using a resin-rich layer next to the core is an increase in weight of the laminate, but its use is considered necessary to create mechanical 'locking' because of the poor adhesive properties of polyester resins. If a laminate is laid-up with an epoxy, however, it is usually unnecessary to use layers of mat, either to increase interlaminar shear strength between layers of cloth or rovings, or between the skins and the core in sandwich construction.

In the case of an epoxy/cloth laminate, the core can be bedded on to a thick, even layer of filled resin or a resin/milled-fibre mix applied to the partly cured outer skin with a serrated trowel or spatula. Enough resin must be laid on the skin to ensure that it will fill the gaps between the blocks of the core as the latter is pressed into place. Laminating of the inner skin then continues normally.

Filled polyester resin is sometimes used as an adhesive layer as described above, but its use, while providing a weight saving, must result in a doubtful bond between core and skins, and should therefore be used only for lightly loaded sandwich mouldings which do not have a long life requirement.

While the use of sandwich construction has many advantages, the limitations placed on it by hand lay-up in female moulds, especially when a polyester/CSM combination is used, do not allow the full potential of this form of construction to be realized. The need to use flexible sheets to cope with the curved areas of the mould results in many gaps, all of which have to be filled with resin/fibre or resin putty, making the laminate heavier than necessary. A great improvement in the properties achieved can be seen when a vacuum bag is used to provide even pressure on plain sheets of the core material. Vacuum-bag and other more advanced methods will be looked at in a later section.

Curing, and removal from the mould

When the laminate has been completed, it needs to be trimmed, allowed to cure and then removed from the mould. Trimming of the edges is best achieved with the laminate in the 'green' or rubbery stage, just after the resin gels. It can then be trimmed accurately and easily with a sharp knife. Any edges that have not been trimmed at this stage will need to be cut with a hacksaw. When cutting, drilling, grinding or sanding a cured FRP laminate, one should always wear goggles and a face mask to prevent eye damage or the inhalation of fibre-laden dust.

Once the resin has gelled and the laminate has passed through the green stage, it becomes tough and hard – a process which, from gelation, can take between thirty minutes and several hours. Although the laminate gives every sign of being cured once it is in the hardening stage, full cure needs a period – the maturing stage – during which it achieves its full physical properties. This process takes several days at room temperature, and during this period the shape of the laminate, if out of the mould, can be drastically altered if it is not well supported.

The gelation, hardening and maturing process depends critically on the ambient temperature and the resin system used, but the process can be speeded up, and the properties of the laminate improved, by an assisted cure at an elevated temperature. All stages of the process can be speeded up by raising the temperature, thus allowing quick removal from the mould, but physical properties can be best optimized by replacing the maturing stage by an elevated-temperature postcure. The length of time and the temperature of the postcure will depend on the resin system and the

supplier should, in all cases, be consulted.

Checking the degree of cure of the laminate can be done only by a comparative test, using an impressor that compares its hardness with that of a known and fully cured specimen – often a laboratory sample. Similarly, it is only possible to measure the physical properties of the laminate by destruct testing a test sample laid-up in the same way and under the same conditions as the moulding.

In some cases it is possible to complete a lot of the interior fitting out while the hull is still in the mould and before the deck is attached. This ensures that the hull is perfectly supported and cannot distort, but in practical production it is often necessary to remove the hull from the mould as soon as possible, and before any interior stiffening, such as bulkheads, are in place. If this is the case, every effort must be made to support the hull both during and after removal from the mould. Hull shape can be maintained during removal by fixing supports at regular intervals at deck level across the hull. Once out of the mould the hull, or deck, must be placed on a solid cradle built to give even and regular support to the whole structure, and capable of taking the extra weight of the interior which is still to be fitted.

Release from the mould is easiest to achieve in the case of split moulds. Not only does this avoid difficulties with release, but it also eliminates the problem of lifting a possibly large and heavy hull several feet out of a single mould. With a hull mould split along the centre-line, the hull can be supported by lifting strops attached to moulded-in strong points, while the mould is pulled away and a cradle brought underneath the hanging hull.

Release from a single mould is usually assisted by the use of wedges, compressed air or water. Shallow wedges of wood or plastic can be tapped

Fig. 9.15 When a split mould is not used, the hull will have to be lifted clear.

Fig. 9.16 Release from the mould is often assisted by the use of wedges.

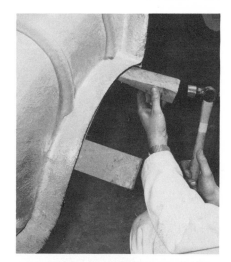

Fig. 9.17 The interior is completed most easily by leaving the deck off until the later stages.

lightly between the laminate and the mould to spring the two apart. They should be positioned close together and must be used with care to avoid damaging the mould or moulding.

Water can be used to dissolve a water-soluble release agent, being poured between the mould and the moulding and left to do its work. When release is likely to prove difficult, it is common to have air holes in the mould which are covered with discs of adhesive paper during laminating. Attaching compressed-air lines to these holes will force the moulding away from the mould, but care must be taken to ensure that too much pressure is not applied to flat surfaces which could be damaged.

When compressed air is not available, or the mould not suitable, a difficult removal can sometimes be aided, if the component is not too large, by striking the mould with the flat of the hand, to spring the two apart at a sticky point. Do not hit the mould with a hammer or wooden mallet as either will crack the mould; even a rubber mallet can cause damage.

With the hull out of the mould and well supported, the interior can be completed most easily by leaving the deck off until the later stages. Obviously this can only be done as long as the fitting out can be effected under cover – as it is in all production building. Amateurs working outside or under a rough-and-ready covering will need to get the deck on once bulkheads and major partitions have been installed, or even before any interior work is undertaken. Because working inside a deckless hull is far easier and quicker than with the deck in place, because of easier access for parts, tools and people, better lighting and ventilation, it is always advisable to work under good cover wherever possible. Even if this means that some time and money must be spent to build a decent shelter, such investment will be well rewarded during the stages of fitting out.

Spray moulding

Spray-up moulding has become very common in recent years, especially for large, simple jobs. This method is an extension of hand lay-up and uses the same mould, but can give greater speed of production when used by an experienced workforce.

Spray-up moulding consists simply of spraying an even stream of catalysed polyester resin and chopped rovings on to the mould and building up the desired thickness, layer by layer. Several different spraying machines are available and fall into two categories: two-component sprays and catalyst injection. The two-component system comprises two equal-sized containers, one of which holds resin with twice the normal amount of catalyst, and the other contains resin with a double shot of accelerator. Catalyst must only be added immediately prior to use, but the accelerated resin may be prepared in bulk or bought in pre-mixed.

Both containers are pressurized equally to force the resin from each to the spray head where they are both atomized and sprayed out, the two resin mixes meeting only outside the spray head. The glass fibre used in spraying operations is continuous roving which is fed through a cutter on the spray gun, is chopped into lengths typically between $\frac{5}{8}$in and 2in (15mm and 50mm), and is then blown from the gun and carried to the mould by the resin spray. Pressure-regulating valves on the resin flow or the chopper can be adjusted to give resin-to-fibre ratios between about 1.5:1 and 4:1 in a typical installation. When spraying has finished, the pre-catalysed resin must be flushed out with acetone.

Catalyst injection equipment uses a large container of pre-accelerated resin which is fed under pressure to the spray gun. Catalyst is fed separately

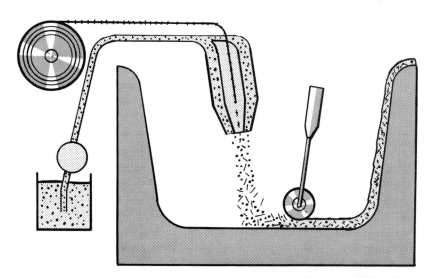

Fig. 9.18 In spray-up moulding, a stream of resin and chopped glass strands is sprayed into the mould where it is consolidated by hand.

Fig. 9.19 The skill of the operator determines the evenness of the moulding and its thickness.

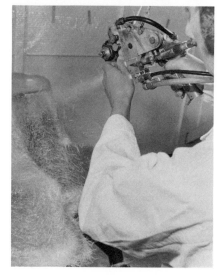

to the spray head by another pump with a calibrating adjustment, is mixed with the accelerated resin and is then forced out of the head under pressure. Glass fibre is chopped and added to the resin spray in the same way as described above. Acetone is used to clean out the spray gun after use.

In use, the mould is prepared exactly as for hand lay-up, gel-coat is applied to it and, preferably, a surfacing tissue is laid-up on the gel-coat. With the spray gun set up for the chosen resin-to-fibre ratio, resin and

Fig. 9.20 A short-hair roller should be used to ensure thorough wetting of the fibres before the laminate is consolidated with a metal roller.

Fig. 9.21 The conventional method of sandwich-construction on a male mould uses a battened jig (*top*) over which is laid the core material. The outer FRP skin is then laminated and the hull removed from the mould before the inner skin is moulded.

Longitudinal Battens   Frames   Outer Fibreglass Skin   Core

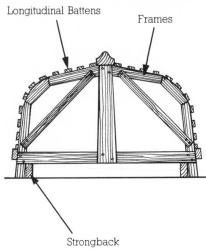
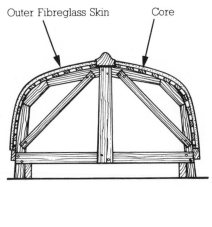

Strongback

chopped rovings are sprayed on to the mould, the operator moving the gun across the mould to avoid overspraying. Each traverse of the area being worked should overlap the previous run slightly to produce as flat and even a surface as possible. As large an area should be sprayed at one time as can be completely rolled and consolidated before the resin begins to gel.

A thin layer (1–2mm) should be laid down first and then rolled. Because of the absence of binder, the fibres will wet-out quickly, aided by the use of a short-hair roller, followed by rolling with a metal washer or spring roller to ensure consolidation. Subsequent layers can then be applied, preferably at 90° to the preceding layer, but no more than 2–3mm should be applied between each rolling. If a thick layer of resin and glass is laid down, it will be impossible to remove all the air pockets and achieve consolidation. Forced ventilation, both general and local, should be provided when spray mould-ing to remove styrene fumes and prevent their building up in deep moulds.

Spray-up is normally used for the quick production of single-skin laminates, but can be used in sandwich mouldings. The method is basically the same as previously described, the outer skin being sprayed, up to the last layer before the core, which is applied just before the core panels are laid in place. Once the core is in position and cured, lay-up of the inner skin can continue as normal.

Spray-up is quicker than hand lay-up but it is not a one-man process; a group of workers are still needed to roll and consolidate the laminate. In many cases the laminate produced is of a lower quality than hand lay-up where there is more control over the laminate. The spray-gun operator is the key man in the process; if he is not very careful, the laminate produced may have a far higher variability in thickness than a hand-laid-up moulding. Thickness variations are very difficult to detect, as are voids which may result if too thick a layer is laid in one operation.

Male moulds

The use of male moulds was pioneered by amateurs using sandwich construction to produce one-off hulls, where the cost of production of a female mould was unacceptable. While the use of male moulds is still most common in amateur, one-off building projects, it is also becoming more and more common for the production of advanced, light-weight, composite structures by professional builders. By definition, such projects do not lend themselves to large-scale production techniques and the use of a male mould is usually the only justifiable approach.

Fig. 9.22 Panels of foam laid over a simple batten and frame mould.

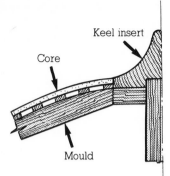

Core

Keel insert

Mould

Fig. 9.23 In areas that will require a solid lay-up, the mould incorporates filler pieces, the same thickness as the foam. These inserts are treated for release before laminating the outer skin.

Fig. 9.24 Once the outer skin has cured, the hull can be removed from the mould prior to laminating the inner skin. In this case the mould and hull have been rolled over before the mould is lifted out.

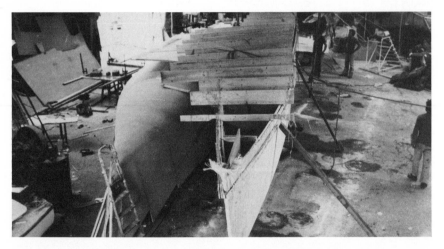

In the conventional method of sandwich construction on a male mould, a battened jig is made as described earlier, to which the core material is attached. The most common core material used in this method is one of the PVC foams, although other cores may be used. The core is attached to the jig by staples, screwing into the core from inside the mould, or by sewing the core to the stringers with nylon fishing line. Plain sheets are used where possible and, in areas of high curvature heat-formed plain or flexible sheets. Once the core has been attached, all gaps are filled with a resin putty and the surface is faired to accept the outer skin. If nylon has been used to sew the core in place, fill the needle holes with putty and, when this has cured, sand off the exposed loops of nylon to leave a smooth surface. If staples have been used these are left in place; they will either pull through the core or out of the jig when the mould is broken out prior to laminating the inner skin.

Lay-up of the outer skin then proceeds as already described. If polyester resin is used, the first layer is usually of CSM to provide reasonable adhesion to the core. The rest of the skin is usually layers of CSM and woven rovings. If an epoxy laminating resin is used, there will be no need for layers of the heavy CSM; the skin is laminated from woven rovings, cloth or other fabrics.

When laying-up the outer skin, be careful to avoid large overlaps as they will cause an uneven surface which will require heavy sanding in the finishing stages. During lamination of the outer skin, its surface should be faired, filled and painted while the hull is still on the mould. Since a gel-coated outer surface cannot be achieved with a male mould, the surface finish is dependent on much work and patience. Remember that if the laminate is weight-critical, as in the case of a high-performance racing craft, the weight can be increased considerably by the amount of filler and paint required to finish the outer surface – an item that is often wrongly ignored in the weight calculations.

Even if a polyester resin has been used to laminate the moulding, serious thought should be given to the use of an epoxy coating, underneath a two-pot polyurethane topcoat, to increase the resistance of the laminate to water absorption (see also Chapter 2).

As much finishing work as possible should be completed at this stage as it is far easier to work on the upturned hull than it will be once it is removed from the mould. It is best if the hull is turned over, complete with jig, and placed on its cradle before the jig is removed. Thus ensures that no distortion can take place. Remember that, with only one skin in place, the hull will be floppy and can be easily damaged or its shape permanently altered.

Once the mould has been removed or broken out, piece by piece, from the hull, the internal surface of the core should be prepared for laminating. If nylon attachment has been used, sand or cut the nylon flush with the surface and fill all holes and gaps. Any areas of the hull that require solid core inserts or a solid FRP lay-up should now be prepared unless the mould incorporated filler pieces in the appropriate areas over which the outer skin was laminated. Cut out the foam in areas where inserts or solid FRP are necessary, tapering all edges to a 4:1 slope in any area where the two skins are to meet. Insert solid wood pieces in the areas where fittings are to be attached and give a final sanding to the whole surface to ensure it is smooth and fair, paying particular attention to the areas where the two skins will meet. A thorough sanding and degreasing is essential in such areas to ensure a satisfactory bond. Once these preparations are complete, the internal skin is laid-up in the way described for a female mould, the final finish being achieved by a layer of surface tissue and topcoat.

Decks can be built in the same way on a male mould or can be laid-up in a temporary female mould made from any suitable available material, prepared for release as described earlier. The latter option has the advantage of allowing one to use the core material only where needed, changing to solid lay-up in other areas, such as vertical surfaces. The female mould also allows the deck surface to be moulded with any finish, such as non-slip, that is desired, and removes the necessity of finishing the outer surface after moulding.

The latest use of male moulds differs from the system described above, by allowing the laying-up of the hull or deck in the exact reverse order to female-mould construction. Thus the interior skin is laid-up before the foam is applied. This method will be described here, although its use does depend on the availability of a vacuum-assisted cure as described in a later section.

This method has several advantages in addition to the increase in laminate properties afforded by the use of pressure during moulding. For instance, the hull is completely finished before removal from the mould, eliminating the risk of hull distortion; there is no need to laminate the inside of the hull after roll-over; and the inside has a smooth finish which can be a gel-coat if desired. In addition, most of the fairing of the hull can be carried out on the (in most cases) more easily faired core material, not the outer skin; inserts are easily laminated in place and the mould may be used for a small number of mouldings.

This method of construction is ideally suited to the production of one-off boat mouldings using advanced materials. The use of epoxy resins, cloths and fabrics, often incorporating the more advanced fibres, and the more advanced honeycomb cores, is made realistic with the employment of vacuum techniques and allows the production of advanced, light-weight laminates without high tooling costs.

The mould used is a normal batten-and-frame jig which is skinned with hardboard, plywood or veneers. Joins in the skins are sealed with plastic tape and the surface is sealed and thoroughly coated with a release agent.

If an internal gel-coat is required, this is applied to the mould in the same way as when laminating in a female mould, and the inner skin is laminated in the usual manner. The benefits of this technique are best achieved with an epoxy laminating resin, rather than polyester, especially when the skins incorporate high-performance materials. If cloth or fabrics are being used and are not too heavy, the reinforcement can be tailored and taped dry to the mould as long as they can be wetted-out satisfactorily through the top surface only. The inner skin is often laid-up in the way previously described for hand lay-up in a female mould, but increased properties can be achieved by using a vacuum bag to consolidate the layer.

When the inner skin is cured, it is sanded to ensure a smooth bonding surface for the core. The tailored pieces of core material are fitted dry at first to ensure accuracy of fit, and are numbered as to fitting sequence before being laid to one side. A layer of CSM will probably be required if a polyester laminating resin is being used and this is laid-up as described earlier. If epoxy is being used, the adhesive layer consists of a filled resin or a resin/milled-fibre mixture into which the core is firmly pressed.

With a section of the core – as large as can be conveniently worked – in position, a vacuum bag is taped over the section, a vacuum pulled and then left until the resin has cured. The bag is then removed and work continues on the next section. Any areas which require high-density inserts or the elimination of the core are dealt with as the core is applied: filler pieces are inserted or the core cut away as required. Remember to taper all edges of the core where the two skins are to meet, such as at the shear or keel.

With all the core in place and the adhesive cured, any gaps should be filled. If a foam or balsa core is used, it may be necessary to use contoured or flexible sheets in areas of tight curvature, and in this case it will be necessary to fill all the gaps between the individual blocks of the core.

The whole surface is now ready to be faired with a power sander or long sanding board. One advantage of this process is that the majority of the fairing required can be done on the core. If the core is fair and smooth, the surface of the outer skin will need little finishing. If foam or balsa is used as the core, the surface should be roughened with a Surform or similar tool after fairing, in order to ensure a good bond with the outer skin.

The outer skin is laid-up in the normal way, avoiding overlaps or thickness variations wherever possible. Higher mechanical properties can be achieved if a vacuum bag is used during cure of the outer skin, and although this makes the process of laminating somewhat slower, it is very worthwhile, especially when high-performance materials are being used. Once the outer skin has cured, it can be sanded, filled and painted before the completed hull is removed from the mould. A less-complicated cradle is needed to support a hull produced by this method since the hull is quite stiff with the inner skin already in position.

The use of pressure

The biggest advance in the production of high-performance, light-weight, one-off racing boats has been achieved by the use of pressure during the curing period. Pressure applied to a curing laminate allows an increased fibre-to-resin ratio through better consolidation, reduces void content and improves interlaminar shear, particularly in the adhesive layer next to a sandwich core. It can be applied by the use of an autoclave, matched moulds or a vacuum bag, the last being the simplest and most commonly used system in boatbuilding.

An autoclave is simply a large oven which can be pressurized. In use the laminate is laid-up and placed in the oven. The temperature is raised (to a level that will depend on the resin system being used) and the autoclave is pressurized. The pressure on the laminate compacts it and reduces the void content, while the elevated temperature shortens the gel-time and the hardening period. Once the resin has hardened, the temperature is usually raised again to give a postcure. While this method provides increased laminate properties and shorter mould times, it also demands a large production run or regular use for one-off, specialized mouldings to justify the cost of the equipment.

The matched-mould method is another one where the expense seldom justifies its use in boatbuilding. In its simplest form, two matching male and female moulds are clamped and sealed together once the laminate has been laid-up in the female part, the cavity is evacuated by vacuum pump, and the two parts of the mould are forced together by atmospheric pressure. The pressure and the vacuum reduce the voids caused by air entrapment, allow a very good fibre-to-resin ratio, and provide a moulding with a good appearance on both sides. The moulds can be heated or put in an oven to give a fast cure and high-temperature postcure. Matched moulds are also used for resin injection and vacuum injection moulding, and can also be used with pre-preg laminates.

Fig. 9.25 The simplest and cheapest way to apply pressure to a laminate is to use a vacuum bag.

VACUUM BAG-MOULDING

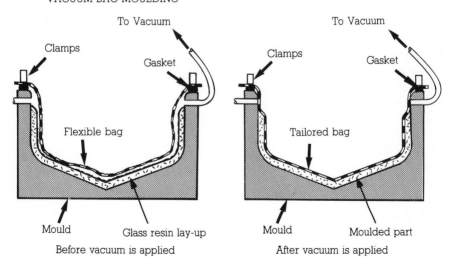

To Vacuum

Clamps

Gasket

Flexible bag

Mould

Glass resin lay-up

Before vacuum is applied

To Vacuum

Clamps

Gasket

Tailored bag

Mould

Moulded part

After vacuum is applied

The simplest and cheapest way of applying pressure to a laminate, and the one most applicable to boatbuilding projects, is by the use of a vacuum bag – a technique that can be used by both the amateur and professional builder. The principle of the technique is simple, consisting of a vacuum bag over the mould, from which air is evacuated by a vacuum pump. The resulting atmospheric pressure then provides a high overall pressure on the laminate in the mould. A vacuum bag can be used on solid lay-ups to reduce void content and to allow a good fibre-to-resin ratio to be achieved, but it is most commonly used on sandwich laminates, the primary aim being to increase core adhesion and to avoid the need to use heavy and inefficient CSM next to the core.

A vacuum bag is made out of transparent PVC sheet and should be at least 2mm thick. When a bag is being used on a female mould, it is best to construct a wooden or metal frame to carry the bag and mate with a flange around the edge of the mould. Sealing the bag to the mould with plastic tape, as has to be done on a male mould, is slow and more prone to leakage. If the moulding is small, it is feasible to use an envelope bag into which the whole mould is placed, but this is not possible with most boatbuilding projects. The bag should be tailored to fit the mould loosely with no tight areas and as few seams as possible. Seams that are necessary can be taped with 2in (50mm) wide PVC tape, but a better and more longer lasting arrangement is to RF weld the seams.

The frame must be designed to seal the bag between itself and the flange, the seal usually being made on a strip of closed-cell, flexible foam stuck to the flange. The flange and sealing area should always be well treated with release agent before laminating.

A proper vacuum pump must be used; not an industrial vacuum cleaner which, while moving a lot of air, is designed to run only under a constant stream of air. The choice of pump will depend on the size of the mould, and the manufacturer's advice should be sought, but a large-capacity pump will help avoid sealing problems.

A resin trap should be installed in the vacuum line to prevent resin reaching the pump, which should be fitted with a bleed valve and a vacuum gauge. The vacuum line should be made of transparent reinforced plastic so that any resin or foreign bodies in the line can be seen. The vacuum line is best attached to the bag through a plastic fitting used normally as a through-hull fitting. This type of fitting has a screw-on backing flange and the area of the bag around the fitting must be reinforced with two or three extra layers of material.

Moulds over about $19\frac{1}{2}$ft (6m) will probably need two outlets at opposite ends, attached to the vacuum line by a Y-fitting, in order to pull an even vacuum across the whole mould. The area of the outlet(s) must be padded in some way to prevent them from bearing directly on the mould, especially if the bag is to be used on a solid laminate as well as a sandwich core. This can be done by taping a $\frac{1}{2}$in (12mm) polypropylene rope to the inside of the bag in a spiral around the outlet(s). The rope stops the outlet sealing itself to the surface and considerably reduces the risk of drawing resin into the line. It is also necessary to provide a bleed path for the air from all parts of the mould to the pump outlet. This can be done by taping some more $\frac{1}{2}$in (12mm) rope in a shallow S-shaped curve from the outlet to the mould extremities. For medium- or large-sized moulds, however, it is best to use an open-weave net of large-diameter plastic fibre to prevent air bubbles forming in pockets under the bag. Remember that all materials used under the bag must be releasable from the resin system being used.

Before using the bag, give it a dry run in an empty mould, checking that a suitable vacuum can be pulled – at least 10psi (0.7kg/cm^2) – and that the bag is in even contact with the mould with no tight spots. If a large mould is being vacuumed, it may help to connect an industrial vacuum cleaner to another outlet to move a larger quantity of air in a short time and so reduce the time necessary to pull the vacuum.

If a sandwich laminate is to be moulded, as is likely, the bag should next be tried over the core laid into a dry mould. If foam is being used it is often possible to use plain sheets; the high and even pressure bending these sheets over quite tight curves. Hold the foam in position, where necessary, by taping with PVC tape over the mould flange. Once the vacuum has been pulled, the foam should be in full contact with the mould; if it isn't, or if a panel snaps on a curve, the template design may have to be changed. If a sheet snaps, move the panel join so that it is in the middle of the curve.

If the foam or balsa in plain sheet form is being used, it is necessary to punch or drill holes in the core to allow air to escape from underneath. These holes need only be about $\frac{1}{8}$in (3mm) in diameter and about 6in (150mm) apart and can be quickly made by a nail board or needle roller. Before finishing with the foam, taper the edges as this will save time later.

Lay-up follows the same procedure as described earlier, bearing in mind that an epoxy/cloth or fabric laminate is likely to be specified in order to maximize the potential of this method. It is not necessary to attempt to lay-up the whole of each layer in one operation – it is quite permissible to work in sections. Often the outer skin will be laid-up and allowed to cure to the green stage without any use of vacuum. The core is then laid on to an adhesive layer, a vacuum is pulled, and the layer allowed to cure, the adhesive thickness and the pressure on the core being confirmed by resin rising in the air holes. Once the core adhesive layer has cured, lay-up proceeds normally.

Although that is the most commonly used method, greater benefits can be

Fig. 9.26 A vacuum bag is just as effective on a male mould but a frame is not usually used and the bag is taped in position.

obtained by vacuuming each stage of the laminate, at the expense of a bit more time and trouble.

A vacuum bag can be used on a male mould and is just as effective, but in this case the bag is usually taped in position, since the use of a frame assembly would be impractical. Taping must be done carefully if the bag is to seal first time: if there is a problem pulling the vacuum, you can usually find the leak(s) by listening for the fluttering of the bag near the leak.

Resin-injection moulding

In this system, reinforcement is laid-up, dry, in a female mould which has previously been coated with gel-coat. A matched male mould is then clamped in place and a measured amount of resin is injected through resin inlets at the bottom of the male mould. As air is driven out of vents at the top of mould, the resin rises and impregnates the reinforcement. A sandwich laminate may be moulded using this system but, depending on core type, it may be necessary to thermoform the sheets prior to lay-up. If plain sheets of the material are being used, they should be punched with holes at regular intervals. In order to prevent an exotherm within the laminate during the process, a resin system with a slow curing cycle should be employed, and the viscosity should be low in order to allow good flow and wet-out.

Fig. 9.27 Resin-injection systems use two matched moulds. Resin is injected through inlets at the bottom of the male mould.

Fig. 9.28 Vacuum-injection moulding incorporates the use of both vacuum and resin injection.

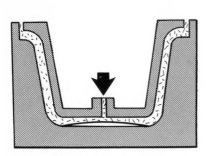

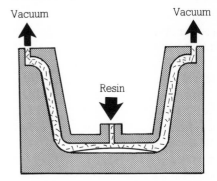

Vacuum-injection moulding

This system combines the use of vacuum and resin injection to try to overcome the problems of void creation, flowpath length restrictions and the need to use low-viscosity resins – all inherent with the basic injection system. The matched moulds, which can be of lighter construction than those used for high-pressure injection systems, incorporate vacuum outlets on the flange edge and a resin reservoir leading to the lowest point(s) of the mould. With the dry reinforcement in the female part and the two parts clamped together, a measured amount of resin is loaded into the reservoir and forced into the mould under low pressure. A vacuum is then pulled through the vacuum outlets and, when the whole laminate is impregnated, excess resin passes through the outlets into a trap and the vacuum is reduced until the resin gels.

Resin- and vacuum-injection systems allow quick moulding times, reinforcement is handled and laid-up dry, both sides of the laminate have a good finish, and a consistent product is produced. Against this is the expense of the tooling and equipment, which can rarely be justified by the low production runs common in boatbuilding. It has also proved difficult to ensure low void contents and to achieve high fibre-to-resin ratios, especially in the larger and more complicated moulds. The development of the moulds, the order of lay-up of the reinforcement, the type and viscosity of resin and the resin flowpaths are all complicated factors that have to be considered, and the possible problem areas fully understood.

Use of pre-pregs

One method that is relatively new but holds considerable promise for boatbuilding is the use of pre-pregs. The materials are simply a fibre reinforcement – usually a woven fabric or UD fibre – which has been pre-impregnated with a very slow-curing (at room temperature) resin system, usually an epoxy. Kept under refrigerated conditions, pre-pregs have a typical shelf life of several months.

Pre-pregs are laid-up in the mould, complete with any core material being used, pressure is applied, and the temperature is raised to cure the laminate. Because the pre-preg is tacky, it is easy to place in position and is clean to handle. Pressure is usually applied by a pair of matched moulds which can be heated – thus obviating the need for an oven – but a vacuum bag can sometimes be used.

The temperature required to cure pre-pregs varies with the resin system, but should be as low as possible for convenience in boatbuilding, especially where a temperature-sensitive core material, such as PVC foam, is being used. The use of acrylic foam with pre-pregs seems likely to grow since this type of foam can accept higher curing temperatures than most core materials and also provides excellent physical properties. The properties of finished laminates using pre-pregs are generally excellent because of the controllability of the fibre-to-resin ratio and the low void content of the laminate.

The use of low-temperature-curing pre-pregs and heated moulds offers a genuine advance for FRP boatbuilding and their use is likely to grow in the very near future. If balsa is, for some reason, being used as a core material with a pre-preg laminate, its surface should be well sealed with resin before lay-up otherwise the amount of resin drawn into the core from the pre-preg could seriously affect the integrity of the layers next to the core.

Pultrusion

Pultrusion is a process for the manufacture of solid and hollow components of small cross-section. Fibre reinforcement is pulled off a spool in a continuous form and is passed through a resin bath. The impregnated fibre then passes through a pre-forming die to rough-form the shape and remove excess resin and trapped air bubbles, and is then drawn through a heated curing die. Postcure can be given in a long heated oven before the continuous profile is cut to the required length. A wide variety of sections can be produced, made from the whole range of fibre reinforcement.

The use of pultrusion has not really been appreciated by boatbuilders, but they could easily find a place for bought-in sections in hull and deck

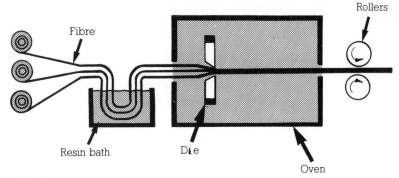

Fig. 9.29 Pultrusion is a process for making components of small cross-section.

mouldings as stiffeners and other reinforcements. These sections would be of known strength and stiffness, making their contribution to the laminate properties easily calculable, and would be easily bonded in position during or immediately after hull lay-up.

Filament winding

Filament winding is another process which could well find an application in the marine industry, especially for the production of FRP masts and other spars. It is used to produce hollow components which require the optimum mechanical properties. A continuous-fibre tow is impregnated with resin and wound on to a supporting mandrel at any angle of wind as dictated by the design loads of the component.

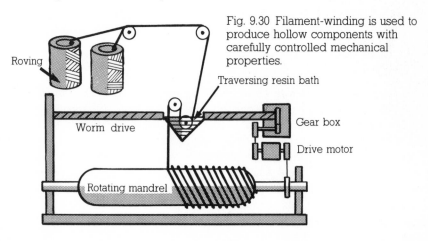

Fig. 9.30 Filament-winding is used to produce hollow components with carefully controlled mechanical properties.

10 BUILDING IN WOOD

As was explained in Chapter 4, wood, far from being a thing of the past, has many advantages that make it eminently suitable for one-off construction and limited-run production boatbuilding. The modern techniques of laminating wood with high-performance adhesives, such as epoxy resin, have ensured a resurgence of interest in this type of construction.

In many cases the use of laminated wood, in one of the variety of construction methods available, can achieve cost/performance results equal to, or better than, those of FRP construction. While timber is still a relatively cheap material, cold-moulded construction is labour-intensive and requires a skilled workforce. FRP construction, on the other hand, can be less labour-intensive and may require less skill, but the material cost is higher. Moreover, when high-performance FRP materials are used, the cost escalates; skilled labour is required, and the job becomes more labour-intensive or requires expensive equipment. So, while the use of high-performance FRP materials and technology can achieve excellent results, if cost is a factor in the equation the use of cold-moulded wood may often be preferable.

Fig. 10.1 A well-finished wood interior can add tremendously to the appearance. This one is the interior of a GRP hull.

The term 'cold-moulded construction' refers in fact not to one method but to a general system of laminating thin pieces of wood with room-temperature curing adhesives. Within this general system there are a number of techniques that can be used to build a hull or deck. Indeed, so versatile are the techniques of working with wood, that the method of building is often tailored to suit the particular requirement with the result that the solution is often as individual as the problem itself.

As with FRP construction, there are basically two approaches to hull construction: a thin skin well supported by stringers, frames and bulkheads; or a thicker, self-supporting, load-bearing skin – a true monocoque – with a smooth interior and an absolute minimum of internal stiffening.

The former, thin-skin approach is, in theory at least, the more weight-efficient, especially for relatively flat surfaces such as the hulls of catamarans and trimarans where there is insufficient curvature to help develop maximum stiffness. The disadvantages, though, are a far more cluttered interior which is difficult to keep clean, and a more tricky building operation if the advantages are to be fully realized.

Although individual laminations of a laminated hull are usually of the same wood species, it is perfectly possible to use sandwich techniques in cold-moulding. Weight can be saved by using a low-density wood for inner laminations, especially in beam-like structures, and using a high-density wood on the edges of the beam. Other cores, including foam, balsa and the various honeycombs, can also be used in conjunction with wood skins of either laminated veneers or plywood. Sandwich construction of this type is mostly used for decks, bulkheads and interior partitioning, although it can also be employed for hulls – perhaps, on a large hull, with frames and stringers fitted in the core to give a smooth interior.

The mould

There is no fixed method for constructing the mould or skeleton on which the laminated hull is to be built. The main difference between a male mould for FRP construction and one for a laminated-wood hull is that usually the wooden hull is laminated over a framework of which some at least becomes an integral part of the finished structure.

The method closest to that of FRP construction employs a closely spaced stringer or frame mould as used for normal foam/FRP sandwich, or a solid mould or plug built in the same way as that described for building an FRP hull, inner skin first, on a male mould. The advantages of these full-mould methods include having a firm mould as a base on which to laminate, and a mould which can be used to produce a number of identical hulls. The disadvantages include the time and cost in materials required to produce the mould, especially if the hull to be built is a one-off; and the problem of not being able to install interior stiffeners in the hull before it is removed from the mould.

This method is most suitable for small boats, where the time and cost of mould making is smaller and may be more easily spread over several hulls. Small boats are also generally of monocoque construction, since even relatively thin skins in hulls of this size can be load-bearing with the minimum of stiffeners.

Another construction method derived from the full-mould approach, is the strip-planking method. This is most suitable for the one-off production of medium to large hulls which are designed to have thick, monocoque skins with a minimum of internal stiffening. This type of construction can give a reasonably light hull with good strength and stiffness properties in boats over about 33ft (10m), and is an excellent approach for the construction of the larger cruising yacht. It requires only a simple framework of temporary and permanent frames, bulkheads, stem, keel and transom, all set upside down on a strongback. One of the advantages of this method is the ease with which a large part of the internal structure can be inserted into the boat before the hull is laid-up, and hence the minimum amount of temporary framework that is needed. The amount of time saved when compared with the full-mould method is large. After all, many full moulds are strip-planked, but with this method most of the work that goes into producing a plug is saved and directed into the building of the actual hull. In addition, since much of the interior structure can be incorporated before planking, when this work is far easier, further time is saved.

When strip-planking has been edge-glued over the framework, thin veneers are laminated as they are over a solid plug. The strip-planking gives strength and stiffness fore and aft, while the laminated veneers provide these properties in the diagonal and athwartship directions. Edge-glued strip-planking is a technique as old as GRP construction but which has only recently been developed, by the use of a laminated-veneer outer skin, because of the need for considerable athwartship interior stiffening to tie the hull together. Because the strip-planking method requires a practical minimum hull thickness of about 1¾in (45mm) when a laminated-wood outer skin is used, a hull built in this way has good sound and heat insulation, plus a very attractive interior surface.

It is also possible to use FRP for the outer skin instead of wood veneer, or to add an FRP inner skin, although under this method the hull would be laminated and no interior structure would be built in until after the inner skin had been laid-up.

The most common building method for use with laminated wood construction is the frame-and-stringer method. Unlike the mould or strip-planking methods, this technique results in a thin skin that is supported by stringers, frames and bulkheads. Originally developed in the aircraft industry before the Second World War, it is suited to building any size of hull and offers the best potential for high strength-and-stiffness-to-weight ratios. Because all the framework over which the hull is laminated is incorporated in the finished structure, and because no relatively time-consuming strip-planking is used, this method is the quickest of the three and is thus the most popular. Like strip-planking, this technique allows the installation and finishing of much of the interior before lamination of the hull begins. Stringer-frame construction is most popular with designers of racing boats, especially multihulls, because their lack of much compound curvature makes the thin skin solution far more weight-efficient than the monocoque approach.

The main disadvantage of this technique is the extra difficulty, when laminating the first layers of veneers, of ensuring a fair hull because of the relatively small amount of support given by the framework. This can cause problems for amateurs unless extra support is incorporated in the form of more stringers. However, such a solution has the disadvantage of adding extra weight since these stringers are only needed during construction and are not required to hold the finished hull together.

Compared to the fully moulded or strip-planked hull, the thin-skinned hull does not give much sound or heat insulation and does have a far more cluttered interior which is harder to keep clean. These disadvantages would be of more concern to the cruising sailor than the racing-boat owner.

The mould method

Although it is quicker and easier to laminate veneers over a solid mould than over one which consists of closely spaced stringers, the latter mould has the advantage of requiring less construction time and will be more attractive for one-off hulls. Laminating is quicker on a solid mould because staples can be shot in anywhere on the surface to hold the veneers, whereas with a stringer mould the positions of stringers and frames must be transferred to the veneers of the first two layers in order to mark where staples can be used. After the first two layers, however, staples can be kept short enough so that they do not penetrate the inner skin. If a vacuum bag is to be employed instead of staples, and there are advantages in this method, it will be necessary to use a solid, airtight mould.

Before laminating begins, the mould must be faired and any permanent keel or stem that is to be fitted at this stage must be recessed into it (and made airtight if a vacuum bag is to be used). All parts of the mould must then be covered with plastic sheet, except for those that are fitted now, such as keel, stem and transom, which must be left so that the veneers can be bonded to them.

When the mould is ready, the veneer stock must be prepared by trimming the edges accurately straight. The width of the veneers that can be used will depend on the amount of compound curvature in the hull, and will vary between the middle – where narrower strips must be used – and the ends, where wider panels are usually satisfactory. On exterior and interior layers that are to be clear-finished, the strips of veneers are sometimes cut the same width so that an attractive pattern is seen. If a veneer proves to be difficult to hold on to the mould at the edges, this is a sure sign that the strip being used is too wide for that part of the hull.

Laminating begins with the location of a reference veneer in the middle of the mould, set diagonally at the desired angle of lay. If the mould has an inset permanent keel, glue the veneers to it and hold well with staples, stapling the rest of the veneers to the mould using just enough staples to ensure good, even contact. Because all of the staples must be removed later in order to allow the hull to be freed from the mould, it is best to staple through a strip of tape, strong enough so that a line of staples can later be removed by simply pulling on the end of the strip. Staples used to attach veneers to permanent parts, such as the keel, can be left in place, but if this is done they should be bronze and not the common steel type.

The amount of curvature will dictate the stapling pattern needed to ensure good contact. In heavily curved areas, few staples will be needed in the middle of the curve since the veneer's resistance to bending will hold it tight on the mould. Either side of the curve, however, the same property will try to move the veneer away from the mould and more staples will be required.

With the first veneer in position, the adjacent veneers, on either side, are fitted to match exactly with the first. If there are enough workers, laminating can proceed towards bow and stern simultaneously. Lay the next veneer in position alongside the first, and it will be clear that the two will not fit exactly because of the curvature of the hull. To rectify this, edge-shape the second veneer to match the reference strip. Because of the shape of most hulls, veneers will need to be tapered at the ends, the extent depending on the amount of compound curvature in the hull. The fit of the veneers in the first layer is most important since this surface is usually given a clear finish, so any mistakes will be visible.

To check the amount of material that must be removed, lay the veneer on the mould and hold in position, as close as possible to the reference veneer, using a few staples, or cramps if a stringer mould is being used. Arrange the veneer so that the gap between the veneers is as small as possible and check that one edge of the strip is not pulled tighter to the mould than the other. Usually a veneer fits with its ends touching those of the previous veneer but with a gap in the middle. If one edge, in the middle area of the

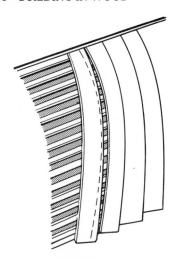

Fig. 10.2 Each veneer must be shaped to fit snugly alongside the preceding veneer.

Fig. 10.3 The veneers in the second layer are laid in the other direction, but at the same angle to the hull, as those in the first layer.

strip, is tighter to the mould than the other, staple the middle area to the mould but leave the ends free. Move the ends slightly until they take their natural positions, then hold them there with a few staples. Do not overdo the number of staples as the aim is only to mark out the veneer. Using a pair of dividers set to the maximum gap between the two strips, scribe a line parallel to the edge of the reference veneer on to the surface of the strip to be fitted. Remove the strip from the mould and trim the edge to this line using a small block plane. Check the fit, then bond the veneer to any permanent keel and staple in position. Fit following strips in the same way.

Although the procedure may sound time-consuming, it is actually very fast, since experience of the amount of material to remove is quickly gained. Be careful not to trim too much off the top or bottom of a series of strips or the angle of the strips on the mould will change from that of the reference veneer. If this happens, fit a tapered veneer to correct the situation.

It is sometimes worthwhile edge-gluing the strips of the first layer as they are stapled to the mould. This has the advantage of giving a more solid first layer and fills any gaps between strips so that the adhesive on the second layer cannot be forced through to the inside surface where it will harden in lumps which are difficult to sand later. The disadvantages of edge-gluing are the time it takes and the difficulty of ensuring that all edges are pulled tight on the mould. If the edges are glued and raised, spots will cause lumps that must be sanded out before the second layer can be laminated. If the edges are not glued, the pressure of the second layer being stapled on top will usually pull the edges of the first down on to the mould.

Once all the veneers of the first layer have been installed on the mould, the process of lamination begins with the laying-up of the second layer. A reference veneer is installed in the same way as for the first layer and at the same angle, but running in the other direction to give a balanced orientation of the wood fibres. Lay the reference veneer in its correct position and mark round it with a pencil on to the first layer. Remove all the staples inside the lines that were used to hold down the first layer. The strips of the first layer should not be disturbed by this since the new strip runs at an angle across several lower strips; and the rest of the staples holding the first layer are usually sufficient to keep them securely in place. Glue the second-layer reference veneer in place, applying adhesive to both mating surfaces, and secure in place with a staple pattern that ensures overall contact. It is best to begin stapling in the middle of the strip, working out towards the edges. This helps to move any air bubbles out towards the edges and also forces out excess resin which can otherwise cause lumps under the veneer. With the first strip of the second layer in position, clean off any of this excess resin that has been forced out at the edges: if this is left to cure, it will get in the way of the next strip and will need sanding off.

The next strips can be fitted in the same way, removing the underlying staples, shaping and gluing each one as you work along the hull; but a better way is to dry-fit the second layer, holding each strip in place with a few staples. When the whole of the second layer has been laid dry, gluing starts with the strips next to the reference strip. Remove each one in turn, apply adhesive and replace with a full staple pattern, then move on to the next strip. This routine is the most efficient because it allows the adhesive to be mixed and laminating to be completed in one quick operation.

Once the second layer has been laid-up, the staples can be removed as soon as the adhesive has reached a partial cure. Staples are much easier to remove when the adhesive, particularly if epoxy resin, is in this state, yet the adhesive is cured sufficiently to hold the veneers quite firmly.

With the second layer finished, the whole surface should be given a light fairing before any more layers are laminated. Most of the fairing will be needed only to remove lumps of adhesive that have been forced up between the joints, but there may also be a few high spots that should be removed at this stage.

Subsequent layers are applied in the same manner as the second, with the difference that short staples which will not penetrate the inner skin should now be used. Since these staples will not penetrate the mould, they can be left in if desired but, if this is done, they should be of bronze and should be shot in so that their tops are recessed, or at least flush with the surface. If a stringer-type mould is being used, it will no longer be necessary to transfer the locations of frames and stringers on to each layer.

Before the last layer is applied, the whole surface must be sanded to a smooth, fair finish so that the amount of finishing on the top surface is as small as possible. This is especially important if the surface is to have a natural finish. Pay particular attention to the fit of each veneer on the final layer, whether the surface is to be clear finished or not, and make sure that the edges are well bonded.

If the surface is to have a varnish finish it is best to apply staples through wood strips rather than the peel strips used previously. Wood stapling strips allow a more even pressure to be put on the veneer, thus reducing the number of staples needed, and prevent the heads of the staples marking the outer surface. If there is a danger that pads could become stuck to the laminate, use a strip of plastic between them and the laminate when shooting the staples.

Final fairing and surface finishing is usually best carried out before the hull is removed from the mould, but in the case of a very light hull that will need much internal stiffening to hold it in shape, it may be best to finish the hull after that stiffening has been installed.

Strip-planking

With this method, temporary frames are again set up on a framework, but permanent members such as bulkheads and frames and any suitable internal items are also mounted on the strongback.

Decide on the amount of permanent members that can be fitted at this stage and then use as many temporary frames as are necessary to provide the required support for the strip-planking. The distance between frames, permanent or otherwise, is determined by the shape of the hull – more frames being needed on a hull with a lot of curvature – and the thickness of the planking that is to be used. While the chosen frame spacing will be suitable for most of the hull, there may well be areas of tighter curves that require closer spacing. Support can be provided in these areas by using temporary frames set up half-way between the station frames, rather than by reducing the overall frame spacing.

With temporary and permanent frames, bulkheads and other interior framework set up on the strongback, the transom, keel and stem are fitted, glued and screwed to all the permanent frames and the bulkheads. Screw these parts to the temporary frames, but cover the whole of the frame with plastic sheet to prevent accidental bonding. A permanent or temporary shear clamp is now installed for the strip-planking to attach to, and the whole framework is faired ready for planking.

Strip-planking, although similar to the traditional carvel type, is simpler and quicker to complete because the planks are not tapered at the ends to allow for the changing shape of the hull, and are not bevelled at the edges to allow the planks to fit flush together. Since planks are being fitted around a curved hull, their outer edges will not fit flush without bevelling but will have a gap between them. This problem is solved by using a filled epoxy resin adhesive to fill the gap and provide structural strength. Since the inner edges fit tightly together, there is no effect on the interior aesthetics. The way around the problem of tapering the planks towards the ends is to allow them to run out at the shear and the keel.

The first step in planking is to locate the position of the master or reference plank. The position of this one plank is most important because it determines the run of the rest. If its position and run is incorrect, the planks on one side of it are likely to be difficult to fit as they approach the shear or keel, because the degree of curvature they are being forced around is too great.

The correct location is found by clamping the master plank to the mid-point of the frames in the middle two-thirds of the hull, leaving the ends free. Move the clamping positions on individual frames as necessary to achieve a fair curve. With the plank temporarily clamped to all the frames in the mid-hull area, measure up and down from it at several points to determine how the rest of the planks will lie. If it looks as if some areas of curvature may cause problems, given the position of the master plank, it can be moved to make the run of subsequent planks more suitable for the curved areas to be crossed.

When the lie of the master plank has been finalized, screw and glue it to all permanent parts of the framework and screw it temporarily to the temporary frames. Carry on planking by similarly attaching subsequent planks, gluing them to previously fixed planks with a filled epoxy resin thick enough to fill the gap between the unbevelled edges.

It is quite usual for the edges of the planks between the frames to be slightly misaligned, but this can be corrected by edge-nailing in these areas, using nails or, preferably, wooden dowels. As the strip-planking progresses, regularly clean the interior and exterior surfaces where resin has seeped out of the joints. It is much easier to do this before the resin cures and saves much finishing time later.

Once the hull has been strip-planked, rough-trim the planks which have run out at the sheer, stem and transom. Rather than cut these accurately at this stage, leave some extension so that there is a solid surface to which the veneers can be glued. Fill any hollows or voids with a thickened resin mixture, then prepare the surface for veneer lamination.

The lamination of veneers is identical to that already described, with the exception that the first layers of veneers are permanently glued to the underlying surface and can also be permanently stapled as long as non-ferrous staples are used and they are well recessed. The strip-planking provides a solid and fair surface on which to laminate the veneers and this process is usually accomplished easily and quickly.

Once laminating has been completed, the temporary frames can be removed and final fairing and finishing can take place. It is often easier to finish the interior surface of the hull with it still upside down on the strongback, since sanding dust will then fall to the floor of the building shed. Once the exterior finishing has been completed, the hull can be rolled over, with the provision of suitable padding, because it does not have to be lifted off a mould.

Thin-skinned hulls with stringers and frames

This method of construction provides a thin hull skin supported by a lattice of frames and longitudinal stringers. The method has the advantage of producing a strong, stiff hull for the minimum weight and also allows the installation of interior bulkheads, frames and interior joinery during the setting-up process. Thus the method has the speed of building advantages of the strip-planking method but produces a more efficient structure in terms of strength and stiffness to weight, particularly when it is used in hulls with large areas of flat panels and little compound curvature such as the hulls of catamarans and trimarans.

While the stringer-frame method is weight-efficient, it does have the disadvantages of giving a cluttered interior and of being a more difficult building operation since the hull skin has to be laminated over a very insubstantial framework when compared to the other methods already described. Because of this latter problem, this method is more difficult than the others for amateur construction.

There are many variations on the basic theme of stringer-frame construction, but the most commonly used method involves the use of sawn-plywood frames and plywood bulkheads rather than the use of laminated frames. The number of frames needed will depend on the shape of the hull – long, lean hulls as found in multihull designs requiring closer spacing than the fuller hull shape of monohulls – but the main determining factor must always be the need to provide adequate support during the building process. Since the stringer-frame method uses far fewer longitudinal stringers than the two methods previously considered, the spacing of the frames is most important if the stringers are not to deform between frames during laminating. Because of the need to support the hull during laminating, the frame spacing is likely to have to be closer than that required to support the completed hull skin. Rather than use permanent frames throughout the hull the builder may, in the interest of weight saving, wish to employ temporary frames, in addition to the permanent ones, to provide the support necessary during construction, removing them once the hull has been completed.

When this building method is being used, time and effort can be saved by pre-finishing and installing major parts of the interior such as bulkheads, frames, stem, keel, transom and major parts of the interior joinery during the setting-up process. The more of the interior that can be installed at this stage the better, since not only is installation usually easier, but every permanent part that is installed at this stage helps support the set-up and reduces the need for temporary frames.

Once all the bulkheads, permanent and temporary frames and any other parts have been installed, the longitudinal stringers can be attached. The only difference in the set-up with this method is that the stringers are notched into all the frames and bulkheads so that their outer edges are flush with the frame faces. The stringers are also fitted flush with the transom and stem, either by notching or by butting flush, so that the hull skin can be bonded flush to all these parts and so help join them together.

In order that the stringers may best be able to withstand the pressures put on them during laminating, it is best if they are fitted on edge with their narrowest edge next to the hull veneers. This makes them stiffer in the direction normal to the hull surface and thus better able to resist the bending loads imposed on them by the bending of veneers over the stringers during laminating. In some heavily compounded areas of certain hulls it may be difficult or impossible to bend the chosen stringer size around a tight curve, and in such instances it may be necessary to laminate the stringer out of two or three pieces. This will have the additional effect of making the stringer far stiffer than its one-piece counterpart and better able to resist the deflection imposed during veneer lamination.

The actual physical dimensions of the stringers are a compromise between the strength and stiffness required to support the completed hull and that required for laminating. In this case the latter requirement will usually dominate and it will have to be accepted that the stringers in the finished hull are oversize for the job of supporting it. It must also be remembered that a certain minimum thickness will be required to ensure that not too many staples miss when the first few layers are being laminated over the stringers: for this purpose, a thickness of about ¾in (18mm) is reasonable.

When the size of the stringers has been chosen, the next decision is their spacing along the frames. Once again the practical problems of providing a reasonable framework for laminating are likely to dominate, and it is probable that more stringers will be needed than are required for hull support. The shape of the hull will determine the actual spacing, areas of tight curvature needing more closely spaced stringers than flatter areas.

Long, lean hulls with little compound curvature allow the stringers to be run parallel to the sheer in succeeding rows which will eventually run out at the keel. In this instance it is possible, and easiest, to pre-notch all the frames on the bench before they are set up on the strongback, simply by measuring up each frame from the sheer. On fatter hulls with more compound curvature, the position of stringers cannot be determined without trial and error and pre-notching cannot be done. The process of finding the best position for the stringers on such hulls depends on practicality; this problem has already been covered in relation to the mould and strip-planking methods. In the stringer-frame method the problem is perhaps slightly more difficult, because the size of the stringers is generally greater and this makes them less easy to bend than in the other methods.

Areas of heavy curvature should be carefully defined by accurately spaced stringers, of which three or four may well be needed to develop a tight curve. With heavily curved hulls it is likely that the stringers will not run parallel but will get closer together as they approach the ends and it may be necessary to stop some stringers short, running them out on a frame near the end. Do make sure that the stringers are spaced so as to divide up the hull with roughly equal spacings between them.

During initial positioning the stringers will have been attached to the frames and bulkheads with clamps, but when all have been attached and adjusted and the fairness of the hull checked with a fairing batten, the frames and bulkheads are notched to accept the stringers, as are the stem and transom.

When all of the stringers are permanently fitted, the faces of the frames and bulkheads are bevelled using the stringers as a guide, and then a final fairing is given to the entire hull surface. Any high spots on stringers or frames should be planed away and any low spots built up with a thin strip of veneer or plywood which is later faired in with the rest of the hull.

It is not as easy to fair a stringer-frame hull as a strip-planked or moulded one since there is so much space between stringers, but the use of a long fairing batten and lots of care and patience will give the required result. Remember that any adjustments made to one stringer or frame can have major effects on the rest of the hull's surface. Check longitudinal fairness by sighting along the stringers and use the fairing batten both at right angles to the battens and diagonally across them to check athwartships fairness.

One advantage of the stringer-frame method of building over the other methods is that the completed set-up, before skin lamination, allows the easy manufacture and fitting of many laminated items such as permanent ring frames, floors or other parts that must follow the curve of the hull skin. By using thin stock, covering the parts not to be laminated with plastic sheet, and by laminating the part close to a suitable frame where the stringers are well supported and will not deflect under laminating pressure, it is possible to manufacture complicated items quickly and simply. Do not allow these laminations to become attached to the stringers at this stage since the finished item will need to be removed for final shaping, sanding and finishing before being permanently installed. When clamping these parts to the stringers during laminating, use plastic sheet between them and use plywood offcuts to prevent clamp damage to the frames. This method can be used to produce elegantly laminated permanent frames which provide excellent support but take up virtually no interior space. This is achieved by laminating an I-beam with the hull skin forming the outer flange, the core being formed by a light-wood blocking, and the inner flange being a laminated frame that is bonded to the core which is fitted between the stringers. The core is fitted first by simply inserting and gluing blocks of a light-weight wood between the stringers after final fairing of the hull. With this blocking in position, it is faired into the stringers and the inner frame is laminated in position over the stringers and the core. This process is much simpler than fitting and shaping the core after the hull skin has been laminated.

Once all the interior fittings that can be installed at this stage have been fitted, it is time to begin final skin laminating. The first lamination is most important since it serves as a mould surface over which further laminating can take place, the fairness of which is determined by that of the first layer.

Veneer can be used for this first layer but it is far easier, especially for the amateur, to use plywood since this is a much more stable laminating material and will provide a more solid and fairer surface for subsequent laminations. Plywood is also more dimensionally stable than individual veneers, so is easier to fit over an inadequate mould and also has the advantage of being pre-sanded which makes pre-finishing with epoxy far simpler if this is desired.

Since the aim of the first lamination is to develop a stiff surface for subsequent laminations, it is desirable to use the thickest plywood that is practical. This layer should be laid in the shortest direction – to help develop stiffness – ideally at 90° to the run of the stringers, since this direction results in the minimum length that is unsupported between stringers.

The best way of using plywood for the first layer is to bevel the ends of a sheet, saw the sheets into conveniently wide strips for laminating, then scarf the strips together into long lengths from which convenient laminating lengths can be cut. If epoxy is being used for finishing the wood surface, much time and effort can be saved by sanding and pre-coating one side of the plywood surface prior to cutting into laminating lengths. Remember, however, that if you have chosen the thickest plywood that will bend around the tightest curves on the hull, a subsequent pre-coating with epoxy will considerably stiffen it and may make it impossible to bend it as planned.

The spiling and fitting of the first layer of laminations is very important with this method, not only for interior aesthetics but also because the edges of the panels must be bonded together to create a rigid surface. There are few stringers to provide support, and if the lay of the strip of plywood or veneer is not correct, pressures will be set up within the strip and the edges will not align perfectly.

Before final attachment, lay the master strip in position at 90° (if practical) to the stringers in the middle of the hull and mark on it the position of the stringers and frames that it covers. Check that the edges sit snugly on all stringers or frames and mark this position of the strip on to the framework so that it can be replaced in that position.

Next, apply a resin mixture to all parts that will be in contact, making this mixture thick enough so that it will bridge any gaps and will not run down any of the parts as it is forced out of the joints. Re-position the plank and fasten with staples through to the stringers and frames, using enough staples to hold the strip flush with all mating surfaces. Staples can be left in place with this method as long as they are non-ferrous and are shot flush or recessed. Spiling subsequent panels is quite easy because of the space between stringers. The fastest way is to fit the subsequent plank to the master unspiled and at a distance away that is slightly less than the width of the planks. Then take the third plank and lay it on top of the previous two, tacking it temporarily in position. Mark the edges of the panel from inside the hull, remove it for shaping and glue and staple it into position between the first two planks, making sure that the edges are well glued.

It is important to work accurately, from the middle of each panel towards the ends, when shaping each plank, since if the plank edges do not fit flush it will be impossible to correct them by the use of extra staples because there is nothing to staple into. This is the main disadvantage of the method: so much time and care is needed to get the first and most important layer to fit correctly.

If some misalignment on plank edges does occur – and that is almost inevitable – this may be corrected by using small pieces of plywood stapled across the misaligned edges to pull them flush. Should this method be used, remember to clean off excess resin from the joint beforehand and use plastic sheet between the scrap plywood and the skin to prevent accidental bonding.

The width of the strips used for laminating will have an affect on the degree of edge-alignment problems, especially in areas of high curvature. If the panel is too wide for the amount of curvature, its edges will tend to curl out and this fault will be difficult to correct. While it is quicker to laminate with wide panels, it is best to reduce the panel width in problem areas.

Take great care when bonding the first layer to the stem, keel, transom and sheer, since any voids or other weaknesses here will compromise the entire structure. Running the first layer beyond the hull slightly at the transom and sheer will give a firmer surface to which subsequent layers can be laminated and will reduce the risk of voids in these areas. As laminating continues, remember to clean up the excess resin squeezed from the joints on the interior and exterior surfaces before it cures. Failure to do this will result in much extra work later and will spoil the interior appearance of the hull.

Once lamination of the first layer has been completed and all the adhesive has cured, any temporary staples or alignment pads should be removed and the hull roughly faired prior to application of the second layer. When fairing the first layer, make sure that you don't remove the marks that indicate the location of the stringers and frames. If using an epoxy resin adhesive, you should give the surface of the first lamination a coating of unthickened resin. This will add stiffness to the layer, and with this layer pre-coated you will only have to put adhesive on to the second layer to be laid. Lightly sand the coated surface prior to fitting the second layer which will now be of veneer rather than plywood.

Begin the second lamination by placing the master veneer at the desired angle in the middle of the hull and fit subsequent panels using whichever spiling method is desired. When stapling the second layer, begin stapling each strip to the marked positions of stringers and frames, starting the stapling pattern at the centre of the veneer and working out towards the edges. Push the veneer tightly against the under layer as you staple and excess adhesive will spread into any voids and will be prevented from building in pools near the centre. Once the veneer is stapled to all the solid areas, short staples that will not break the inner surface are applied over the rest of the strip. Since it will not be possible to recess these staples, you should use a stapling strip to facilitate removal. You can usually tell which areas between stringers require extra staples by pressing with your fingers. Any areas where the veneer is not lying snugly will move under finger pressure and should be stapled. Use plenty of staples along the edges of the veneers between the stringers to ensure a flush fit and prevent the edges curling.

Once the second layer is on, the hull surface will be very rigid and subsequent layers can be laminated quickly and easily in the way described for the mould or strip-plank methods. Like the strip-planked type, a stringer-frame hull can be rolled over after final fairing, painting or varnishing since it does not have to be lifted off a mould.

Plywood construction

It was the introduction of low-cost plywood panels that revolutionized wooden boat construction and created the boom in readily available small dinghies, cruising and racing boats, both power and sail. Despite develop-ments in FRP and wooden construction, plywood is still a very useful building material. After its initial popularity, plywood construction devel-oped a bad reputation based on the high cost of maintaining some plywood boats and the short life-span of some designs. This reputation was one of the main reasons for the original introduction of GRP as a production material. Many boats originally designed for plywood were later built in GRP simply because of the reduced need for maintenance and despite the fact that GRP was heavier and less stiff than plywood, especially since the flat panel design necessary for the latter (although some designs do incorporate developed compound curvature) increased the problem of panel stiffness when GRP was used.

Plywood still has a place in boatbuilding today because of the develop-ments in resin adhesive and coating technology which can successfully protect it from the deterioration to which it was previously susceptible. The great advantage of this material is that it is the easiest and quickest to work with, but its disadvantage is that its use is essentially restricted to the building of single- or multi-chine hulls where the panels have to be curved only in a single direction.

Plywood chine hulls are generally built over a simple permanent frame-work consisting of frames, chine pieces, a few stringers, stem, keel, sheer and transom. Frames are often cut from plywood sheets, although they can also be simply made up from solid timber or laminated pieces. Much time can be saved by pre-finishing and rounding the interior edges of all permanent parts of the set-up.

The hardest job during the building operation is likely to be the installation of the chine pieces. This area is most important because it provides structural strength and support at a potentially vulnerable part of the hull and has also to be large enough to join two panels and provide a vital structural joint. The chine pieces are notched into the frames, stem and transom and are then faired to match the changing angles between the frames. The installation of the few stringers needed for hull support (and they are not needed for much support during the building process) are installed next. Once the stringers are fitted they can be used as accurate guides to the fairing of the chine pieces. A fairing batten can be laid across the stringers and will show the bevel required on the chine piece. Fore-and-aft fairing along the chine piece can be checked by clamping the fairing batten along the chine and then sighting along it to identify high and low spots.

With all the framework in position, final fairing should be done, and special attention should be paid to ensure that at no point is any part on any frame above the fore-and-aft member: it is better if the frames are slightly low, since any protrusion will show up in the finished hull surface.

Before fitting the plywood panels, decide on the largest panel of ply that

Fig. 10.4 Plywood still has many advantages, not least that it is quick and easy to work with, but its use is mainly restricted to single- or multi-chine boats.

can be worked with. When building small boats, it is normal to apply a complete panel, probably made up of scarfed pieces, in one operation; but with larger boats it will be found easier to apply smaller panels and perform the scarfing operation in place. If you have two scarf panels together on the framework, make sure that you plan the lay of the panels so that the scarf joint falls over some strong part of the framework so that it will be well supported.

It will often be found much easier to use a template to transfer the outline of the panel shape to a plywood sheet rather than trying to mark up the plywood *in situ*. Panel installation can begin either on the bottom or topsides, whichever is most suitable for the individual project. With the first panel shaped and ready for fitting, the position of all frames, stringers and chines that it covers should be marked on the surface and, if so desired, an epoxy coating should be applied. With this pre-coat applied and lightly sanded before fitting, much finishing time is saved later and it is also not necessary to apply adhesive to the ply, only to the framework. Before applying the adhesive, mark the panel and surrounding structure so that the panel can be replaced on to the coated structure with the minimum of positioning.

Hold the panel in position on the adhesive-covered area with a few locating staples while its exact fit is checked, then apply pressure with staples exactly as described for the other methods, using non-ferrous staples countersunk so that they do not need to be removed. In places that will require a lot of shaping, this method of stapling will not be possible and it will be necessary to remove the staples once the adhesive is cured. In areas where more pressure is required than can be provided with staples, nails or screws through a piece of scrap ply can be used to provide temporary pressure.

Once the first panel has been bonded, all the excess resin squeezed out of the joint should be cleaned off before it has the chance to cure. The fitting of subsequent panels is slightly more tricky since it becomes necessary to bond at least one scarf joint at the same time as fitting a panel. To make sure of an exact fit, always dry-fit to check the alignment of the scarf joint after final shaping of the panel.

When fitting the next panels, apply extra pressure on the scarf joints by stapling an offcut of ply along the line of the joint to provide even pressure, making sure that the offcut does not bond to the hull. When maximum pressure is needed on a joint, use screws or nails rather than staples into the solid area that should be underneath. Getting a flush fit on the interior of the scarf joint is not usually a problem as long as enough pressure is used to bring the exterior edges together, since the curvature of the hull usually ensures that the interior edges are held tightly together.

Once all the panels have been installed, all temporary fastenings should be removed and the areas of the keel and chines shaped, with care being

Fig. 10.5 The well-known stitch-and-glue method uses copper wires to hold panel edges together, while glass-fibre tape and resin are used to bond the joints.

Fig. 10.6 A fillet of thickened epoxy can be used to bond panels. The epoxy fillet is spread using a shaped stick and the excess scraped off. Once the resin has cured the joint may be stronger than the wood itself, depending on the density of the resin filler.

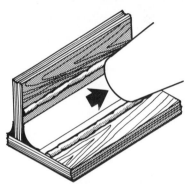

taken that not too much material is removed from these important structural joint areas. Finishing of a plywood hull is usually the easiest part of all since if the framework was fair the sheet ply should produce a fair and even surface that requires little more than sanding and painting before being turned over and the interior finished.

Not all plywood-built single- or multi-chine designs use the framework described above. Many designs, usually of small craft, get rid of the chine pieces altogether and join the edges of the plywood panels with glass-fibre tape or a filled epoxy fillet, or both.

The now well-known stitch-and-glue method of construction made popular by the Mirror dinghy uses copper wire ties to hold the panel edges together while tape and resin are applied to one side of the joint. Once that has cured, the copper wire is cut and removed and the other side of the joint is faired, filled and taped to produce a strong structural joint. An even easier method is the use of a thick mixture of epoxy resin which is shaped along the joint to form a structural fillet that should be at least as strong as the wood itself. Chine boats, usually dinghies, can be easily and quickly built on a female or male jig that is used to hold the panels in position while the joints are taped or a fillet is applied. Such dinghies can have the minimum of permanent interior framework; all that is required is enough support to provide structural stiffness to the finished hull. A female mould is preferable to a male for this simple form of construction since it allows one to tape or fillet the inside of the joint first. Once this has been done, the dinghy can be removed from the mould and the outer joints can be rounded and faired before it is taped over, thus producing a fairer exterior than a hull fashioned on a male mould.

Given the simplicity of plywood construction and the protection it can now be given with epoxy resins, it is likely that we will see more designs produced which are suitable for this form of construction.

Hull sheathing

In the early days of GRP construction some owners of wooden boats thought that they had discovered a material that would be ideal for hull sheathing, would protect and waterproof their hulls and would, perhaps, even increase the structural strength of the hull. Their experiments inevitably led to trouble, with glass sheathing peeling off and other tales of woe abounding.

The fact is that polyester resin is not a good adhesive and is not suitable for bonding cloth to wood which is invariably damp and dimensionally unstable. The developments in epoxy resin technology for boatbuilding use have, however, led to the reintroduction of sheathing for wooden hulls. If a wooden hull has been glued and coated with epoxy, its rate of dimensional change due to water absorption will be reduced to a near-insignificant level and sheathing a new wooden hull with a glass or other form of cloth, again using an epoxy adhesive, becomes a practical proposition.

The advantages of sheathing include increased abrasion resistance, a possible increase in strength and stiffness – depending on the type and amount of cloth used and at a penalty of an increase in weight – and the ability of the cloth to act as a screed to ensure a minimum thickness of coating resin that is not easily sanded away. During the final finishing process a light-weight cloth also helps fill staple holes and other minor imperfections that would otherwise have to be filled individually. While the use of cloth sheathing with an epoxy adhesive is now a worthwhile consideration when building a new wooden hull, it must be said that applying such a sheathing to an older hull is still of dubious value unless great attention is applied to stripping the hull surface and allowing it to dry thoroughly before beginning the process, which should always be done under controlled conditions under cover.

11 OSMOSIS

In the last twenty years glass-reinforced plastic – glass fibre, as it is commonly known – has become the most widely used material for the construction of marine pleasure craft. The reasons for this shift away from the traditional materials such as wood and steel are quite clear. Glass fibre is strong with a good strength-to-weight ratio and it can be moulded to suit intricate shapes. The materials used are easily available and relatively cheap and, even more important, the labour costs of producing a glass-fibre boat are less than the same boat in timber. Glass fibre is ideally suited to long production runs of identical boats and it is in these cases that the advantages over other materials become most apparent. Another benefit is that it is a material created when the boat is moulded and results in a monocoque hull produced without elevated temperatures or pressure. While wood can rot and steel can rust, glass fibre was claimed to be totally impervious to such forms of attack.

So it was claimed, at least until the first few crops of blisters were found on glass-fibre hulls. Often called 'boat pox', this phenomenon is frequently caused by a process known as osmosis, although not all such cases will be brought about in this way. Blisters may appear on the surface of painted boats after application in poor working conditions or because of faulty application. They can also occur in a dark-coloured gel-coat if an air bubble is trapped behind it: when the surface heats up in sunlight, the air expands and can cause a blister on the outer surface.

The mechanism of true osmotic damage will be explained shortly, but first it must be made clear that the sole primary cause of this damage to glass-fibre hulls is nothing more than water. Glass fibre may not rust or rot, but it can still be damaged by the water in which it floats. This fact often comes as something of a shock to many boat owners who imagine that, because their hull is monocoque and doesn't leak, it must therefore before impervious to water. The truth is that polyester resin is not completely impervious to the passage of water and can allow molecular water to pass through. Technically speaking, a polyester gel-coat (or the filler or fairing compound on a male-moulded hull) can act as a semi-permeable membrane by allowing the passage of these small quantities of water and it is this action that is at the root of the osmosis problem.

Next to the gel-coat or surface filler, the glass-fibre laminate contains within its structure many cavities. The majority of these are micro-cavities and they are most likely to be found within the glass-fibre strands. These strands are composed of bundles of glass filaments held together by a flexible binder. Because the strands must be flexible, these micro-cavities can exist within them. Since polyester resin has a relatively high viscosity, it is not possible for it to fill all of these cavities, no matter how much rolling or stippling takes place. As well as these unavoidable cavities, there may also exist larger voids in the laminate, caused by air being trapped during laminating, and dry areas where resin wet-out of the glass fibre has not occurred. It is the surface finish of the glass-fibre hull, usually a gel-coat, that has to protect the rest of the laminate from water penetration.

If minute amounts of water penetrate the gel-coat by the process described earlier, the water molecules collect to form droplets inside a cavity. This can then dissolve any water-soluble materials present from the glass-fibre binder, components from undercured resin, free peroxide catalyst and the like, and so form a solution. This solution is usually acidic and can become highly concentrated.

Osmosis is the term used to describe the process where two solutions of differing concentration, separated by a semi-permeable membrane, cause liquid to flow from the weaker to the stronger solution to even out the concentrations. By the process of osmosis, the concentrated solution in a cavity within the laminate draws in more water from outside and so more water enters the cavity. As this process continues, osmotic pressure builds up within the cavity and can reach values approaching 100psi ($7.0kg/cm^2$). This pressure begins to distort the gel-coat or outer skin if the cavity is near the surface, and will eventually show up as a bump or blister. In the case of a large cavity deep within the laminate, the pressure can cause failure in the interlaminate bond, leading to serious delamination problems.

Eventually the pressure inside the surface blister will become so great that the gel-coat can no longer withstand it and the blister will burst. The pressure is then released, but water is now able to affect the laminate directly and continue its attack on the structure. The osmosis effect just described is likely to occur more quickly in boats kept in fresh water than sea water. This is because the difference in concentration between fresh water and the cavity liquid is greater than between sea water and the cavity liquid since sea water is a solution containing sea salt. Hence the osmotic pressure generated by a boat in fresh water is greater and blistering is likely to occur more rapidly.

The effect just described might appear alarming and may seem to imply that no glass-fibre boat is safe. In practice, of course, the situation is not so clear-cut and the writer has no wish to alarm present boat owners into thinking that it is only a matter of time before their boat suffers from 'pox'. However, quality control in the moulding and curing process and the correct choice and use of materials will seriously influence the tendency to osmosis damage. All factors that affect the resistance of water absorption of the gel-coat and laminate must be controlled carefully if future problems are to be avoided. There is little doubt that there are boats on the market that have been produced in less-than-perfect conditions, using materials and methods that are less than ideal. If the prospective owner is to minimize the risk of osmosis damage to his pride and joy, it is necessary for him to choose carefully and to understand something of the preventative measures that should be taken before the boat ever sees the water. If the known problem areas are dealt with during manufacture, there is a very high chance that no future difficulties will occur.

Since the gel-coat is the surface barrier that keeps water away from the laminate, it is obviously vital that it too should do its job as well as possible. There are many basic polyester gel-coat resins that can be used, but there are two major types known as orthophthalic and isophthalic resins. Of the two, it is well known that isophthalic types have superior resistance to water absorption to the orthophthalic types and so must be the first choice for use at least for the underwater areas of the hull.

Laminating resins can be of many different types designed to suit varying applications. Many are of different flexibility and a rigid resin used with a more flexible gel-coat could cause adhesion problems. As with gel-coats, both isophthalic and orthophthalic laminating resin are available, the former being the more expensive. It is claimed that the water resistance of the laminating resins is not so critical but many manufacturers of resin do recommend a matched system. Some laminating systems contain wax to exclude air from the surface and so allow the resin to cure. Heavily waxed resins should be avoided for laminating as they can cause poor interlaminate adhesion and lead to eventual failure. Epoxy laminating resins are also available, although more expensive than the polyester resins that are commonly used. They do, however, have far superior resistance to water absorption than polyester and when they are used, usually in conjunction with specialized fibres in the production of one-off craft, osmosis damage is very unlikely to occur.

The composition of the glass-fibre reinforcement can also have an effect on the development of osmosis. To produce a cloth or mat, a binder is used to hold the strands of glass fibre together. Two basic types of binder are used: a polyester resin powder and an emulsion binder. The emulsion binder is much more sensitive to water than the powder type and tests have shown that this can have a significant effect on the development of osmosis when water has penetrated the gel-coat.

Even when materials chosen for the lay-up are the best available, there are still a number of other factors that will affect the performance of the finished hull, ranging from the conditions in which laminating takes place to the methods used and the amount of maturing of the hull that takes place. Naturally the application of the gel-coat to the mould is critical. The thickness of the gel-coat is most important and is normally in the region of 550 microns (22 thou). If too thin a gel-coat is used, it cannot fulfil its function as a water barrier completely; on the other hand, if it is too thick, it may crack or craze and be prone to impact damage. Gel-coat is best applied in two layers and the thickness controlled by using a simple wet thickness gauge after allowing for the shrinkage that occurs when polyester resins cure. By applying the gel-coat in two stages, the risk of trapped air is reduced and the finished coat is more likely to be of even thickness. If air bubbles are present in the gel-coat, its thickness is seriously reduced at that point and hence water permeation is more likely to occur. Air can also be trapped in the resin by high-speed stirring and this should be avoided as should the use of too viscous a gel-coat resin. Air bubbles that are trapped near the surface of the gel may burst and reveal themselves as pinholes which the partly cured resin is unable to fill.

The accurate measurement of catalyst for both the gel-coat and the laminating resin is absolutely vital. If too much catalyst is used, a residue will be left when the resin has cured and this is very sensitive to water and will dissolve in it to form a concentrated solution. If too little catalyst is used, the resin may never reach optimum cure and its resistance to water absorption will be drastically reduced. The rate of cure of the resin should never be adjusted by varying the catalyst or the working condition. If it is necessary to alter the rate of cure, an accelerator should be used.

If too long a delay occurs between the curing of the gel-coat and the application of the next resin layer, the result can be a poor bond between the two, allowing an easy passage for water that enters the laminate. To obtain a correct bond, the styrene in the laminating resin must be able to soften the gel-coat slightly, so allowing good adhesion. If the gel-coat has cured for too long, however, this softening cannot take place. On the other hand, if the first layer of laminating resin is applied too quickly, the styrene in the resin can attack and oversoften the gel-coat. Styrene may be trapped or the softened gel-coat may allow the first layer of glass fibre to penetrate and end up too close to the surface. If this occurs, wicking can take place in which the fibres of glass absorb water and transmit it through into the laminate.

To ensure optimum water resistance, there should be a resin-rich layer next to the gel-coat. This is best achieved by the use of a light-weight cloth or tissue mat which is easy to wet-out without heavy rolling. Hard rolling at this stage can have the effect of removing much of the resin and may also drive strands of glass into the gel-coat. Using a heavy reinforcement immediately behind the gel-coat may also have the effect of trapping air bubbles immediately next to it, which must be avoided. Throughout the laminating process it is vital to avoid dry spots which are not thoroughly wetted-out. Should such areas exist and water find its way through them, it will easily wet the dry glass, dissolve the binders – especially if of the emulsion type – and form a concentrated solution.

The conditions in which the hull is moulded are absolutely critical if the full performance of the materials is to be realized. The moulding shop should be heated and well ventilated, and maintained at the levels of temperature and humidity recommended by the resin manufacturer. A hygrograph should be mounted in the shop to show relative humidity and temperature and all materials should be allowed to come into equilibrium with the workshop conditions before use. If the mould is stored outside, this too must be allowed to reach the working temperature before being used. Glass fibre should always be stored in clean, warm and dry conditions. If damp glass fibre is used, water will be immediately introduced into the lay-up. Draughts should be eliminated from the workshop and direct sunlight should also be excluded. Either can lead to uneven curing areas of the hull and this can set up stresses within the laminate which may result in cracks.

The period after the hull has been moulded and hardened is very important to the water-resistant properties of the hull. Ideally, a postcuring treatment should take place to allow the hull to reach optimum cure. The length of time this takes is dependent on the temperature in which the hull can be stored. At 20°C a minimum time of two or, better still, four weeks should be allowed. During this period the hull must be kept dry and well supported to avoid distortion to the shape. A final test for hardness should then be carried out using a Barcol hardness test. In this a simple instrument is hand-held against the gel-coat, a pressure applied and a reading of the resulting indentation obtained. This really tests only the gel-coat, but it does give some measure of hardness and hence of the cure of the hull.

While the prospective or actual boat owner may question why he should have to concern himself with the actual production process, it must be realized that an understanding of the problems by the buyer can greatly help him in search for a conscientious boat builder. The fact that a hull carries a Lloyd's Hull Moulding Release Certificate is a good guide to the conditions in which it was moulded, its scantlings and so on, but it is still no guarantee that the best materials possible have been used in the manufacture. Often the only way to ensure that these materials are used is for the buyer personally to specify them on order – and how many buyers are technically qualified to do that? Some care and understanding of the problem at this early stage will go a long way to making certain that the problem of osmosis does not occur.

At the stage just described, the vast majority of new boats are considered ready for the water after an application of antifouling (in the case of those to be kept permanently afloat). However, there is another stage that can and should be undertaken by the owner who wishes to avoid the expensive and worrying problems of osmosis damage. Although a polyester gel-coat is the best water-resistant coating that can be applied to a female-moulded glass-fibre hull, its performance is not as good, thickness for thickness, as two-pot polyurethane or – even better – epoxy painting systems. Therefore the owner who requires the best protection possible should specify a full painting schedule. It is true that glass fibre was originally described as a virtually maintenance-free material which did not need painting. However, the modern paint systems, properly applied in the correct conditions, will last at least as long as the polyester gel-coat before needing repainting, when the job will be relatively easy. Although the underwater surfaces are the most important, ideally the painting should cover the topsides as well to reduce the risks further. The inside areas of the boat are often totally ignored, but water can be absorbed into the laminate at least as easily from the inside as from the outside. The inside surfaces should therefore also be painted with one of the high-performance systems if total protection is required. While this may seem excessive and expensive, it is much more easily done and cheaper than the repairs that may be necessary after osmosis damage makes itself apparent.

For the exterior of the hull a good choice of system would be three coats of a high-build epoxy coating below the water-line before antifouling. When applying antifouling, the maker's recommended primer should first be used to prepare the epoxy coating. Many people believe that the antifouling alone will aid the water resistance of the polyester gel-coat, but this is not true, since all antifoulings must be water-sensitive to release their toxins. If a painting system is to be used above the water-line, good protection and finish can be achieved by two coats of a high-build epoxy followed by two undercoats and two topcoats of an aliphatic two-pot polyurethane. An aliphatic type should always be chosen because of its resistance to yellowing and chalking when used on exterior surfaces.

For interior surfaces not on view, a high-build epoxy tar composition could be used, but for other surfaces two coats of epoxy followed by two or three coats of a two-pot polyurethane would be the ideal solution. For interior surfaces an aromatic polyurethane would be perfectly acceptable since chalking and yellowing will not be a problem.

So far, female-moulded glass-fibre hulls have been the subject. In the case of a male-moulded boat, a gel-coat will not be used and the surface will need final finishing and painting. Blistering has been known to occur on some new boats, one possible explanation of which lies in the type of filler that is used for final fairing. This surfacing filler is important since it is part of the system keeping water away from the laminate. Commonly used fillers are often of silicate and their performance when over-painted may be suspect. For this purpose a better solution would be to use a phenolic filler with either polyester or epoxy resin, depending on the resin used in the laminate. After final fairing, a painting schedule as already described should be undertaken to provide the best possible barrier to water absorption.

In the future we may well find that the risk of osmosis damage is further reduced as ways are discovered to improve the water resistance of the surface of the glass-fibre laminate. At the present time at least one company is working on the development of a polyurethane finish that can be applied into the mould before the gel-coat, so producing a hull that is, in effect, pre-painted. Until then it is up to both owners and builders to make sure that the risk of osmosis is kept to an absolute minimum.

GLOSSARY

accelerator: catalytically increases the curing rate of a thermosetting resin.

angle ply: a laminate in which alternate plies are laid at an angle to a reference direction.

anisotropic laminate: a laminate which has different properties along different in-plane directions.

balance laminate: a laminate in which the lay-up is symmetrical about its mid-plane.

carbon fibre: graphite fibres are more commonly used in high-performance composite structure nowadays. Despite their high cost they provide the best specific stiffness generally available.

catalyst: promotes the curing cycle when added to the synthetic resin.

composite: a material consisting of two or more constituents which combine to give properties different from those of the individual constituents.

crossply laminate: a laminate in which the layers are oriented at right angles to one another.

CSM: a mat created by randomly distributing and binding together chopped strands of E-glass fibre.

cure: the stage at which the properties of a thermosetting resin are irreversibly changed by a chemical reaction.

delaminate: breakdown of a laminated material arising from separation of the layers.

denier: the weight, in grammes, of 9000m of roving, tow, yarn or strand.

drape: the ability of a woven fabric to conform to surface irregularities such as double curvature.

E-glass: the most commonly used fibre reinforcement. It is relatively cheap, easily available and has adequate physical properties.

end: an individual roving, tow yarn, thread or filament.

epoxy resin: one of the three most commonly used thermosetting resins. Epoxies generally provide the best properties for high-performance structures.

filament: a single fibre of reinforcement.

filament winding: a method of winding an impregnated fibre tow on to a supporting mandrel at any desired angle to produce a hollow tube with readily defined properties.

folded yarn: a yarn formed by twisting together two or more single yarns. (*American:* plied yarn.)

gel-coat: the surface resin finish of an FRP moulding designed to resist chemical and environmental attack. A gel-coat resin is significantly different from a laminating resin. A gel-coat is usually only used on female moulded components.

glass fibre: filaments drawn from molten glass of varying chemical compositions. E-glass being the most commonly used fibre material.

hybrid: a cloth, woven roving or unidirectional material composed of two or more different fibres, the properties of the hybrid material being a proportional combination of the properties of the individual fibres. Thus a carbon/Kevlar hybrid has the stiffness of the carbon and the impact resistance of the Kevlar, depending on the proportions used of the two materials.

isotropic: a laminate with uniform properties in all directions.

kevlar: the Du Pont trade name for aramid fibre. Kevlar is a low-density fibre with excellent specific strength and good specific stiffness properties. It also has excellent impact resistance.

lamina: a single layer of reinforcement impregnated with resin.

laminate: a moulding consisting of two or more laminae.

lay-up: the description of the components of a laminate and the order and arrangement of reinforcement in a laminate.

matrix: the resin component of a composite which surrounds the reinforcement, protects it from damage and transfers loads to and between the reinforcing fibres.

modulus: a measure of the stiffness of a material. The relationship between stress and strain.

orthogonal: having two principal directions at right angles, such as the yarn directions in a woven fabric.

polyester fibre: fibres of polyester are not commonly used in marine structures because of their low physical properties, but they do give excellent impact resistance to a laminate and so have some use in sheathing applications and in small hulls such as canoes.

polyester resin: the most commonly used thermosetting resin.

postcure: a second-stage cure undertaken at elevated temperature to improve the properties of the resin system and to give a complete cure.

pot-life: the length of time that a mixed resin and catalyst retains a low enough viscosity to be worked.

pre-preg: a pre-impregnated reinforcement. Reinforcement is impregnated with the correct quantity of resin with a slow catalyst for curing at an above-room temperature, and is stored under refrigerated conditions. This method allows accurate measurement of the correct resin to fibre ratio and allows clean working.

pultrusion: a system in which reinforcement impregnated with a suitable resin system is drawn through a die and cured at an elevated temperature.

quasi-isotropic: a laminate in which laminae are oriented in several directions to give approximately equal properties in all directions in the plane of the laminate.

R glass: a glass fibre with different chemical composition to the commonly used E glass, giving higher properties but at a higher price.

resin injection: a moulding system in which resin is injected into the reinforcement-filled cavity between two matched moulds.

roving: an untwisted assembly of strands.

S glass: similar to R glass in composition. (S glass is an American product, while R glass is European.)

size: a compound which is applied to a reinforcement to assist handling and to improve the properties of the laminate.

specific modulus: the modulus of a material divided by its density.

specific strength: the ultimate strength value of a material divided by its density.

strand: an untwisted, compact bundle of filaments.

surfacing tissue: a lightweight mat used next to a gel-coat or on the surface of a male moulded component to help protect the underlying laminate.

syntactic resin: a resin mixed with a low-density filler to produce a structural filler or core material.

tack: the stickiness of a pre-preg resin.

tex: the weight in grams of 1000m of roving, tow, yarn or strand.

thermoplastic resin: a resin system whose state is reversible between liquid and solid on the application of heat.

thermosetting resin: a resin system which, once solidified, cannot be changed back to its original state. All the commonly used resins for boatbuilding are in this class.

tow: a loose, untwisted bundle of filaments.

unidirectional: a reinforcement which has the majority of its strength properties oriented along one axis.

vacuum injection: a moulding method in which resin is injected into a cavity between two matched moulds, the cavity being evacuated to increase resin penetration and help ensure thorough penetration of the reinforcement.

vinylester resin: a resin system, similar to polyester, with improved chemical-resistance and elongation properties.

warp: the yarn that runs lengthwise in a woven fabric.

weft: the yarn running across the width of the fabric, usually (but not always) at right angles to the warp.

woven rovings: a fabric woven loosely from rovings.

yarn: a twisted strand of continuous or discontinuous fibres used for fabric weaving.

INDEX